# Life Is a Little Better

# Conflict and Social Change Series

## Series Editors
Scott Whiteford and William Derman
*Michigan State University*

# Life Is a Little Better

## Redistribution as a Development Strategy in Nadur Village, Kerala

Richard W. Franke

Westview Press

BOULDER • SAN FRANCISCO • OXFORD

*Conflict and Social Change Series*

Cover drawing by M. Subramanian Nambudiri, a retired art teacher in Nadur Village

Published in 1993 in the United States of America by Westview Press, Inc., 5500 Central Avenue, Boulder, Colorado 80301-2877, and in the United Kingdom by Westview Press, 36 Lonsdale Road, Summertown, Oxford OX2 7EW

A CIP catalog record for this book is available from the Library of Congress.
ISBN 0-8133-8591-1

Printed and bound in the United States of America

The paper used in this publication meets the requirements
of the American National Standard for Permanence of Paper
for Printed Library Materials Z39.48-1984.

10    9    8    7    6    5    4    3    2    1

# Contents

# Tables and Figures

# Acknowledgments

This project was made possible primarily by Joan Mencher's generous sharing of her 1971 household survey from Nadur Village. Our field research was funded by National Science Foundation Grant BNS 85-18440. We were also aided by Separately Budgeted Research Grants from Montclair State College and the Montclair State Distinguished Scholar Award (1988). Our research in Kerala was facilitated by the Centre for Development Studies in Thiruvananthapuram. Among the many persons at the Centre who aided our research are former Director T. N. Krishnan, Research Associates K. N. Nair and T. M. Thomas Isaac, and Mr. Phil Roy. Researcher Nata Duvvury also provided many helpful ideas. Kannan Nambiar and Manu S. gave excellent Malayalam lessons.

In Nadur Village, M. S. Ravikumar Nambudiri, M. Subramanian Nambudiri, Raman Nambudiri, and Sreekumari M. G. supplied expert research assistance. We are also grateful to Nadur residents Mukhami Amma, Narayani Amma, and the late Madhavan Nair.

In the United States, Mira A. Franke and Lorraine Zaepfel did much of the computer data entry. We received excellent statistical advice from Professor Gil Klajman of the Montclair State Sociology Department. Deirdre Stapp ably prepared the maps. Barbara H. Chasin gave invaluable support throughout the project.

The tables in Chapter 1 and some of the general history of the Kerala workers and peasants movements appeared earlier in *Kerala: Radical Reform as Development in an Indian State* (San Francisco: Institute for Food and Development Policy, 1989, co-author Barbara H. Chasin). Much of Chapter 7 and parts of Chapter 12 appeared in the *Journal of Anthropological Research* 48(2):81-116, 1992. We thank again the many critics and commentators on that book and article. We assume full responsibility for all data and analysis presented here.

*Richard W. Franke*

# 1

# Development, Inequality, and Redistribution

Is redistribution of wealth an effective third world development strategy? Despite an ongoing expert debate about growth versus reform and the widespread occurrence of reform and revolutionary movements among the third world poor in the 20th century, this question has attracted little social science research at the local level. Most analyses refer to national level statistics. Few regional or village studies are available to assess the impact of reform strategies on the lives of the world's poorest people—most of them third world farmers and farm laborers.[1]

### Kerala's Achievements

This book is an attempt to fill part of the gap by measuring the achievements and limitations of a large-scale reform process. It is a study of Nadur Village in central Kerala. We chose to conduct a detailed anthropological village study in Kerala State, India, because radical peasant and worker movements there have brought about one of the third world's most extensive experiments in the redistribution of wealth and productive assets. Per capita income in Kerala in our study year 1986-87 was only about $182 in 1986 compared with the all-India figure of $290. Kerala's income increased little from its early 1970s level of $126 per year. If Kerala were a separate country in 1986, it would rank 9th from the poorest of 130 (Morris 1979:64; GOK 1988; World Bank 1988).

Though not intended or desired by Kerala's planners or its people, this income stagnation has the effect of making Kerala a controlled scientific laboratory of the consequences of the reforms which become the most likely explanation for any material improvements in people's lives. Just how substantial these improvements are can be seen from Table 1.1.

Table 1.1
Physical Quality of Life Indicators: 1986
Kerala State Versus All-India,
Low-Income Countries, and the USA

| Indicator | Kerala | India | Low-Income Countries | USA |
|---|---|---|---|---|
| Per Capita GNP | $182 | $290 | $200 | $17,480 |
| Life Expectancy in Years | 68 | 57 | 52 | 75 |
| Infant Mortality Rate Per 1,000 | 27 | 86 | 106 | 10 |
| Birth Rate Per 1,000 | 22 | 32 | 43 | 16 |
| Adult Literacy Rate Percent | 78 [a] | 43 [b] | 48 [c] | 96 [b] |
| PQLI (0-100) | 82 [d] | 56 | 59 [a] | 96 [a] |

Sources: World Bank 1988:222-223, 276-277, 286-287; GOK 1988;GOK 1989:82; and Nag 1989:417.

Notes: Data closest to the 1986-87 study year were used in all cases. Kerala's per capita GNP was calculated at the rate of 13 rupees per U. S. dollar, the approximate rate of exchange in 1986-87. "Low-Income" refers to the average of 37 countries so designated by the World Bank and excluding China and India. The PQLI figure for the low-income group is for 143 countries so designated by Lewis et al (1983).

In the USA, we find major discrepancies among population groups. In 1985, infant mortality for whites was 9.3 per 1,000 while for blacks it was 15.8 (Boone 1989:47). Effective literacy in the USA should be defined differently from the U.N. 3rd grade equivalent. Education critic Jonathan Kozol (1985:5) estimates effective U.S. illiteracy at 33%, making the U.S. 49th out of 158 U.N. member nations in the mid-1980s. See also The New York Times 7 September 1988.

a.    1981 data are from Government of Kerala (GOK) 1985; GOK 1984:28; and Lewis et al 1983:210-220.
b.    1985 data from Grant 1988:64 and 71.
c.    1985 data from World Bank 1990a:xiv, using a slightly different set of countries from those noted under unmarked data below.
d.    Kerala PQLI computed by the author from 1981 data in sources listed above.

From Table 1.1 we can see that Kerala stands out both among low-income countries and in comparison with the rest of India. These particular indicators are important because—except for GNP—they all measure things that must be available to wide sections of the population to show up statistically. The GNP per capita is an average of *all* income divided by the number of persons. If wealth is highly concentrated in the hands of a few, the average could be high while most people have little. But the literacy rate can only improve as more and more people learn to read and write. Average life expectancy will also not go up much if only the elite live longer, because even *they* can only live about 75 to 80 years no matter how rich they may be. Similarly, infant mortality and birth rates change only when large numbers have received the benefits of modern medicine. Thus, these four indicators (literacy, life expectancy, infant mortality, and birth rate) reliably measure the impact of social and economic development as it spreads to large sections of the population.

One of the striking features of Kerala's development is that quality of life benefits are fairly equally distributed among men and women, urban and rural areas, and low and high castes. This can be seen on Table 1.2.

Literacy, for example, exhibits a 9 point spread between males and females in Kerala, while for all-India males have a 22 point advantage. Urban India is nearly twice as literate as the rural areas, while in Kerala the disparity is only 76% versus 69%. Kerala's low caste population is now as literate as India's urban people, while low castes in the nation as a whole are still nearly 80% illiterate. Even for tribal groups living mostly in the mountains, literacy is nearly twice the all-India average although it remains far below the level of Kerala's other groups. In Kerala, tribal groups account for 1% of the state's population, while for India as a whole, they make up nearly 8% (GOK 1985:1).

Kerala's rural infant mortality and birth rates are only slightly behind the urban centers where medical care is easier to provide. For all-India, urban-rural differences in 1981 were especially severe in mortality, with the incredibly high figure of 124 infants per 1,000 dying before they reached the age of one year. Kerala's *rural* infant mortality rate is about one third less than the all-India *urban* rate, a remarkable achievement. And, while Kerala's rate has continued to fall—from 37 in 1981 to 27 in 1986 and 22 in 1989—India's has fluttered about, dropping to 86 in 1986, but rising in 1990 to 92 per thousand (World Bank 1988:286; 1992:272).[2]

Another way to see Kerala's unique development profile is via the Physical Quality of Life Index (PQLI), a composite of literacy, infant

Table 1.2
Physical Quality of Life Indicators: 1981-82
Distribution Across Various Social Groups
Kerala State Versus All-India

| Indicator | Kerala | All-India |
|---|---|---|
| **Percent Literate (all ages)** | | |
| Males | 75 | 47 |
| Females | 66 | 25 |
| | | |
| Urban | 76 | 57 |
| Rural | 69 | 30 |
| | | |
| Low Caste | 56 | 21 |
| Tribal Groups | 32 | 16 |
| **Life Expectancy in Years** | | |
| Males | 64 | 57 |
| Females | 68 | 56 |
| **Infant Mortality Rate Per 1,000** | | |
| Urban | 34 | 65 |
| Rural | 41 | 124 |
| **Birth Rate Per 1,000** | | |
| Urban | 23 | 27 |
| Rural | 26 | 36 |

Sources: Government of India 1983.:xxv; Government of Kerala 1984: Tables 1.12, 1.13, 2.1.2, 2.1.4; World Bank 1988:Table 33; Government of Kerala 1985:1-2.
*Note: Some figures on this table will not coincide precisely with those from Table 1.1 because of variation in years for which different kinds of data are available.*

mortality, and life expectancy (see Table 1.1) that is widely used as an indicator of development. By the early 1970s, Kerala's PQLI was 70 on a scale of 0 to 100, making it equal to countries such as Brazil and Thailand which had many times its per capita income (Morris 1979:90; Morris and McAlpin 1982:58). For the early 1980s we have computed that Kerala's PQLI had increased to at least 82, compared to an all-India figure of just 56. Kerala's PQLI has continued to improve as fast as India's, despite

Table 1.3
Provision of Basic Services in the Late 1970s
Kerala State Versus All-India

| Feature | Rank of Kerala Among All Indian States | Percent of Villages With Service in | |
|---|---|---|---|
| | | Kerala | All-India |
| **Within Two Kilometers** | | | |
| 1. All-Weather Roads | 1 | 98 | 46 |
| 2. Bus Stops | 1 | 98 | 40 |
| 3. Post Offices | 1 | 100 | 53 |
| 4. Primary Schools | 1 | 100 | 90 |
| 5. Secondary Schools | 1 | 99 | 44 |
| 6. Fair Price (Ration) Shops | 1 | 99 | 35 |
| 7. Health Dispensaries | 1 | 91 | 25 |
| 8. Health Centers | 1 | 47 | 12 |
| **Within Five Kilometers** | | | |
| 9. Higher Education Facilities | 1 | 97 | 21 |
| 10. Hospitals | 1 | 78 | 35 |
| 11. Fertilizer Depots | 1 | 93 | 44 |
| 12. Water Pump Repair Shops | 1 | 65 | 19 |
| 13. Veterinary Dispensaries | 1 | 82 | 45 |
| 14. Credit Cooperative Banks | 1 | 96 | 61 |
| 15. Other Banks | 1 | 96 | 40 |
| 16. Seed Stores | 2 | 63 | 40 |
| 17. Storage and Warehouses | 4 | 34 | 21 |
| 18. Railway Stations | 8 | 23 | 18 |
| **In the Village** | | | |
| 19. Drinking Water | 5 | 96 | 93 |
| 20. Electricity | 3 | 97 | 33 |

Sources: Kannan 1988:18-21, based on surveys of the Government of India, Central Statistical Organisation.

Note: At the 1981 census, India had 22 states, 9 Union territories including the capital city, New Delhi, some island groups, and other small units. Villages surveyed: 558,519 of which 974 were in Kerala; Number of states compared 22.

the fact that PQLI is more difficult to raise as it approaches 100. Kerala's PQLI of 82 in 1981 was far above that of all African countries, all Asian countries except Sri Lanka (82), Mongolia (81), and the high-income nations of North Korea (81), South Korea (85), Taiwan (87), and Japan (98). It was well above the total world average of 68, and the average of just 59 for 143 developing countries that had an average per capita GNP of $772, far above Kerala's $182 (computed from Lewis *et al* 1983:210-220). In addition, Kerala's PQLI was nearly equal across rural and urban areas and between males and females, in striking contrast to *all* other parts of India, including even the high-income states of Punjab and Haryana (Morris and McAlpin 1982:71,90-94).[3] Kerala has clearly found a way to deliver high development indicators at low incomes. Our research in Nadur village attempts to explain how this has come about.

A different way of looking at Kerala's development achievements comes from a series of studies done by various Indian agencies on productivity and basic services. In 1980-81, Kerala ranked 7th among Indian states with a per capita GNP of Rs 1,421 compared to the all-India average of Rs 1,559 (GOK 1985c:24). In agriculture, Kerala ranked first among all Indian states in the rupees value of output per unit of land area. In addition, the state was first in India on 15 of 20 measures of basic services within two or five kilometers of villages, and very high on five others as shown in Table 1.3.

From Table 1.3 we can see that Kerala stands above other Indian states in providing basic services to its people. Among the most impressive figures are those showing 91% of Kerala's villages having health dispensaries compared to the all-India average of just 25%; 47% having health centers compared to just 12% countrywide; 99% having fair price food shops within two kilometers versus 35% for all-India; and 99% with secondary schools as against the all-India average of 44%. In later chapters we shall provide more details regarding people's access to these services and their use.[4]

Kerala's striking performance in raising certain living standards and providing access to basic facilities, combined with the low per capita income, give the state an important place in the ongoing debate about growth versus redistribution. We call this the "redistribution debate."

## The Redistribution Debate in Development Policy

Since World War Two economists and other development experts have offered various ideas on how to achieve rapid economic development. Modernization theorists looked to private sector economic growth as the mechanism for development. Radical alternatives began to appear in the late 1960s. In response to the evident failure of economic growth alone to provide a decent standard of living to large numbers of people in the third world, radicals argued that lessons should be sought in China, Cuba, and North Vietnam where growth had been supplemented with redistribution of wealth and expanded health and education services even while per capita incomes remained low.

To this challenge, establishment economists offered two modifications of modernization theory: (1) equitable growth and (2) special targeting.

## Equitable Growth

In Taiwan and South Korea rapid growth in agriculture and manufacturing combined with land reform and spending on public services to raise incomes, life expectancy, literacy, etc. all at once. These success stories engendered the theory of *equitable growth*. But how replicable are the experiences of Taiwan and South Korea? Evidence suggests that both countries had unusual colonial histories with substantial industrial and infrastructural development before World War Two (Shalom 1989:94).

Furthermore, Taiwan and South Korea entered their phases of most rapid growth during the big postwar upswing in the U. S. economy (Shalom 1989:96). Can the wealthy nations today absorb enough textiles and electronics products to support a third world full of Taiwans? Would Taiwan's landlords have gone along with the land reform without the fear of China's communist revolution gaining support on their nearby island (Reitsma and Kleinpenning 1985:372)? And can these two countries maintain their equitable patterns? Evidence indicates that South Korea at least has become less equal since 1965 (Shalom 1989:96; Bello and Rosenfeld 1990).

If Taiwan and South Korea are not likely paths for present-day countries, are there other ways to achieve equitable growth? Can heavy investment in agriculture do it? The northwest Indian states of Punjab and Haryana may be examples (Westley 1986), but their quality of life indicators remain below Kerala's despite massive growth in farm output. Growth seems rarely very equitable. Skepticism about the possibility for equitable growth in most third world countries has led to a second alternative: basic needs theory and special targeting policies.

*Basic Needs and Special Targeting for the Poor*

The World Bank and other Western lending agencies have come to embrace special targeting or "investing in people" (World Bank 1991:69) where growth is not generating equity quickly enough to satisfy the restless poor. Among its four major recommendations to developing countries, the World Bank (1991:11) lists first:

> Invest in people. Governments must spend more, and more efficiently, on primary education, basic health care, nutrition, and family planning. That requires shifts in spending priorities; greater efficiency and better targeting of expenditures, and in some cases greater resource mobilization.

Despite these high-sounding words, we have reason to doubt the commitment of the World Bank and major Western lending agencies to a program of targeted benefits to the poor. We note that "shifts in spending priorities" lies buried in the midst of a list that includes a double reference to "greater efficiency," often a code for cutbacks in the very spending priorities supposedly being called for. Nowhere does the World Bank proclaim targeting to be a higher priority than growth. The practice of the World Bank, USAID, the IMF, and other foreign aid establishments never seem to force the issue of equity. Debt repayment, however, *is* forced, along with adjustment packages imposed by the IMF which often undercut programs for the poor. Contrary to the World Bank's rhetoric, UNESCO's Director-General stated in 1989 that "The past few years have witnessed an unprecedented halt in the growth of basic educational services" (Grant 1990:9).

In two of every three developing countries spending per student declined from 1980 to 1989 (Grant 1990:9). Health statistics indicate that more than 3/4 of the nations of Africa and Latin America have reduced per capita spending on health. Clinics have closed, vaccines have not been purchased, low birth weight babies have increased in numbers, and more (poor) children die of malnutrition and hunger-related diseases (Grant 1988:28; Grant 1989:1; Grant 1990:8). Special targeting seems not to be very special.

The theory of special targeting derives in part from the World Bank's own sponsored study on meeting basic needs. But that study (Streeten *et al* 1981:20-21) concluded that it is "...an empirical fact that the only societies that have been successful in meeting basic needs are those that have also reduced inequalities."

## Long-Term Redistribution Via Development

How are inequalities reduced? Early development literature took its cue from a 1955 paper by economist Simon Kuznets who argued that development led first to higher degrees of inequality later followed by a more egalitarian distribution of wealth than before the development process started.

Why did development and inequality patterns correspond in this way? Kuznets compared trends in income inequality of Germany, England, and the United States to conclude that early accumulation by entrepreneurial elites created greater inequality that was then reduced by increased output of industry, urbanization, greater skill levels of the work force, and government policy ("legislative interference" 1955:9) such as progressive taxes. Kuznets did not apparently consider the role of unions or worker militancy to be important despite the fact that the periods he identified as those with reductions in inequality correspond with the periods of greatest labor militancy in all three of the countries he used for his study.

How long would the process take? Kuznets' three-country sample required more than 100 years to complete the "long swing" from preindustrial inequality to early industrial greater inequality to later industrial lower levels of inequality. Can the poor countries of today develop within the one to two centuries needed by their Western predecessors? David Morawetz found that at average annual growth rates between 1960 and 1975, poor countries containing the majority of the developing world's population, will never close the gap in GNP per capita with the developed countries (1977:29). In 1986 Jerome Segal made a similar calculation using 1965-1983 growth rates. He concluded (1986:55) that four countries would close the gap in less than a century, eight would close it in 100 to 1,335 years, and 49 countries would never close it. We must wonder whether Kuznets' long swing will ever occur for most people.

Even if it does, is a wait of a century acceptable? In the present world with rapid communications and the idea of social justice widespread in both the developed and underdeveloped countries, can we expect people to wait more than four generations to achieve a decent standard of living? Given the extreme inequality of many of the poorest countries, the spread of egalitarian ideologies, and access to weapons, shouldn't we expect the poor to organize, rebel, and attempt to seize and redistribute the wealth of their society?

## Redistribution by Popular Demand

Much of the history of the third world since 1945 has been of popular movements for redistribution of wealth. Where the movements have been destroyed or brought under control such as Guatemala and Indonesia, high rates of inequality remain. Where the movements have gained state power such as China and Cuba, substantial redistribution has occurred. In a recent survey of 123 countries, Cereseto and Waitzkin (1988:115) found that socialist countries had substantially less inequality than capitalist countries at the same level of economic development. They further found that "at the same level of economic development, the socialist countries showed more favorable outcomes than the capitalist countries" on basic needs/physical quality of life variables such as literacy, life expectancy, infant mortality, per capita calorie supply, and access to health care. The relative advantage of socialism was greatest at the lowest levels of economic development (1988:108).

The analysis by Cereseto and Waitzkin shows that capitalist, growth-oriented development requires greater income increases and thus a longer wait in order to achieve high physical quality of life statistics than socialism which makes possible such achievements in the early stages of economic growth. For the third world's hundreds of millions of poor, illiterate people living short, unhealthy lives, redistribution offers more immediate improvements than growth-oriented market capitalism. In its 1991 report focussing on "The Challenge of Development," the World Bank (1991:10) seems to have accepted part of this argument: "...for many of the world's poorest countries, decades of rapid growth will be needed to make inroads on poverty."

Kerala fits into the debate precisely at this point. Kerala has not had a socialist revolution like China and Cuba. Redistribution in Kerala is substantial, however, and results not from policy directives of Western development agencies but from popular demand exercised through petitions, marches, strikes, and election campaigns (Franke and Chasin 1989).

As we noted earlier, per capita income in Kerala has remained very low. Kerala's economic stagnation was not consciously chosen by its leaders or its people who want consumer goods and the other trappings of development just as much as everyone else. But the stagnation is a fact which renders Kerala a laboratory to study the effects of redistribution in isolation from growth.

## Inequality in Social Science Theory

In addition to its importance for development policy, Kerala's experiment in attacking inequality carries broader implications for social science theories of inequality. Five main questions present themselves:

1. How did inequality arise?
2. How is inequality sustained and perpetuated? What have been the patterns of inequality over time?
3. How much inequality is justifiable?
4. Why do people sometimes rebel against inequality? Why do they sometimes fail and sometimes succeed?
5. How much can inequality be reduced?

Kerala's recent history does not provide data on the first question. For the other four, Kerala offers valuable case study material. Let us examine these questions briefly in order to set the context for our study of Nadur village.

### Why Did Inequality Arise?

Modern anthropological and sociological studies indicate that the earliest hunting and gathering cultures were egalitarian. Humans probably lived without inequality for thousands of years (Lenski 1966:102-112). With the invention of agriculture, surplus production and the rise of inequality became possible. Anthropologists still debate which specific features of early agricultural societies led to inequality—management of water, management of land, organization of military defense—but there is general agreement that more technologically and organizationally complex societies tended to develop positions of coordination that led to authority of some over others (e.g. Fried 1967; Kerbo 1991:11; Lenski 1966).

### How Is Inequality Perpetuated?

Once implanted, inequality seems to be self-perpetuating and self-expanding. "When some people control what others want and need, they are able to demand additional goods and services in return for distributing these necessities" (Kerbo 1991:11). This so-called "Matthew Principle" (To those that have it shall be given) leads to a hardening or institutionalization of inequality so that some groups have regular, patterned power over others. Individuals are recruited from the same layers of the hierarchy, further hardening the structure to prevent both mobility within it and any attempts to reduce the inequality.

Comparative history indicates not only perpetuation but a general increase in inequality from early agriculture to a high point in the most advanced agricultural societies (Lenski 1966:437). The wealthiest, most powerful, and most privileged groups were remarkably similar in percent of the population and in amount of wealth controlled within their respective societies. In the Roman Empire, 18th century France, 19th century China and Russia, and 17th century England, the privileged nobilities all made up 1-2% of the total population (Lenski 1966:219-220). These ruling elites seem to have held about 25% of the total wealth generated by their production systems, while the top ruler may have had another 25%, meaning an elite of 1 to 2% of the population held 50% of the total wealth (Lenski 1966:228-233). Twelfth and 13th century English kings had incomes averaging 24,000 times that of peasants (Lenski 1966:212; Kerbo 1991:74). The great wealth of the nobility and the fantastic wealth of the king contrasted sharply with the lives of most English peasants whose

> ...diet consisted of little more than...a hunk of bread and a mug of ale in the morning; a lump of cheese and bread with perhaps an onion or two to flavor it, and more ale at noon; a thick soup or pottage followed by bread and cheese at the main meal in the evening. Meat was rare, and the ale was usually thin. Household furniture consisted of a few stools, a table, and a chest....Beds were uncommon and most peasants simply slept on earthen floors covered with straw. Other household possessions were apparently limited to cooking utensils (Lenski 1966:271).

Conditions for peasants in other areas were sometimes far worse.

The apparent tendency for inequality, once implanted, to grow to similar extremes in diverse regions, has not been fully explained. For now we note a pattern of increase from the earliest farming villages where inequality was still limited, to its high levels in the great agricultural states, some of which lasted into the 20th century.

India fits this pattern. Chandragupta, first king of the north Indian Mauryan Empire from 326 to 301 B.C., took from 1/4 to one-half the produce from the lands under his control. His counselors received 800 times the annual incomes of unskilled laborers (Wolpert 1989:58,60). By the time of the Mughal Empire (1526-1764 A.D.), north India's Emperor Shah Jahan built his Peacock Throne out of materials worth more than one million pounds sterling (Moore 1966:327). The famed Taj Mahal cost even more, yet both were built during one of India's worst famines during which only 5,000 rupees per week could be found for the relief of millions of starving and plague-infected peasants in the Deccan region Jahan was attempting to subdue (Wolpert 1989:153). The construction of lavish palaces, mosques, and tombs along with the expensive lifestyles of the Mughal rulers led "peasants to risk death from rebellion rather than accept inevitable starvation" (Wolpert 1989:159).

Conditions in south India may have been less extreme. We could not locate quantitatively comparable materials, but we discovered that rulers and aristocrats often made large grants of land or other goods to temples (Majumdar and Srivastva 1987, esp. 192), suggesting they had a lot of surplus to distribute as they chose (Sastri 1966:133-140, 204-206, 315, 325-329).

We also cannot say with certainty whether the British conquest raised or lowered overall levels of inequality. Direct English plundering of 5 million pounds sterling from the Bengal treasury (Wolf 1982:244) after their victory at Plassey in 1757 and other massive "repatriations" of wealth accumulated by the Mughal rulers (Wolf 1982:246) may have had the temporary statistical effect of lowering inequality within India by shifting it to the international sphere. We can say with some certainty, however, that British colonial rule hardened the most basic component of Indian inequality: **land ownership**. In northern India, the British strengthened the Mughal emperors' local tax collectors or *zamindars*, after 1793 by making them private property owners with the power to buy and sell their land, and to throw off unwanted tenants. During the 19th century, absentee Calcutta bankers and money-lenders eventually became the absentee landlords replacing the Mughal ruler and aristocracy (Wolpert 1989:197; Wolf 1982:247). One result of the combination of extreme inequality and the control by landlords was the starvation of about 1.5 million people during the great Bengal famine of 1943 (Sen 1981:52-85).

In south India a different British policy produced similar effects. Here the British forced peasants to pay their land taxes directly. Intermittent bad harvests slowly pushed much of the land into the hands of Madras moneylenders (Wolpert 1989:207; Moore 1966:364), except in parts of Kerala where a resident landed elite held power in the village economy until 1969. In Chapter 7 we shall examine Kerala's land reform history in more detail. We shall see in other sections of this book that farmers and farm laborers in Kerala and in Nadur village lived much like the medieval English peasants until quite recently.

While we cannot explain the perpetuation and expansion of inequality, we can conclude that *the natural processes of unequal societies tend to increase the level of inequality, and that only sustained, conscious, organized struggles by the victims of inequality can undercut these natural processes.*

### How Much Inequality Is Justified?

Following economist Kenneth Boulding, Marvin Harris (1988:399) argues that inequality produces exploitation when four conditions are met: (1) The subordinate groups suffer deprivations with respect to basic necessities such as food, water, air, sunlight, leisure, medical care, housing, and transport, (2) the ruler or other higher classes enjoy an abundance of luxuries, (3) the luxuries enjoyed by the rulers depend on the labor of the lower groups, and (4) the deprivations experienced by the lower groups result from the failure of the rulers to apply their power to the production and distribution of necessities. A quick look at the data on inequality presented above for England, China, and India should make it clear that exploitation was present. In the course of this book we shall show that inequality in Kerala and in Nadur Village also meet Harris's criteria for exploitation.

Many U.S. social scientists ignored exploitation, leading to unqualified acceptance of inequality. In 1949 the American sociologist Kingsley Davis summed up the argument that inequality is necessary and desirable:

> Social inequality is thus an unconsciously evolved device by which societies insure that the most important positions are conscientiously filled by the most qualified persons (quoted in Lenski 1966:15).

In opposition, anthropologist Gerald Berreman asserted in 1981 that stratification

> ...is humanly harmful in that it is painful, damaging, and unjust, and it is consistently experienced as such by those who are deprived and oppressed (1981:4; for India see also Mencher 1974).[5]

We agree with Berreman. Those he calls "deprived and oppressed" are those whom Harris calls "exploited." In our view, deprivation, oppression, and exploitation, can and should be replaced by egalitarian, cooperative, non exploitative, environment-sustaining communities. As Berreman (1981:4) aptly puts it, inequality

> is responsible for hunger even when there is plenty, for high mortality, high fertility, and low life expectancy, for low levels of education, literacy, political participation, and other measures of quality of life (1981:4).

Recasting his statement, we take as an ethical premise for this study the proposition that *if there is poverty or misery of any kind coexisting with enough wealth or resources to provide a decent life for all, then inequality is leading to exploitation.*

Under such circumstances, people have the moral right to rebel to seek to reduce the inequality by redistribution of wealth. Social scientists can support such struggles to reduce inequality by helping to discover its causes and the conditions under which it can most effectively be reduced. For this purpose, Kerala's people in the 20th century have provided some of the world's most valuable experiences. Their achievements and failures deserve to be recorded for study by those still denied the decent life which the wealth and resources of the world are now able to provide. We hope this study of one village in Kerala will aid in the understanding of what can and cannot be accomplished by such struggles.

## Why Do People Sometimes Rebel?

Social scientists continue to debate why people usually put up with inequality, oppression, and injustice and why they sometimes organize to overcome it (Moore 1978; Skocpol 1979:3-43). In an earlier study (Franke and Chasin 1989:22-27) we suggested a few of the reasons for Kerala's success in building movements for spreading the benefits of modern life to most of its people despite low per capita incomes. Kerala's natural geographic access to water and good land have led to an even distribution of its population that lowers the cost of delivery of education, health care, and other public services. Kerala's favored location on major trade routes has resulted in lengthy and intense contacts with many cultures producing a sophisticated, cosmopolitan people. Kerala's spice, tea, and coffee potential led British colonial rulers to introduce plantation agriculture earlier than in most parts of India, creating a working class more free of caste and religious identity and more able to develop class consciousness than in most other parts of India—and this development took place at a crucial historical juncture when revolutionary movements were producing optimism about the possibilities of radical change. This last factor helped lead to Kerala's development of a body of committed radical cadre whose principles, dedication, and sacrifice gave leadership to caste improvement associations, trade unions, peasant organizations, the independence movement against British rule, and the Communist Party.

All these factors helped foster Kerala's radical tradition and implant in its people a sense of their power and effectiveness that stands out in the world today.  In Chapter 14, we shall see that activism remains strong in Nadur village—a heritage of Kerala's past and a continuing promise for its future.  We shall also see that the energy and strength of the reform movements offers potential for a new generation of Kerala actions for development which some leaders have called "The New Democratic Initiatives."

### How Much Can Inequality Be Reduced?

How much reduction in inequality is possible?  How much redistribution is necessary to produce how much welfare?  These questions cannot be answered by our Kerala research alone.  We hope that our Nadur data will stimulate more of the long collection process that will be necessary to formulate general hypotheses about the relationships among inequality, redistribution, the standard of living, and human welfare.  We hope this study of redistribution versus inequality in Nadur village will help expand the policy discussion regarding development to the larger arena of overcoming deprivation and oppression, of creating a world where inequality cannot make life painful, damaging, or unjust.

## Why a Village Study?

Most people in Kerala live in villages.  Here inequality displays its most salient features.  Within the village, elite groups live in luxury, give orders to their subordinates, and humiliate and exploit those farthest below them.  Within the village, oppressed groups suffer poverty, obey their superiors, and experience humiliation.  Regional and national struggles force people to act at the village level where they come face to face with the inequality that has endured for centuries.  Programs to reduce inequality must therefore show results at the village level.  For these reasons, we believe a single village study is appropriate for shedding light on Kerala's reforms.

Furthermore, village-level research is what anthropologists know best.  By living in one small community, we try to bring a level of detail and a perspective that unites the most general research techniques —questionnaire surveys—with their most specific counterparts—life histories.  Our research in Nadur attempts to combine these anthropological techniques in the context of Kerala's radical history and development achievements to show how the people of one village—Nadur —have fared in one limited period of time—1971 to 1987.

## The Study Hypothesis

This book is organized around the hypothesis that *in Nadur Village from 1971 to 1987 a major reduction in income inequality occurred because of specific radical reforms and this redistribution resulted in modest but measurable improvements in the lives of the poorest villagers despite only small overall income gains in Kerala.*
We shall attempt to verify and expand upon this hypothesis in the next several chapters. In Chapter 2 we describe the field surveys and methods of data analysis used to test the hypothesis. In Chapter 3 we describe Nadur village and the annual cycle of life its people have built around the farming seasons with their corresponding religious rituals. Chapter 4 lists and defines the castes found in Nadur. Chapter 5 examines the class categories we have assigned to the sample households.

The main analysis begins in Chapter 6 where we argue that inequality has declined in Nadur over the period between the 1971 and 1987 surveys. Chapter 7 shows how the land reform contributed to this decline. In Chapter 8 we look at the problems of laborers in Nadur and the attempts of unions and reform governments to improve their lives. Chapter 9 looks at pensions and other special programs designed to supplement the land reform by extending some of its precepts to landless laborers. Chapter 10 surveys Kerala's extensive public food distribution system while Chapter 11 examines access to literacy and the levels of education among the castes and classes. In Chapter 12 we consider how much mobility has been fostered by the reforms.

Throughout the middle part of the study, our independent variable is the redistribution of wealth. Chapters 7 through 11 are structured according to our understanding of what has happened in Kerala. Put simply, we believe the reform struggles reduced inequality which in turn improved the material lives of the poor. Chapters 7 through 11 are introduced by historical descriptions of the Kerala-wide movements for redistribution of land (7), wages (8), development resources (9), food (10), and education (11). Each chapter continues with statistical data on the redistribution in Nadur, along with village-level descriptions such as a sample nursery (Chapter 10) and the village library (Chapter 11). The consequences of the redistribution are then examined by caste and class. Chapters 9 and 12 include household case studies to carry the effects beyond statistics to individual households and the lives of their members.

Chapter 13 provides a summary of the available evidence on changes in the absolute standard of living among Nadur sample households as well as respondents' statements about how they view their lives and futures. Their most common response gave the title to this book. We heard it first from Govindan Nair—Household Case 1—who is introduced in Chapter 9. "Life is a little better." Nadur's people see and appreciate the changes brought in their lives by Kerala's redistribution programs. Like people everywhere, they want life to be better still.

Chapter 14 concludes our study with examples of local Nadur struggles for improvements in the village and some assertions about equality, democracy, and development that we believe link Nadur and its people to you who are reading this book.

## Notes

1.   Hunters-gatherers, pastoralists, and urban slum dwellers make up the other main categories of the world's poorest.

2.   The provisional results of the 1991 Census of India give Kerala a birth rate of 20 versus an all-India rate of 31 (Bose 1991:52-53); a female-male ratio of 1,040 females per 1,000 males in Kerala compared with 929 for all-India (Bose 1991:67); and for Kerala, a literacy rate of 91% for persons 7 and over versus 52% for all-India (Bose 1991:69). Kerala's male literacy rate in 1991 was 94%, the female rate 87%, keeping the state in 1st place among all Indian states with the lowest male-female disparity (Premi 1991:70). India's rates in 1991 by gender were 64% for males and 39% for females (Premi 1991:69).

3.   From the 1991 Provisional Indian Census results and Government of Kerala statistics (GOK 1990:93), we computed Kerala's 1989 PQLI at 88. From the same census report and the 1992 World Bank Report (1992:218,272), we got 1989 and 1990 data to compute the all-India PQLI at 60. Kerala's PQLI advance since 1981 seems to be even faster than the all-India rate despite the greater difficulty of raising PQLI the closer one gets to 100. We are grateful to our colleague Stephen Rosskam Shalom for designing a computer program to compute PQLI's from the indicators.

4.   A brief comparison of Kerala with all-India and with socialist China appears in Drèze and Sen (1989:221-225).

5.   An earlier set of objections to Davis came from Melvin Tumin (1953 [1966]) with reply by Davis (1953 [1966]). Tumin's logical and functional critique could expand substantially Berreman's argument, but it goes beyond the needs of the Nadur village analysis here.

# 2

# Methods of Research and Analysis

Our study compares household surveys of Nadur Village in 1971 and 1986-87. Three major assumptions provide its foundation: (1) Joan Mencher's 1971 survey in Nadur produced rich, detailed, and reliable data, (2) the baseline year 1971 captures Nadur just before many important Kerala reforms entered the village and (3) therefore the 1986-87 survey captures the effects of the reforms 16 years later.

We employed the standard anthropological participant-observation method to gather narrative information combined with detailed household questionnaires administered by research assistants to derive quantitative data on the households. In this chapter we will explain why we chose Nadur, how we conducted the field research, and what methods we used to analyze our data.

## Why Nadur Village?

Five major reasons justify our choice of Nadur: (1) how it fits into Kerala's village types, (2) how it fits into Kerala's geographical diversity, (3) how it fits into Kerala's history, (4) its relatively small number of Middle East remittances, and (5) the outstanding research assistants living there.

### Nadur Fits Kerala's Dispersed Village Type

Most Indian villages fall into 1 of 3 types. *Nucleated* villages have houses close together in a well-defined site. Such villages are common in western Uttar Pradesh, Delhi, the Punjab, and some parts of southern India and are associated with wheat, barley, and millet production.

*Hamleted* villages are found in the middle and lower Ganges plain and some other areas. They are composed of "a central settlement, several hamlets, and satellite settlements scattered over the fields" (Cohn 1971:142). Hamleted villages occur generally where rice and other grain agriculture are mixed (Cohn 1971:143). In Kerala, villages correspond to the third pattern: *dispersed*. This pattern is also found in some of the hill regions and in the lower delta of the Ganges, and in other areas of intensive rice agriculture. Dispersed villages have homesteads spread across the landscape in such a way that one cannot always tell where one village begins and another ends. In many parts of Kerala, villages are more like extended suburbs of towns with no clear boundaries between urban and rural areas.

Why is Kerala's settlement pattern different? In many parts of India, the difficulty in getting water compelled people to settle in compact villages where they could construct large irrigation facilities under the political centralization of a monarch. Kerala's easier access to water may have offered the possibility of more local and small-scale political development (Fuller 1976:25-27; Mencher 1966:144).

Kerala's villages have been described as lacking true centers (V. K. J. Menon 1953:46 as quoted in Mencher 1966:141):

> In general the settlement has no distinct core, nor is there any residential area or shopping street....Here and there, there is a small hut....an occasional large house with a garden gate-house and outhouses probably belonging to an important landlord. In some cases there is a ....tea-shop where some of the men might meet. There may be a temple, village tank, or court of justice but none of these form the core of the village which is altogether rather loosely knit.

This description, which has influenced much of the thinking on settlement patterns in Kerala, may exaggerate the looseness of Kerala villages, however. Hamleted and dispersed villages do not differ from each other as much as they both differ from the nucleated type. Despite their apparently random dispersal across the landscape, many Kerala houses *are* grouped into fairly distinct units in which people interact with each other more frequently than with outsiders. Nadur constitutes a geographical and political locale, with distinct shopping streets, a post office and government center, a main temple, an artisan caste compound, and a cluster of landlord estates. The main temple and landlord houses may have constituted the traditional authority center of the village which has now passed to the government *panchayat* office. Within Kerala itself, the degree of dispersion probably varies from the highlands where villages tend towards nucleated to the coastal areas where populations are dense and villages seem more dispersed. Nadur lies about half-way between the two extremes, but has many features of the hamleted village type.

## *Nadur Fits Midway into Kerala's Geographic Diversity*

Kerala can be divided into 3 broad regions, running north to south: (1) a narrow low coastal area a few miles wide, (2) low laterite plateaus and foothills from 62 to 185 meters elevation, and (3) the Western Ghats mountain highlands with peaks rising to 2,817 meters (Mencher 1966:137; Menon 1979:4-7). These regions are shown on Figure 2.1.

Each region has its own agricultural features. The lowlands provide abundant rice and coconut harvests, often planted in depressions close to or below sea level (Tharamangalam 1981:25-29). The highlands harbor tea and coffee plantations. Nadur lies in the central region, in the lower foothills of the Western Ghat Mountains. It contains intensive irrigated rice fields similar to the lowland areas, hillsides with cashew and coconut gardens more common in the central area, and some upland rubber and forest land like the higher elevations. Nadur thus incorporates geographic and production features found in a large number of Kerala villages.

## *Nadur Fits Midway into Kerala's Historical Types*

Kerala is made up of 3 pre-independence regions—Travancore, Cochin, and Malabar—each with a somewhat different history. Figure 2.2 shows the locations of these 3 historical units.

In Travancore, or southern Kerala, 19th century royal policies spread education and land ownership widely among the population. To the north in Malabar, British rule ignored education and enacted laws that benefited landlords, resulting in bitter struggles between tenants and rulers. Cochin followed behind Travancore both in education and land reform, but was ahead of Malabar. Nadur lies in the northern part of Cochin. Nadur is not a major center of Kerala's radical political movements. Peasant organizations and farm worker unions are not strong there. During the height of the land reform struggle in the 1960s, forcible seizures were not undertaken in Nadur, although they did occur in one nearby village and may have convinced Nadur's landlords of the inevitability of the reform. Nadur has supporters of both radical and conservative political parties. In the context of Kerala, Nadur has a

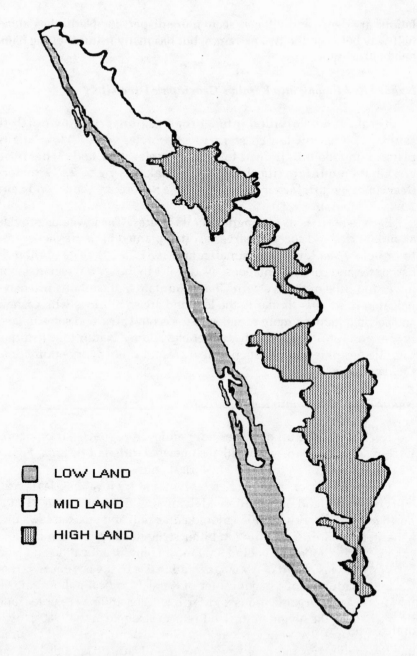

Figure 2.1  Geographical Zones of Kerala

medium level of political action with neither extreme apathy nor the high level of mobilization and polarization resulting from decades of militant caste and class conflict that characterize some parts of the state.

## Limited Middle East Remittances

In one important way, Nadur is at one end of a spectrum. Many Kerala coastal villages have been dramatically influenced by money earned in Middle East Gulf countries during the 1970s and 1980s. Workers sending back remittances or returning with savings that are enormous by Indian standards have built mansions and purchased VCRs, refrigerators, and other expensive consumer goods. The impact of this money on some villages statistically overwhelms any measurable consequences of Kerala's social and economic reforms.

In Nadur, only a few households have reaped the benefits of "Gulf Money," as it is often called in Kerala. Many Nadur villagers do work in nearby towns, in other parts of Kerala, or in the Tamil Nadu State metropolis of Madras. As we shall see in Chapter 6 (Table 6.3), remittances accounted for 11% of sample income in 1971 and 9% in 1987. We shall see in Chapter 8 how important these remittances are for particular groups. We shall also see that the levels of pay are within the range of local incomes and thus do not overwhelm the structural reforms.

## Outstanding Research Assistance

Nadur contains some of the finest and most experienced researchers an anthropologist could hope to find. Mencher's 1971 survey utilized the expertise of an art teacher whom she had come to know in 1962 and who supervised the household survey. In 1987 we were able to engage the same researcher to conduct the restudy. His son, who holds a B.A. in physics, became our major household interviewer while the father aided us in interpreting the data and developing follow-up questions for selected households. These researchers gave valuable insights and critical scrutiny to our data and analysis throughout the field study and afterwards via detailed correspondence and careful reading of our initial drafts. Midway during our fieldwork, we also benefited from the excellent research assistance of an economics graduate student from Calicut who lived from February through July with us in Nadur.

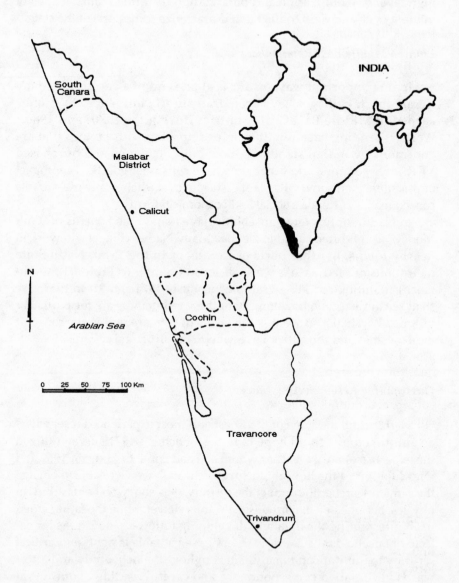

Figure 2.2   Historical Regions of Kerala

## The 1971 Household Survey

Mencher's 1971 survey covered 356 (63%) of 565 households listed in the Nadur census block by the 1971 Indian census (Government of India 1971:78). The questionnaire contained 84 items, several of which had multiple parts so that about 200 pieces of information were obtained. The survey included the following sections:

1. General information: caste, household size and composition, gender and ages of household members (10 questions).
2. Family planning practices and attitudes (13 questions).
3. Land ownership (13 questions).
4. Employees hired (16 questions).
5. Employment for others in agriculture (8 questions).
6. Other sources of income (2 questions)
7. Size and condition of house and other property owned (2 questions).
8. Adoption of new agricultural methods (13 questions).
9. Water and irrigation problems (5 questions).
10. Relation to government agricultural officers and attitude towards recent changes (2 questions).

Mencher's survey provides a "set of core baseline data" sufficient for a successful restudy (Wadley and Derr 1989:80-81; Foster *et al* 1979). The questionnaires retrieved enough quantitative information for statistical comparisons. They also include much narrative data that allowed us to construct economic histories of several households. These narratives appear in the household case studies in Chapters 9 and 12.

## The Sample

Mencher's 356 households do not make up a true random sample. A quantitative study should start with the drawing of a sample that can be assumed to represent the population of which it is a part without any unusual features (Rudra 1989). The only way to assure this is to follow formal random sampling techniques.

In the absence of a formal random sample, we employed 3 techniques to achieve the most representative sample possible: (1) we used the same approach to finding households that had been used in 1971, (2) we held caste ratios the same for both surveys, and (3) we compared the samples statistically with larger populations whenever possible.

(1) The 1971 survey was organized outwards from the house of the principle research assistant. In resurveying the 1971 households, we made an expanding set of circles outwards from the same house. When we saw that time was running short, we added outcaste households from 3 of the 4 outcaste colonies in Nadur by going to each from the closest to the farthest and interviewing whichever household heads or spouses were available. Any other sampling technique might not have been successful without greater time availability as the low-caste households are mostly made up of laborers who are not easily reached at home until late in the evening.

Our 8 months in Nadur allowed us to resurvey a 1987 subset of 170 households from the 356 households surveyed in 1971. For these 170 households, there were 160 data sheets for 1971. Ten new households had been created by partitioning when adult children moved into separate houses. We left the partition households in the 1987 sample; they represent a real process that took place between the 2 surveys.

(2) We held caste ratios constant across the 2 surveys. This limited the number of the categories to be compared. We shall see in Chapters 6 through 11 that the comparisons by caste are easier to make and to understand than those by class where the numbers do vary between the 2 surveys.

(3) We compared Mencher's sample and our 1987 sample with other populations. Because the 1971 survey was done in a year of the Indian census, we can compare her 356 households with the demographic data on the entire census block and the census block with larger nearby units such as the entire Taluk, or administrative region in which Nadur is located. Although these comparisons still do not create a true random sample, they increase our confidence that both surveys are fairly representative of Nadur and nearby areas.

One available comparison is the literacy rate. For the 160 households in the 1971 sample also resurveyed in 1987, the 1971 sample included 917 persons of whom 476 were literate, or 52%. For the entire census block of 565 households 1,676 persons were literate out of 3,343, or 50%. For all of the Taluk with 74 villages, there were 403,795 persons with 227,051 literate, a rate of 56%.

Another available statistic is household size. The 160 households of 1971 had 5.7 members on average while the Nadur census block as a whole had 5.9 (3,343/565). The Taluk included 68,515 households with 403,795 persons, or 5.9 per household.

The only available dispersion statistic from the census is the percent of the population belonging to "Scheduled" (former untouchable) Castes and tribal groups. (Other caste breakdowns are not given in the 1971 census.) For the 1987 sample, 10% of persons were from Scheduled Castes; for the 160 baseline households of 1971, the figure was 9%, for the entire 356 households of 1971, 8%, for the Nadur census block, 9%, and for the entire Taluk 14%.

We made several additional statistical comparisons. All convinced us that the sample population is representative of the local area. In Chapter 4 we consider the Nadur sample breakdown by caste compared with the most recent all-Kerala figures. In Chapter 5 we compare the occupational and ownership class distribution in Nadur and the Cochin region of Kerala. For both comparisons, we use the most relevant of available statistics.

### The 1986-87 Field Study

Prior to selecting Nadur, we examined data on 30 Kerala villages that had been studied between 1917 and 1971. We visited 3 other villages that had detailed baseline data. One factor in choosing Nadur was that the data on other villages did not lend themselves to following the histories of particular households. During preliminary visits to Nadur in October 1986, we took copies of the 1971 survey sheets and asked follow-up questions of 6 households. Because the principle village researcher from 1971 accompanied us and knew many of the households well, we could locate them easily, and he could explain our purpose to the potential respondents. Our initial visit convinced us that a direct, detailed, and meaningful comparison was possible in Nadur, despite the problem of the sample which we described above.

On 15 November 1986 we moved to Nadur. We lived there until 15 July 1987. Our household survey consisted of 6 separate parts: (1) the general survey, organized like the 1971 survey, (2) a general nutrition survey, (3) a food intake survey in February-March, 1987, (4) a food intake survey in July 1987, (5) height and weight measurements on 722 Nadur children both in and outside the sample households (which also helped verify the representative nature of the 1987 sample), and (6) second-round surveys of about 20% of the households to clear up inconsistencies, fill in missing pieces of information, or amplify the data. All questions were asked in Malayalam—the language of Kerala—but responses were written in English by our research assistants.

We phrased many of our questions in the same way as Mencher had. This reduced the problem found in some restudies where researchers are not certain they are measuring the same thing as the previous researchers whose questionnaires may not have been available (Wadley and Derr

1989:114). Our main questionnaire asked for about 300 pieces of information in 13 parts:

1. General information: caste, household size and composition, gender and ages of household members (27 questions).
2. Family planning practices and attitudes (10 questions).
3. Land ownership and land reform (15 questions).
4. House size and condition and other property (40 questions).
5. Marriage and dowry (8 questions).
6. Participation in government welfare programs (14 questions).
7. Income, debt, and savings (22 questions).
8. Organizations and attitudes (18 questions).
9. Rice land gained or lost in the land reform (land owners only: 40 questions).
10. Employees hired (34 questions).
11. Water and irrigation problems (27 questions).
12. Farming costs and returns (26 questions).
13. Adoption of new agricultural methods (18 questions).
14. Employment and wages in agriculture (agricultural laborers only: 27 questions).

### Quality Control of Data

One of the most difficult problems in anthropological research is the control over accuracy and reliability of data. We attempted to solve this problem by our questionnaire design, questionnaire review, a few "trick" questions, second-round interviews, and careful data entry and proofreading.

### *Questionnaire Design*

We phrased the 1987 questions so that the answers would be in small pieces such as "yes or no", or "how much," and as precise as possible except in a few cases where we wanted open-ended responses. For example, we did not ask the research assistant to find out how much rice land the household owned. Instead, we asked a series of questions: "How many cents of 3-crop (2-crop, 1-crop) rice land does your household own? Where is this land located? Do you own land in any other village?" For each question eliciting quantitative data, we attempted to direct the respondent to the precise information we desired. This made the questionnaire long and detailed, but reduced the chance of misunderstanding by the respondent or of carelessness by the research assistant.

## Questionnaire Review

Within a week of each questionnaire, we went through all the responses, typing summaries and looking for vague, missing, illegible, or seemingly impossible entries. We went over all problem answers with our research assistants. They would explain or correct what was written, or we would mark the information for a second-round interview.

## Quality Control Questions

We also asked a few questions designed to trick respondents who were possibly giving uninformed or misleading information. The most difficult area was household income. On the main questionnaire, we asked several questions to elicit this data. On the nutrition surveys, we asked respondents how much money they had spent on food during the previous 7 days. Part-way into the research, we entered the income and expenditure data onto our field computer and compared responses on these questions. In some cases, the amount spent on food multiplied by 52 weeks was far greater than the household earned or too little for the number of household members. This led to second-round questions that produced upward revisions of the household income or downward revisions of the food expenditures so that the ratios fell within an acceptable range.[1]

## Second-Round Interviews

One of the most valuable techniques was the revisit to about 20% of the sample households. In some cases we corrected data, and in most we gathered much additional information. Some second-round interviews were based on the interest which the household held rather than on data inconsistencies. We reinterviewed the landlords who lost in the land reform as well as several farm laborers who were participating in government programs to improve their lives—all these because of their inherent interest for our study. The nutrition surveys gave us a chance to ask even a few "third-round" questions to certain households.

## Limiting Emic/Etic Discrepancies

Answers given by respondents cannot be automatically considered the most appropriate for the outside researcher's needs. Marvin Harris calls the respondent's answers "emic" or internal data and the explanation of the outside researcher "etic" (1979:esp. 32-35). While emic and etic are often the same, they can be very different, even opposed. Finding a difference is itself of scientific importance. Respondents could be lying, unconsciously repressing uncomfortable information, or interpreting the interviewer's questions differently from what the interviewer thinks he or she is asking.[2]

Through our questionnaire design and in our observations, we attempted to keep emic and etic levels separate. We experienced 3 important emic-etic discrepancies. In Chapter 5 we will see that our definition of social class leads us to label some households differently from their own perceptions. Some households gain most of their income from sale of house compound crops such as coconuts, but no member of the household considers himself or herself to be a farmer. In Chapter 7 we show that former tenants often describe only part of the pre-land reform rent for house compound land. The records of 1 important landlord indicated that money was demanded and paid along with the vegetables recalled by informants. Failure to include the money results in underestimating the redistributional effects of the reform. In Chapter 8, we will see that household membership can include or exclude an absent member working outside Nadur but sending money. As we will show, for some purposes it is more informative to include the members, for others we leave them out. Finally, in Chapter 8, we shall also see that respondent perceptions of unemployment do not sufficiently indicate its harmful effects. By creating an etic definition of the unemployment level for each rural labor household, we can more accurately pinpoint relations with other household variables such as income and number of dependents.

Other emic-etic discrepancies include membership of some Nair households where husbands live part of each week in their maternal homes (are they household members or not?), and whether the coconut trees owned by a household are yielding or not—an important emic distinction which we had not considered in drawing up the questionnaire.

### Limiting Researcher Bias

One of the most difficult problems to solve in field research is that of researcher bias. Our research assistants were thoughtful, educated, intelligent, and scrupulously honest. They were all from high caste, well-off households, however. Could their own social position influence their interview techniques? We attempted to check for this possibility by frequently going over questionnaires and probing for possible influence of the researchers' attitudes towards the people they were interviewing. This seemed especially important for the lowest caste households where the likelihood would be greatest for prejudices to creep in. In a small number of instances, we uncovered minor examples of such bias and arranged to redo some questions with careful preparation in the second-round interviews.

Researcher bias is just as important in the analysis stage. With narrative notes it is tempting to ignore contradictory statements and emphasize remarks that support our hypotheses. With quantitative data, bias can also be introduced by skewing assumptions or manipulating variables.

To reduce or eliminate our own bias, we employed 2 techniques: blind data entry and conservative assumptions. By blind data entry, we mean that we collected and entered into our notes and computer database all quantitative data without knowing what it would tell us on most major points. We entered and proofread the income data prior to making any runs to see whether income inequality had declined in the period between Mencher's survey and our own.[3]

After seeing that inequality indeed seems to have declined as we show in Chapter 6, we to set up the analysis in Chapters 7 through 11 with conservative assumptions. This strategy should be most apparent in Chapter 7 where we limit our analysis of the land reform to what we think could be the minimum possible effects. Since those minimum effects are strong, we consider our conclusions justifiable. We also state the assumptions underlying our statistics so that the reader can judge independently whether we have produced a minimum-effects analysis. Much recent anthropology has touted non-scientific and non-objective orientations.[4] We hope our methods will help students and others see the rewards of a research strategy where the process of data-gathering, data-analysis, and conclusions are spelled out explicitly.

### Time and Language Constraints

Many anthropologists consider that 2 years is about the appropriate amount of time for conducting village research in a culture distant from one's own. We were able to live in Nadur for only 8 months. We could not gain the degree of confidence or the experience with people in Nadur that would have come with a second year there. Part of this liability may be offset by the skill of our research assistants, the fact that 2 of them were lifetime residents of Nadur, and our frequent correspondence with them, to correct and supplement our data.

Anthropologists also know the importance of speaking and understanding the language of their informants. We began our study of Malayalam in 1985, and achieved limited speaking, reading, and comprehension before our arrival in Nadur. But our very limited knowledge of the language means we had to rely primarily on the English translations of our research assistants. These may have been precise, but we cannot independently assure it.

## *Data Entry*

The computer can manage enormous amounts of data. It can also be a mechanism for error. The "1.5" that gets entered as "15" or ".15" affects all kinds of quantitative conclusions. We used database entry control techniques wherever possible, such as putting maximum and minimum levels on data entry that would flag or refuse to enter data outside the range. In addition, we entered our data slowly and carefully, although this delayed by several months the beginning of our data analysis.

We also proofread every data file with 2 people. One read the entries aloud from either the questionnaire or the computer print-out while the other watched for mistakes the computer could not be programmed to catch. Despite all these procedures, we still found a few errors late in the analysis and had to correct some of our tables and other statistics. Because we employed quality control procedures throughout the study, we believe the data are substantially accurate.

## Units of Analysis

Measuring inequality over time requires choosing appropriate units to compare with each other. First the basic unit must be chosen. The main 3 possibilities are (1) the household, (2) the person (per capita), and (3) the standard person (adult equivalent).

## *Why the Household?*

We chose the household because total household income captures the phenomenon of "start-up" costs which a household of any size must cover: a house, house compound, cooking equipment, etc. The household is also the unit which directly experienced the land reform. Household income is the easiest of the units to understand. With the household as our unit of analysis, we can also construct combination indicators such as the ratio of workers to dependents within the household.

We shall use these combined indicators, especially in Chapter 8, to connect households' membership patterns to their economic conditions.

Choosing the household blurs the effects of variations in household size and composition, however. A way around this problem is to divide household income by the number of household members. This choice has the disadvantage of blending the start-up costs into the per capita income.

An even more refined unit is the "Adult Equivalent" (AE). As defined by the Indian Council of Medical Research (ICMR), 1 adult equivalent is equal to 1 "average adult male doing sedentary work" (Gopalan *et al* 1985:10). Additional units in tenths of an adult equivalent can be added for moderate and heavy labor. Tenths of an equivalent are subtracted for individuals using less energy such as females and children ages 12 and below. To these official designations, we added units for pregnant and lactating females to reflect their greater energy needs. The adult equivalent ranges from a maximum of 1.6 units for an adult male heavy worker to 0.4 units for a child 1-2 years. Because rural third world households spend most of their income on food, the adult equivalent is especially useful for nutritional computations. In Chapter 10, we substitute the adult equivalent as the unit of analysis for the Nadur nutrition surveys (especially Tables 10.9, 10.10, and 10.11).

To check for effects of the choice of units, we ran almost all computations for households, per capitas and adult equivalents. The 3 units produced very similar outcomes.

## Quintiles

To measure inequality among households, we chose the quintile, or 20% unit of the sample population. For the 1971 data, the 160 households divide into 5 quintiles of 32 households each; the 1987 sample of 170 divides into 34 households per quintile. These are ranked from richest to poorest, or from largest landowner to smallest. Because each quintile has the same number of households, we can use its percent of total sample income to measure the overall degree of inequality. If perfect equality existed, each quintile of households should have 20% of the total sample income. The degree to which the various quintiles diverge from that assumption measures the degree of inequality.

## Caste and Class

Beyond the general mathematical measurement of inequality among quintiles, we are also interested in the degree of inequality among actual socioeconomic groups. In Nadur the main forms of inequality are **caste** and **class**. The definitions and sizes of the castes and classes will be given in Chapters 4 and 5.

## The Statistics Used in the Study

We used a variety of statistics in analyzing the data. Some points could be argued with raw numbers, averages, and percents, that will be familiar to all readers. Other points required more complex statistics including correlation coefficients with significance numbers, regressions, analysis of variance, the Gini coefficient (Gini index) of inequality, indexes of change over time, and ratios of a group average to overall sample average. Readers who know about these statistics may wish to skip to Chapter 3.

### Raw Numbers, Averages, and Percents

The numbers recorded directly into the questionnaires are raw numbers. They include the household incomes, land owned, calories by household, and amounts of land received in the land reform. Averages appear throughout the study: average household income in 1971 and 1987, average income, land ownership, education, or land received in the land reform by caste, class, or income quintile or other group where relevant.

### Correlation Coefficients

Raw numbers, averages, and percents cannot tell us the degree of association between 2 variables. Correlation coefficients do this. Correlation coefficients appear as numbers between minus 1 and plus 1. The scale below can be used to explain how we interpret them:

-1................-.45.........0.........+.36................+1

A correlation of minus 1 is shown at the far left. This means that 2 variables are perfectly correlated in a negative way: for each acre more of land, there is 1 kilogram less of low-cost ration shop rice. At the far right we have plus 1, a perfect positive correlation: for each year more of education of the household head, the household might have 1,000 rupees more income. In the middle stands zero: no correlation at all. The age of marriage of children in the household bears no relationship to the number of coconut trees owned. The use of correlation coefficients usually involves 3 steps: (1) the suspicion that a relationship exists based on general knowledge of the variables, (2) the computation of the mathematical degree of the relationship—the correlation coefficient—and (3) confirmation or rejection that the suspected logical relationship is the one actually being measured by the coefficient.[5]

Perfect 1-to-1 correlations are very rare. We shall see in Chapter 7 that the 2 large landlord households had almost a plus 1 correlation between land owned and income in 1971 and almost a minus 1 correlation in 1987. Zero or near-zero correlations are common, however: much statistical research ends up showing that not much of a relationship exists between 2 variables. Zero and near-zero correlations are often not presented since they indicate lack of relationship. Sometimes the absence of a relationship is important, however. In Chapter 7, we shall see that the correlation between land owned and income was nearly zero for the main landowning Nambudiri caste in 1987. This near-zero correlation, combined with other information, indicates that the land reform pulled loose the ties between that caste's income and its land owned.

More common are correlations from about ±0.20 to ±0.60 in social science data of this kind. On the scale above, we see a correlation coefficient of plus 0.36. This coefficient is taken from Chapter 7 where we see that the amount of rice land owned correlates +0.36 with income *for the 61 rice land owning households in the sample*.

To the left of the zero, we see the correlation coefficient minus 0.45. This coefficient from Chapter 10 expresses the relation between years of education and number of children borne by females in the Nadur sample.

*Understanding Correlations.* Correlation coefficients are measures of statistical association. They do not consist of actual units of either of their variables. They are not pieces of land, rupees of income, or numbers of children. We can best describe them as high (about 0.8), medium (about 0.5) and low (0.3 and below) (Downie and Heath 1983:103). In social science research, medium correlation coefficients are common (Downie and Heath 1983:104).

What do these coefficients mean in terms of the variables, then? With at least a medium coefficient and some other information, we can assume a significant linear relationship.[6] If we can also reasonably assume which variable is independent (causal) and which dependent (caused), we can compute a 2-variable regression equation. This equation does estimate the relationship in units of the variables.[7] We also get some additional information.

Let us consider the coefficient of +0.36 above. Regression analysis shows that the relationship between rice land owned and rupees is such that each cent or 1/100 acre of rice land creates 45 rupees income after or on top of an income of 4,306 rupees.[8] The income of 4,306 rupees is the income we expect if the household owns no rice land.

For the birth and education correlation of minus 0.45, we find that each year of education produces 0.3 fewer births below 5.1 births.[9] We expect women with no education to bear 5.1 children. A woman with 3 years education would have 4 children instead of 5. A woman with 6 years of education will have only 3 children; with 9 years education, 2 children. The correlation coefficient and the regression equation operate only within certain limits. No matter how many years of education, no women will necessarily have zero children. Somewhere at the extreme of the pattern, the correlation effect will break down. Because the interpretation of each and every correlation coefficient requires that we interpret at least 1 regression equation, we often prefer simply to discover whether we have a high, medium, or low correlation coefficient. In later chapters we will give the regression equations when they add important information to the analysis; otherwise, we will only present the correlation coefficients to indicate statistical support for our statements.

*Statistical Significance of Correlations.* Correlations can tell us the degree of association between 2 variables. A medium or high correlation coefficient—interpreted carefully—usually means that 1 variable is influencing another enough to be of interest, to require an explanation. One way to verify this is to compute the *significance* of correlation coefficients. Significance numbers tell us the probability that the correlation coefficients we computed might be due to chance rather than a likely causal relationship. The lower the chance probability, the higher the probability of causation.[10] Significance numbers are based on the sample size and other factors in the computation. We make use of 2 common significance levels in this study. For probability of -.01 we mark the correlation number with a single asterisk*. This means that in fewer than 1 case in 100 cases is the correlation due purely to chance. For probability of -.001 (fewer than 1 in 1,000 cases due to chance) we mark the correlation coefficient with a double asterisk**. The correlation coefficients in the examples above—on land and income and on education and births—with their significance markers attached, are 0.36* and -0.45**.

## Multiple Regressions

Correlation coefficients work best with only 2 variables. Sometimes we need to examine the relationships among 3 or more variables. A common procedure is called multiple regression. This statistical procedure results in a formula with a dependent variable that is partially explained by about 2 to 5 independent variables which are adjusted in relation to each other as well as to the dependent variable.[11] Multiple regressions can be very complex to put together in a reliable way even though the microcomputer can quickly come up with the computations.[12]

We ran multiple regressions on most of our data, but decided to present and discuss them only in a few places where they add meaning beyond what we can get from correlation coefficients. In Chapter 10, we employ multiple regressions to produce a formula explaining calorie intake in the 2 nutrition surveys. In Chapter 11 we go beyond the 2-variable relationship between years of education and number of children. With years of education alone we can explain 20% of the variance of births. The multiple regression in Table 11.10 shows that 41% of the variance in number of births can be accounted for with a combination of 5 interacting variables: age, age of marriage, years of education, household income, and whether the mother is a member of the Ezhava caste. Greater age, greater income, and Ezhava caste membership pull towards having more children. Greater age of marriage and more years of education pull towards fewer children. Older women have had more children than younger women, Ezhava caste women have more children than we would expect based on the other factors, and women in higher income households have a slight tendency to have more children. The later the age of marriage and the greater the number of years of education, the fewer the children. However, since only 41% of the variance can be explained with this regression, we must also conclude that other important factors remain to be discovered.[13]

## Analysis of Variance

Sometimes we want to find the significance of differences among groups. Analysis of variance, usually called ANOVA, allows us to compute this. ANOVA provides a statistical method to identify forces similar to correlations when the independent (causal) variable is a group such as a caste or class rather than a number. Although it is named "Analysis of Variance," ANOVA is really a method of comparing averages among groups (Downie and Heath 1983:198).

In Chapter 8 on Table 8.4 we see that several household demographic components vary significantly by the caste membership of the household. Correlation coefficients cannot be used to show this since they require that both variables be numbers. On Table 8.4, we have only 1 potential independent variable, so we call the analysis of variance a One-Way ANOVA.[14]

The one-way ANOVA consists of a ratio of the mean square of the deviation between groups to the mean square within groups. This ratio provides a value for what is called the "F-statistic," which has a known probability distribution that can be looked up on standard statistical tables.

On Table 8.4 we see that the number of dependents in a household varies significantly by caste. This is shown by the 2 stars above the dependents column. The actual significance is 0.0009.** This tells us that something about caste strongly influences the number of nonworking dependents in a household. With multiple regressions, we could eventually identify likely aspects of caste such as average income, traditional land ownership, age of household head, or some other factors or combination of factors that make caste such a force in influencing the number of dependents. Such an analysis, however, would be very time-consuming. The choice of whether to continue an analysis to deeper levels depends on what we want to explain. Since analyzing household structure is not a major goal of our study, we note in Chapter 8 simply that caste plays a statistically significant role in somehow generating the distribution of dependents.

An intermediate follow-up for a significant ANOVA is to specify which groups are responsible for generating most of the statistical significance. One method for doing this is called the Scheffe Procedure Multiple Range Test. Using this test for the dependents data on Table 8.4, we find that the Muslims on the one hand versus the Nair and Craft castes on the other, are the main sources of the statistical significance. This finding could lead us to a more detailed consideration of why these particular castes differ more than any of the others in the average number of dependents.

Chapter 8, however, is concerned with work and income, not primarily with household structure. Therefore, we pass over the ANOVA from Table 8.4 to concentrate on the etic dependents-to-worker ratio, which the ANOVA gave us cause to suspect would be significant also. Indeed, we find a significance of 0.0004** on Table 8.10 for etic dependents-to-workers by caste. The Scheffe procedure identifies the Pulaya caste as the major group, differing significantly from Nambudiri, Nair, Ezhuthasan/Chetty, and Craft castes. This finding verifies the underemployment of field laborers originating in part from their caste heritage as we will explain in Chapter 8.

## The Gini Coefficient

To measure inequality among the quintiles, we employ 2 procedures. First, we compute the total income per quintiles as percents of total sample income at each survey period. These percentages can be directly compared. By simple addition or subtraction of percentage points, we can see what has happened to the share of income garnered by each quintile. These statistics are used by many economists to measure the degree of inequality. We present these figures in Chapter 6 and examine them more closely in Chapters 7 through 11.

A more general statistic is the Gini coefficient. This coefficient provides in a single number the degree of inequality on a scale from 0 to 1, or—as more commonly presented to limit the number of decimal points—from 0 to 100.

What is the Gini? Technically, it is the area between the diagonal of perfect equality and the Lorenz curve of measured inequality. The standard formula for the Gini coefficient is $G = 1/2 \sum |X - Y|$ where X and Y are 2 sets of percentage frequencies (Reitsma and Kleinpenning 1985:374-375) that is, "half of the relative mean difference—the average of the absolute values [indicated in the formula above by the vertical bars] of the differences between all pairs of" whatever is being measured—relative to the mean (Jenkins 1991:15). The Gini coefficient can be computed more simply by taking any set of equal units such as quintiles or deciles (10% units) of a population. The cumulative sum of these percents is subtracted from the cumulative sum of observed percents of the total income or landholdings—the 2 features we shall examine in this study. The remainder is then divided by the product of 100 times the number of the equal units (10 for deciles, 5 for quintiles, etc.) minus the sum of the cumulative percents of the equal units.

With 10 percent units inserted into the formula the Gini becomes:

$$\text{Gini} = \frac{(\text{Sum of Cumulative Observed Percents}) - 550}{1{,}000 - 550}$$

The number 550 is the cumulative sum of 10%, 10 + 20 (10 + 10) + 30 (20 + 10)... + 100. The number 1,000 is the line of perfect *inequality*, or 100 times 10 (Smith 1979:364). Because both the 1971 and 1987 samples can be divided by 10 and we can get whole numbers, we can use this convenient formula. Our Gini computations are all done with deciles for greater accuracy, but we present the tables below in the quintile versions for easier reading. We have multiplied all Ginis by 100 to give numbers between 0 and 100.[15]

How do we interpret the Gini? A Gini of zero means perfect equality among the units measured (deciles, quintiles, etc.) while a Gini of 100 means perfect inequality, that is, the top unit has 100% of the income while those below it have none. The closer the Gini to zero, the less the inequality; the closer to 100 the greater the inequality.

*Understanding Ginis and Quintile Tables.* The Gini coefficient is a complex statistic. But it allows us to capture in a single number the measure of inequality overall for a sample population, making comparisons simpler. We will see in Chapters 6 through 9 how the Gini helps us measure the overall degree of inequality in the Nadur sample households.

Along with the Gini, we must keep a watch on the actual quintile tables, however. Since the Gini is an overall measurement, it does not tell us in which parts of the inequality distribution any changes have taken place. If wealth is redistributed from the upper quintile to the second highest, we are essentially measuring shifts from upper class to middle class. The Gini may indicate less inequality overall, but the poor have not benefited. Therefore, when comparing the Ginis, we shall also consider which quintiles have gained or lost income or land. In this way we can use the Gini to give a quantitative measure of overall inequality changes (if any) and derive from the quintiles which economic levels experienced those changes.

### Absolute Gain, Index, Ratio to Average

Groups such as castes and classes do not distribute themselves equally among a sample population, nor do they necessarily fall in correct ascending or descending order across inequality distributions to allow computation of the Gini. For these groups, we must employ other techniques.

One way to compare the 2 sample populations is to compute the average absolute rupees gain in income for each caste and class between the 2 survey periods. This tells us which castes or classes have improved their income the most or the least. But the groups did not have equal starting points. We can refine our measurements by dividing the groups' incomes in 1987 by that of 1971, and multiplying by 100.

This index tells us which groups have gained the most or the least *relative to their incomes in 1971*. Those groups with the highest indexes have improved their position compared to the groups with lower indexes. If the lowest groups in 1971 have the highest indexes, while those with the highest incomes in 1971 have the lowest indexes by 1987, we can say that inequality has declined, although we cannot say statistically how much in the absence of a Gini coefficient.

One further refinement is to compute the ratio of the average income for each caste and class to the average for the sample population overall at both survey points. If the lower groups have raised their ratio to average while that of the higher groups has declined, we can again say that inequality has declined. We shall make use of these indexes and ratios in Chapters 6 through 12.

## Data Analysis: The Basic Structure

Four types of analysis make up the basic structure of our study: (1) comparisons between 1971 and 1987, (2) comparisons with and without government programs, (3) program descriptions, and (4) household case studies.

### Comparisons Between 1971 and 1987

We take 1971 to be a year before the land reform was implemented. It is also before the Kerala Agricultural Workers Act (KAWA) was passed in 1974. Comparisons of the degree of inequality in 1971 and 1987 therefore tell us the effects of those 2 programs. The inequality data are presented in Chapter 6, the land reform is analyzed in Chapter 7, and the KAWA in Chapter 8.

### Comparisons With and Without Other Programs

Besides the land reform and the KAWA, we were able to assess government welfare programs, school and nursery feeding programs, and the subsidized food distribution in Nadur's ration shop. We make the assessment by showing the 1987 income inequality distribution in Chapter 6 first without and then with each of these programs. First we add welfare which is analyzed in Chapter 9. We then add the rupees value of school and nursery feeding programs to those households benefiting from them, adding last the rupees value of the food price subsidy from the ration shop. The different inequality patterns are introduced in Chapter 6. The effects of the food programs are analyzed in Chapter 10.

## Program Descriptions

We describe programs that do not lend themselves to the same statistical analysis appropriate for the land reform, the KAWA, welfare, or food distribution. In Chapter 9 we describe loans for house construction, purchase of animals, and public health improvements that are mostly available to low income households in Nadur. In Chapter 11 we show how education has expanded among Nadur households, but we did not find the expansion to be directly related to the changes in inequality by any simple statistical procedures. For that reason, we present the educational data and analyze it by itself.

## Household Case Studies

In Chapters 9 and 12, we examine the effects of reforms by summaries of the recent histories of several representative households. These histories show much about the conditions of household members that could not be derived from statistical analysis. The case studies are particularly useful for enhancing the statistics of the land reform, the workers' act, and wages and employment. We bring educational levels in a narrative way into these case studies to show that education is playing a role in household income histories. The case studies also illustrate more random factors such as timing, good or bad luck, all of which play roles in the lives of individuals and families.

Having summarized our methods, we are ready to look at the data. But first, we will describe Nadur village and watch its people living through a typical agricultural year.

### Notes

1. We resurveyed all households where reported food expenditures were greater than 90% of income. We also resurveyed those with expenditures below 50% if the total household income was below the sample average. We arrived at the 50% limit after calculating that households at about the sample average were spending about 75% of income on food, both as stated on the questionnaires and according to our computed ratio. Very high income households could obviously spend less than 50% of income on food.

2. One of Harris's own examples comes from Kerala where respondents

insist that they do not kill male calves—emic data. The etic ratio of 67 male calves per 100 females, however, can only be explained by selective male bovicide. The discrepancy led Harris to investigate further and discover that owners keep male calves away from their mothers' teats so they are more likely to die in the first year of life. Harris explains the pattern by the low demand in Kerala for male traction animals (1979:32-33).

3. We deposited copies of our original data at the Centre for Development Studies in Thiruvananthapuram (Trivandrum).

4. Clifford Geertz (1973 and 1983) proposes what he calls "interpretive theory" based on "thick description." Marvin Harris (1979:281) rightly describes it as a version of the "cultural idealism" of Talcott Parsons. Paul Shankman (1984) offers a sustained critique of Geertz's approach to which Geertz has chosen not to reply. Harris (1979) sets forth a case by case attack on what he calls the "obscurantism" of Marshall Sahlins and others whose work resembles that of Geertz. The essence of these and similar debates is whether the anthropologist supports his/her analysis with evidence and methods that could be verified by other researchers or whether one simply "interprets" whatever one chooses and leaves the reader to decide somehow if the data are representative, accurate, relevant, or appropriate.

5. This final step is necessary to reduce the chances of a false correlation where the numbers indicate an association being produced by other variables than the one chosen by the researcher. This step can include running additional variables separately, running multiple regressions with detailed residuals analysis to check for multicollinearity, and other techniques.

6. The technical definition of significance is given a few paragraphs below under "Statistical Significance of Correlations." We confirmed linear relationships by examining scatterplots of the data; we do not consider non-linear relationships in this study.

7. The correlation coefficients turn up as the standardized regression variables, or betas in the 2-variable regression results.

8. The constant is 4,306. The T-value is 2.938 (significance .0047**) for the rice land. The adjusted $r^2$ for the equation equals 0.11.

9. The constant is 5.13, the T-value of the years of education is -8.3 (significance 0.0000**), and the adjusted $r^2 = 0.24$.

10. We usually need to carry out additional tests to check for influence of other variables.

11. After 5 variables, additional explanatory power is rarely provided by further variables.

12. The once time-consuming computational work is easily automated on the computer. As a result, multiple regressions are likely to appear with greater frequency in social science literature.

13. We ran all regressions as forced entry, stepwise, and combination. The

stepwise regressions are presented in the text. We assumed a linear relationship (tested with scatterplots) and a least-squares regression line. Other more sophisticated techniques might raise the $r^2$ value, but might not add to our verbal understanding of the relationships. For example, we did not make variables into polynomials to straighten out the regression line and increase the $r^2$ since we cannot explain the common-sense meaning of such terms.

14. Statisticians recognize the ANOVA as functionally equal to a series of paired t-tests that are also often used to examine differences among averages (Downie and Heath 1983:199). When we need to evaluate more than one independent variable per dependent variable, we must use the multivariate analysis of variance, or MANOVA. ANOVA closely resembles single-variable regression while MANOVA closely resembles multiple regression (Pedhazur 1982). For this study, we use ANOVA for a single category variable with a single numerical variable, but we use multiple regression for more than one variable. We do this because once multiple regression is employed, we usually have both numerical and categorical variables, while with one variable, we can choose the correlation coefficient for numbers and ANOVA for categories.

15. Tables 7.1 and 7.4 use quartiles instead of quintiles. As we explain there, the sample of 48 landowners divides into whole numbers by 4 but not by 5. We used 1/8 units for the Gini calculations.

# 3

# Nadur Village

Kerala's capital city is Thiruvananthapuram (Trivandrum). From most of its hotel terraces or housetop gardens one can see in microcosm Kerala's 3 major geographical regions that we introduced in Chapter 2: the coast, the midlands, and the mountains, each a narrow strip running north-south for the 576 kilometers length of the state, which lies between 8 and 12 degrees north latitude. Looking due west to the Arabian Sea, one's eyes are drawn to an unbroken mass of coconut trees, their bright green leaves in rounded tops one next to the other. They are thick and almost uniform in shape and size, each tree about 100 feet high, some standing straight, others at nearly a 45 degree angle, bending gracefully over streets and housetops or towards the water's edge.

When one looks to the south or towards the central and northern parts of Kerala, the endless mass of coconut tops continues, up and down the beach as far as the eye can see. To the south is Kanyakumari (Cape Comorin), 86 kilometers distant where the Indian subcontinent gives way to the Indian Ocean on multicolored beaches. To the north, one sees Kerala's narrow alluvial coastline, only a few kilometers wide. The soil is rich and supports a substantial harvest of rice and coconuts. Farther up the coast, at Alleppey, the sea invades the land at many points, creating backwaters where boats are the main form of transportation and long canal-like seaways are dotted with the retting piles of coconut husks that are left for 6 to 9 months in the salt water and then dug out and scraped clean for the fibers that are spun into rope and woven into mats. Kerala's coir, or coconut fiber, industry, was one of its 19th century attractions to British and American investors, but today the industry languishes because of the competition from synthetic fibers. Farther north, the alluvial coastline is known as the Malabar coast, one of Kerala's most ancient areas of contact with the outside.

Farther east one sees the central strip of Kerala, a series of low laterite plateaus from 62 to 185 meters alternating with hills and valleys. In the valleys more rice is grown, while on the hillsides one finds gardens of coconut, bananas, pepper, ginger, jack fruit and mango. Cashew nuts and rubber are also grown in this area which extends most of the length of Kerala. Until recently the hills were covered with large patches of forest. Elephants carried lumber and wild pigs and deer could be hunted. Today, most of these forest areas have been cut for crop land. Some areas have been denuded by impoverished peasants or workers turned forest wood gatherers. These areas are now a source of soil erosion. Unlike most of India, which uses cow dung for fuel, Kerala cooks with wood fires. In this central region, a day's journey to the north, lies Nadur Village.

Farthest towards the east, stand the magnificent Ghat ("step") mountains. Peaks rise to more than 2,300 meters and harbor important temple and pilgrimage sites for the state's 60% Hindu population. The mountains were formerly the home of various tribal groups. During the 19th century these mountains were intensively developed by British tea and coffee plantation investors. Like the hillsides of the central strip, the mountains today are seriously denuded of their tree cover, and may be losing soil at a rapid rate. In 1905, 44% of Kerala was forested. By 1965 this had dropped to 27%, in 1973 to 17%, and in 1983 to only 7-10%. Experts fear that Kerala's decreasing rainfall may be due to the loss of mountain forests. Average rainfall has declined from the 1960s through the 1980s. Soil studies seem to confirm severe erosion in the Ghats. Kerala's once abundant water supply may have been destroyed by intensive 19th century capitalist plantation production combined with the desperate search for income from firewood sales by impoverished peasants and workers (Kannan and Pushpangadan 1988:A125-A126).

To get to Nadur, one can best take the train. Although Kerala's road length of 2,010 kilometers per 1,000 square kilometers is 5 times the all-India average and nearly twice the nearest competitor state of West Bengal (Westley 1986:313), congestion and the many forms of traffic make bus and taxi commuting both slow and dangerous. Kerala has the highest road accident rate in India.

Half an hour north of Thiruvananthapuram's Central Station we arrive at Varkala. Along the tracks some of Kerala's homeless squatters have put up cardboard shanties. Behind these are sturdier structures, and a central business district. Just down one of the main streets to the east, in front of a row of high hills, we see a sparkling dome of an unusual looking temple.

This is the burial site of Sri Narayana Guru, Kerala's great early 20th century social reformer and founder of the Ezhava Caste Improvement

Association, described in Chapter 4. Narayana Guru is commemorated at this large temple. All across Kerala one finds smaller neighborhood shrines with a seated figure of the guru inside and his famous slogan—"One Caste, One God, One Religion for Mankind"—painted outside.

An hour later, at Tiruvalla, north of the ancient coastal city of Quilon, the tracks turn inward and the train moves slowly along the edges of the central hill area, bypassing Alleppey and the heart of the lowland rice and coconut backwaters area. After 4 1/2 hours, it arrives at Ernakulam-Cochin, Kerala's major port, a city of more than 750,000 people, and, after 2 more hours, it reaches Thrissur (Trichur), the "town of the name of sacred Siva" (GOK 1962:1), a major tile producing industrial town and a center of traditional high caste Nambudiri Brahmin culture.

The Thrissur area contains some of Kerala's most ancient sites, known back to at least Roman times. Historians equate the ancient pepper and cinnamon port of Muziris with the modern Thrissur coastal town of Cranganore (Menon 1984:49). A little farther up the coast, near the town of Chavakkad, one comes to the Palayur Church. According to Kerala tradition, it was founded in 52 A.D. by the Apostle St. Thomas, making it one of the oldest Christian communities in the world. Nearby are the remains of a Jewish synagogue.

In Cranganore, one also finds the Cheraman Juma Masjid, or mosque. Built in 629 A.D. as an extension to a Hindu temple, it is considered the oldest mosque in India. The founder, Cheraman Perumal, is said to have met the prophet Mohammed on a trading mission to Jeddah where he was converted to Islam. (GOK 1980:41)

A few kilometers distant stands Guruvayur temple, one of the most famous in India. This temple is more than 6 centuries old, with sculptures of heads of elephants and bulls, and fresco paintings depicting the adventures of the Hindu *avatar* Arjuna (GOK 1981:38). In 1931 Guruvayur was the site of a famous *satyagraha* or "truth struggle" which involved the Indian nationalist leader Mahatma Gandhi. Low caste Hindus and their high caste supporters pressed for the opening of the temple to all castes. This was finally achieved in 1946 (GOI 1966:82). Guruvayur Temple hosts almost continuous prayer services and festivals and is a popular place for expensive marriages and celebrations of other major life cycle events for Hindus from throughout India.

From Thrissur the train continues north through the central midlands of Kerala. In the low areas are rice paddies, flanked as always, by coconut trees, but many of the hillsides have lost their tree cover. Thirty minutes north of Thrissur, we arrive at the Shoranur railway junction.

Now it is time for a bus or taxi ride to Nadur. The asphalt highway winds out of town towards the southeast and crosses over the *Bharata-puzha* river to the south. During the major monsoon of June to August, the Bharatapuzha is a giant muddy wash; in the late dry season from March through May the river dies down to a thin, clear stream in the sandy bottom. Trucks descend to the river bed to retrieve sand for concrete mixing. *Mahoots* lead their elephants into the pools of the wet bottoms where the giant animals are coaxed to lie down sideways to be brushed and scrubbed clean.

Across the bridge one passes a long series of shops, schools, and a hospital. As in so much of Kerala, the street bustles with the activity of small vendors with their metal pots hanging out in front of their shops. In the air are the pungent smells spices and, of meat hanging under the rafters of the butcher counters, of a large pile of limes standing next to a blender in which various fruit drinks can be concocted. At the right time of day, what seem to be thousands of students pour from the school ground on their way home. Many walk, while others with longer trips stand at the bus stops.

The drive continues south, passing the *Kerala Kalamandalam*, a traditional dance and music school established by the state's famous poet Vallathol Narayana Menon. Vallathol (1878-1958) was a man of many talents. He translated the *Rigveda* and *Ramayana* from Sanskrit into Malayalam. He wrote fiery nationalist poems including an homage to Mahatma Gandhi. He also strove to preserve and enrich the traditional arts of *Mohiniattam*—a folk dance genre—and *Kathakali*, Kerala's most famous dance-opera with its intricate movements, elaborate costumes, and plots from traditional Hindu literature. The Kalamandalam today is a major training center for Kerala's thriving traditional dance and music scene. Its students come from many parts of India as well as from Europe to learn the highly disciplined dance routines of ancient Kerala.

### Entering Nadur

A few kilometers south of the Kalamandalam, a large open field appears at a road junction. Here on Tuesdays is an animal market. It is surrounded by various house compounds enclosed in plaster walls on which are painted the ever-present Kerala political slogans and drawings including numerous hammers and sickles of Kerala's 2 major Communist Parties.

At the junction, the vehicle turns east toward the mountains. After a kilometer, the road becomes choppy and wet; a water pipe alongside has been broken for some time. We are entering the Moslem neighborhood at the western edge of Nadur. Women in brightly colored patterned skirts and blouses with colorful lacy scarves over their heads are lined up at a faucet. Each holds 1 or more aluminum pots that come to nearly a close at the top and then open again with a wide pouring mouth. These pots allow the women to carry water for long distances without spilling. If it is late in the dry season, many have walked 1 or 2 kilometers to the road from more inland house sites for a few liters of water for drinking and washing. Some are accompanied by young girls; men and boys rarely carry water.

We see a *madrasa*, a religious school on one side of the road. Although the Moslems in this part of Kerala are poor, many attempt to offer Arabic education to their children. For those who cannot pay for the religious school, the government public school is open to them, but is 2 kilometers away near the center of the village.

The vehicle now passes houses with mud walls. Every half kilometer or so is a small shop with tea, warm soda, plastic cups and buckets, and a few other household items, along with some local food supplies such as gourds and squashes. Most shops are at small junctions where dirt paths lead off from the main road. These paths are often wide enough for a taxi to enter, but they may not be passable at the height of the rainy season.

After a turn in the road we have a magnificent vista of rolling hills and valleys, and suddenly we realize that the vehicle is moving along a ridge top. Below in the distance we see rice fields lined with coconut trees. Houses stand scattered on the hillsides. Most appear to have permanent tile roofs, and a few are clearly quite large. Some have 3 stories and 1 or 2 boast water tanks on their roofs. Both telephone and electric power lines lead along the roadside into the village.

After 2 kilometers the road comes to a 3-way junction with a large and beautiful banyan tree as a divider. To the left a dirt road branches off and a small thatch-roofed shop stands with the word *arrack* written in Malayalam. This road connects 1 of the Pulaya outcaste colonies to the village. The arrack shop serves a locally grown rice or coconut liquor.

The vehicle turns right along the paved road and we arrive at a small business district: 2 tea shops, a 1 room post office, and the village Panchayat, or government headquarters. Here the village Chief Executive Officer works with his staff and a number of elected counselors from the village neighborhoods. A few hundred meters and a Y-junction is reached. To the left the road passes the village library and the school. Farther down that road is another outcaste colony on rocky terrain where even coconut trees do not thrive.

The 2 tea shops at this junction are small, 1-room stalls with open front walls giving them a porch-like appearance. On the meter-high front wall are brightly colored posters advertising Malayalam movies. Most have mildly titillating scenes of scantily-clad Indian women. In the morning, many men stop at these shops on the way to work for a glass of tea costing 1/2 rupee. Some also purchase fried flour dumplings called *dosai*, or steamed flour *iddilies* for another rupee, served up with a spicy vegetable sauce called *sambar*. An even spicier thin "pepper water" called *rasam* is often part of a Nadur meal. The well-known south Indian *mulligatawny* soup is derived from the Tamil-Malayalam word *mulaku*, meaning "pepper," and Tamil *tawni*, meaning "water."

Although the village library subscribes to several daily and weekly papers, it is in the tea shops where most men seem to do their reading. The shops subscribe to 2 or 3 Malayalam language papers brought by the early morning bus. While sipping their tea and eating their doshas, men talk about the weather, the harvest, recent movies, and what is in the papers.

The availability of newspapers in the tea shops and the high literacy rate in Kerala are part of the state's lively and active political life. Party leaders spend much time in the shops defending the views put forth in their papers and attacking those of opponents. Women are mostly absent from the tea shops.

Our vehicle turns right and we begin a kilometer long descent of a hill with spectacular views of the rice fields below and row after row of hills in the distance behind. Near the bottom we pass Nadur's *Ayurvedic* Pharmacy, run by a former low-caste household that now does well from this business. Ayurvedic medicine derives from ancient Hindu theories about the nature of the human body, going back to well before 500 A.D. when they were more or less formalized in texts. According to the Ayurveda, good health depends on balances of 3 "humors" within the body: wind, fire, and water. Diet, enemas, induced vomiting, surgery, life style advice, and various pills and powders are used by ayurvedic physicians (Jefferey 1988:43-44; Murthy and Pandey 1985). To Nadur villagers, as to many rural Indians, ayurvedic medicine is more available and substantially cheaper than Western medicine. In addition to the pharmacy, there are at least 2 ayurvedic doctors in Nadur. Although there is no clinic or hospital within the village, hospitals are located within 2 to 5 kilometers in neighboring towns.

After passing the pharmacy, the vehicle crosses a lowland rice field. We stop to inspect the electrical transformer on the main post in the middle of the field. This is the Nadur substation, the last link in a long line of wiring that brings limited current to the village. In the 1987 Nadur sample, only 24% of households actually had electricity.

Looking up the valley, we see it is flanked by the most splendid of Nadur's houses, many of them 2 and 3 stories tall with tile roofs and large front and side gardens. These are the homes of the Nambudiri Brahmins, the Thrissur area's traditional landed elite and temple priests for Kerala Hindus. These Brahmin houses have the best views, access to cooling winds during the hottest part of the year, and, because of their low placement on the hills, wells that never run dry. The houses face onto the rice fields traditionally owned by that family so that they could watch their tenants and farm laborers from the verandahs.

One section of the hillside is crowded with smaller houses and fewer coconut trees. This is the craft caste neighborhood. Here live the carpenters, blacksmiths, and goldsmiths. Some of the Pulaya farm labor caste houses are grouped on hillsides behind the Brahmin mansions. The laborers' household names are derived from their former Brahmin overlords.

## Nadur's Main Temple

On another side of the field, we see a 3-storeyed building several hundred feet long built in a square around a central pond. This is Nadur's Hindu *ambalam*, or major temple. Like many village temples in India, it is several hundred years old and contains beautiful stone and wood carvings. Part of the temple building was used for rice storage prior to the Kerala land reform. Temples in Kerala sometimes served as conduits for Brahmin households to control rice land. Brahmin priests were fed at the temple from the produce of the lands it controlled. Today the temples are run by a government-appointed temple board and have significant secular input into their management. They are gathering sites for the many festivals of the agricultural year. Nadur's ambalam is dedicated to Lakshminarayana, another name for Vishnu. As with many Indian temples, this one has associations with local deities that can be incorporated into the Hindu pantheon without difficulty. Alongside the Vedic Siva and Vishnu, Nadur residents also worship Baghavati (Kali), the Malabar-Cochin goddess of war, smallpox, and soil, and Ayyappan, the god of forests, hills, and wild animals. Some households venerate ancestors at shrines inside their houses and others have set small outdoor stones on platforms for gods specific to their caste. Nadur's ambalam was opened to all castes in 1951 along with the 5 smaller temples dispersed across the village.

The temples also provide certain community services. Nadur's Lakshmi temple has a large pond in the center courtyard where people

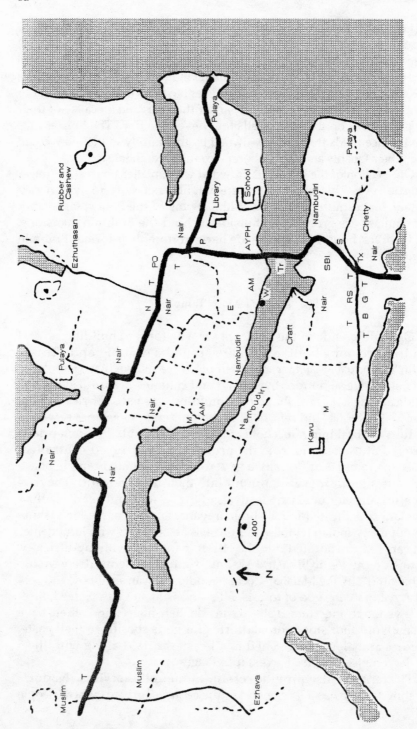

Figure 3.1  Nadur Village

# Key to Symbols on Figure 3.1 as Described in Chapter 3

| | paved road | P | Panchayat office |
| | dirt road | Tr | Electrical transformer |
| | rice fields | PO | Post office |
| – – | pathways, lanes | RS | Ration shop |
| AM | Ambalam (major temple) | SBI | State Bank of India office |
| Kavu | Kavu (minor temple) | T | Tea shop |
| A | Arrack shop | Tx | Taxi stand |
| AYPH | Ayurvedic pharmacy | W | Well open to community in dry season |
| B | Barber shop | | Hilltop |
| E | Ethnographer's residence | | |
| G | Goldsmith's shop | | |
| M | Maidan or open field for animal grazing and public events | | |
| Nair, etc. | Caste neighborhooods in residential areas | | |

can bathe. Another large temple, farther up the valley, has a pond outside the walls as well as a large grass field that provides a grazing area for animals.

Our vehicle crosses the rice fields and climbs up a gently sloping hillside. We pass the village branch of the State Bank of India and several small newly-built houses that are part of Kerala's ambitious program to build decent quarters for its poorest farm laborers. With 250 square feet of floor space, 3 rooms, a hard foundation, cement floor, sun-dried brick walls, and a tile roof on hardwood beams, each house is a vast improvement over the mud floor, 1 room, thatch walls and leaf roof structure it replaced.

## Nadur City

After 1/2 kilometer we arrive at another hilltop. A 4-way junction appears with a taxi stand and 1 taxi waiting at the corner. Nadur's only taxi and 1 of 2 automobiles in the village, it is owned by a local merchant. A business area with about 15 shops heralds our sighting of what villagers call "Nadur City." A mailbox, a tailor's shop, a goldsmith, the village ration shop, and several tea shops and provision shops line the dirt road. There is also a barber shop, complete with a real barber's chair, an electric fan to cool the customer, and life-size girlie wall posters with Western women in various stages of undress and mildly erotic poses.

The paved route follows the hillside down towards the interior and on to the next village. At the far end of the shopping area—only about 200 meters long—there is a small rise in the ridge, some grazing land, and at the very top a small Hindu shrine to Siva.

The shrine, a *kavu*, or minor temple, is built on the top of one of the highest hills in Nadur, in the shade of a large banyan tree. The outer platform is about 2 meters high and 20 meters on a side. In front to one side is a large carved linga. The temple itself is an L-shaped structure 5 meters wide at the front, 10 meters at back, and another 10 meters across at the longest part of the L. In the front is a gate behind which a small platform stands which has the altar. To the side is a latticed wall with 3 linga-shaped tablets inside. In the back is a small porch. During festivals kerosene or coconut oil lamps are hung all along the edges and around the gateways, somewhat as American-style Christmas lights are strung along the roofs and sides of homes and businesses. The flickering oil lamps create a more mystical touch than electric lights.

## A Walk Through the Lanes

From the temple we walk down the hillside to a narrow lane flanked on both sides with mud walls. Part of the descent is steep; rough steps have been cut in the soft rock. We pass houses with tile roofs and cement foundations with plaster over brick walls. Smoky fires at the back signal women working in the kitchens. Quarters are close and the wood fires produce serious air pollution. Respiratory diseases are a major problem for Kerala women. Plans have been made for high-efficiency *chulahs* or ovens, but few have yet been introduced.

Each courtyard in this area is about 10 meters per side. These are the craft households. The goldsmith's house is by far the best in appearance with glass windows in the front and a newly painted verandah. Just behind are 2 blacksmith houses, 1 with thatch roof, the other tiled.

At the bottom of the hill we look straight across the rice fields to the opposite hill. About 100 meters of rice plants are crisscrossed by a few narrow dikes and a 5-meter-wide *thodu*, or canal that provides water for the minor monsoon crop planted in October and harvested in January. As we start across the fields we notice a stream of people walking in small groups along the middle of the fields toward the road where they branch off in several directions. Some carry umbrellas to ward off the hot afternoon sun. Even at 4:00 or 5:00 p.m. it can be punishing. Others have 40 kilogram sacks on their heads, filled with rice, or several liters-full containers of kerosene for lighting their electricity-less houses at night. Many of the items were purchased at the ration shop.

We come to the middle of the rice valley and see that it extends nearly as far in both directions as our eyes will take us. In the far eastern edge some low hills break up the valley. To the west we see only rice flanked by coconut trees right to the horizon. As the sun sets, a spectacular light show takes place in dry season Nadur above the rice fields and the coconut trees. The rice fields glow a brilliant fluorescent green while the sky lights up with opalescent blue, pink, red, and purple.

We come to the edge of the fields and notice a large open well. It is 2 meters on a side. In the rainy season, water is almost at ground level. As the dry season progresses, this well is one of the few in this section of Nadur that continues to have accessible drinking water. The table may drop to 7 meters below the ground, and people will leave a bucket and rope for public use. But many will walk 1 or 2 kilometers twice daily by April and May to get a few liters of water to drink and wash with. The well is on the property of a wealthy Nambudiri Brahmin household. Nothing is charged for its use.

We look up the hillside and see the large house of the high caste family whose well this is. The Nambudiri house is 1 of the largest in Nadur. Like most other Brahmin caste homes, it is multi-storied, with a fine verandah with tile floor and a wonderful cool breeze off the rice fields even in the hottest time of year. Inside are 12 rooms including one filled entirely with religious artifacts and used for prayers. Behind is a private pond for bathing. The house stands on 2 acres of land with many coconut, mango, teak, and other trees.

In front of the verandah of this house has been set a group of stones shaped like an eagle. On a platform like this in a nearby field in 1975 a 12-day vedic "ritual of the fire altar" was performed by local priests at the request of foreign researchers who filmed the event. More than 10,000 people attended the final day of the ritual (Staal 1983).

As we continue up the hill, the lane turns left and we enter a much poorer neighborhood. The houses here have 2 or 3 small rooms and courtyards of only 5 meters on the front and 10 to the back. The house must fit in this area, leaving room for only 1 or 2 coconut trees and only rarely enough for a mango or other economically valuable tree. Yet here and there we see a slightly finer house, and sometimes a cow or goat tethered at the side. This neighborhood is mostly Nair caste households whose adults work as field laborers in the rice season or house compound workers during the dry season. Here many houses are without verandahs or have only a small patch of hardened earth in front under a roof overhang to use as a place to catch a cool breeze during the hottest times. We see no electrical lights here; only the dim flickering of the oil or kerosene lantern. Looking through the front doors and glassless window openings, we see almost no furniture, not even chairs or tables. People sleep on coir mats and eat sitting on the ground.


### The Seasons at Nadur

Our visit shows us Nadur's beauty along with its dependence on the land. Life in Nadur is governed by 2 major sets of events: the agricultural cycle and the Hindu festival year. Nadur villagers have several methods of time reckoning. Following Hindu traditions, they consider overall time infinite. To Vedic priests, one year for the God Brahma equals 311 trillion human years. Many such Brahmas have been and will be (Padmanabha Menon 1986:262). The more modest Kerala Malayalam calendar dates from the Christian year 825 A.D. or Hindu Kali year 3,926 when King Udaya Marthanda Varma revised certain elements of the traditional Hindu calendar then in use, based on astronomical observations combined with the signs of the zodiac, (Padmanabha

Menon 1986:265). By subtracting 825 years from the Christian calendar, we arrive at the year in the "Malayalam Era," or M. E. The calendar established in 825 created a year with 365 days, corresponding to that now in use in the West, but maintained many other features of local Hindu and Kerala traditions. Days are broken down into 60 *nazhikas* of 24 minutes each, the precise opposite of the Western way of thinking of 24 hours each of 60 minutes. The Malayalam nazhikas are broken into 60 *vinazhikas* then 10 *gunitam*, 4 *muhurtha*, and 8 *noti*, or "snappings of the fingers." Because the Malayalam months are grouped by the signs of the zodiac, they fall almost exactly in between the lunar months used in the West. Thus, the Kerala new year begins in the month of Chingam under the sign of Leo and corresponds to the last half of August and first part of September. Dhanu is governed by Sagittarius, starting in mid-December and running into mid-January. High-caste priests are responsible for the knowledge of the Malayalam months that govern Hindu rituals. Moslems follow their religious leaders for ritual events. Both the Western and Malayalam calendars are used for government records.

Agricultural and religious events are coordinated through the Malayalam calendar. Here is how the year proceeds at Nadur.

### Onam: The New Year and Harvest Festival

The Malayalam new year comes in late August or early September. The major rains have fallen during June to August, on average 2,200 mm. (GOI 1966:8). This southwest monsoon produces the *virippu*, or autumn rice crop. It is the largest. People have been waiting for the skies to clear and the harvest to be brought in. The *Onam* new year festival spans several days with games, sports, festive meals, special food and clothing allowances at the ration shops, and beautifully arranged flower designs at the house front or in the courtyard.

The floral patterns are said to be welcoming signs for Maveli, an ancient Kerala king whose story lies behind the Onam events. During Maveli's reign, Kerala was free of inequality, crime, injustice, poverty, and all other social evils. So just and successful was this king that the gods became jealous. Vishnu incarnated himself and tricked Maveli. Appearing as a small boy, he asked the king to grant him all the land he could cover in 3 footsteps. The generous king agreed, but then the small boy grew suddenly to such a size that he covered the entire universe in just 2 footsteps, placing his foot for the third step right on top of Maveli's head. Before being pushed down to the underworld, Maveli asked for, and received, the right to visit his people in Kerala once each year (George 1983:184; Iyer 1981, vol 2:67-68). Thus, when the granaries are full, the skies are clear, and the flowers and trees are in their fullest bloom, Kerala's people celebrate the harvest, the new year, and the memory of a glorious past.

## Mundakan: The Little Monsoon Rice Season from October to January

Soon after Onam, it is time to plow, hoe, dike, ditch, smooth, and plant the rice fields for the *mundakan*, or winter crop that will be harvested in January. In October and November, the retreating northeast monsoon deposits an average of 469 mm. of rainfall in Thrissur District (GOI 1966:8). A stream runs down the long valley between Nadur's 2 ridge tops, providing irrigation water for 2/3 of the fields. With a smaller area to cultivate, farm labor opportunities are less than in virippu. Yields average only 69% compared with the virippu season planting.

Field preparation, planting and cultivating costs are paid at 20 rupees per day for men and 12 for women. Plowing costs 50 rupees per day for bullocks and 80 rupees per hour for a tractor that farmers can rent with driver from a nearby village. Farmers say the tractor does a better job and is ultimately cheaper; one result has been a severe decline in plowing opportunities that previously had supported some low caste households. Preharvest cash outlay runs at about 1/6 of the gross return if rains are normal and if insects or birds do not get too large a share.

Harvesters are paid in cash or unhusked rice that averages about 1/6 more of the gross. Planting, transplanting, weeding, and harvesting are done mostly by women; men do the plowing, ditching, diking, and smoothing. In January the women harvesters return from the fields with their heads nearly hidden by the sheaves of rice they are bringing in for threshing. Their pay is measured in fixed containers held by the owner. The *para* (7.2 kilograms) is the standard unit. For smaller amounts, owners use the *idangazhi*, 1/10 para, and the *naazhi*, 1/4 idangazhi.

## Tiruvatira

The January harvest does not produce such a grand celebration as Onam. The end of the mundakan rains brings on the long dry season that lasts until late May or early June.

During the Malayalam month of Dhanu (December and January), Nadur villagers celebrate *tiruvatira*. This festival commemorates the death of Kamadevan, the Hindu Cupid, who gave up her life for love (Fawcett 1985:299). In Nadur, it is a special ritual of the Nair caste and is understood also as the birthday of the god Siva. The festivities also contain elements of an American Halloween in the taking of food or money by children and of "Mardi Gras" in the disobeying of certain traditional caste rules.

In Nadur, the 1987 (M.E. 1162) tiruvatira began on the 30th day of Dhanu, January 14, at 2:00 a.m. Twenty Nair caste boys from our local neighborhood arrived on the verandah of our Nambudiri landlord's house, shrieking and making dramatic begging motions of the hands. They were dressed in elaborate costumes of dried banana leaves. One carried a cane, wore a mask, and acted crippled. Our landlord made a contribution of 10 rupees. The contribution was duly noted in a ledger book which the youths suddenly produced. In earlier times, such children would not have been allowed on the premises of their higher caste neighbors. But in costume, and with a special religious purpose, the caste barrier could be temporarily lifted. In 1987, the caste barriers had long been officially abolished.

The following day, the festival passed to the women. In some villages, tiruvatira is celebrated by loud singing of groups of women at the bathing ponds, the use of bamboo swings, and generally gay and unrepressed behavior from the gender that does not usually act in such ways in rural Kerala. Nadur held a more sedate ritual. In mid-morning, women gathered at different homes where they chewed betel nut preparations that are normally only for men. The betel nut produces a mild high after which the women turned to some altars in the home and prayed for long lives for their husbands. Taking betel once a year is said to be good for one's married life.

Later that second evening, women gathered again and sang and danced on the verandahs both religious and secular songs. The dancing was initially subdued: the women took 2 or 3 steps in 1 direction, bowing in rhythm to the singer's beat, sometimes clapping hands together with the woman next to them, then returning only 1 or 2 steps backwards so that a circle slowly wound round clockwise.

After 20 minutes, things livened up. Secular, happier, faster, and more rhythmic dancing started. There was much laughter and clapping of each others' hands now. This went on for more than an hour.

At this dance, 3 different castes were present, touching each other, dancing, and singing together. In the distance we could hear wilder drum sounds from other neighborhoods.

## The Early Dry Season: January and February

During and just after tiruvatira, farmers harvest the mundakan rice crop. January gives several days' harvest and threshing labor to Nadur farm workers. As the grains turn brown and the plants begin to bend and sag on the fields, harvesting women appear in small groups. They work the fields of landowners. Of 61 rice-land-owning households in the Nadur sample, 33 do only supervising work. They own on average 1.1 acres each compared with 0.63 acres for the 14 households that both work on and supervise other laborers on their rice fields and 0.55 acres for the 14 households that do all the work on their rice fields. Those who only supervise work no days on their fields as laborers; households combining supervision with household labor average 13 days agricultural labor on their fields. Those who do all the work themselves put in 31 days labor to produce their crops. Harvesters' children miss several days of school at peak labor times to help their parents. The long dry season is beginning: it is a time of plenty tempered with anxiety.

Days begin to warm up through February. Wealthier households hire laborers to repair fences, plant vegetables in the house compound land, or pull down coconuts or the ripened mangoes from the compound trees. For the poorest farm workers, February and March are 2 of the most difficult months. Days are hot and dry, work peters out. Food is mango stew, mango curry, mango pickle, fried mango, mango snacks, and mango dessert. From December through February, only 52 mm. of rain fall; from March to May there will be 403 mm., but most of that falls in May. As the dry season progresses, water tables fall. Some wells dry up altogether on the highest parts of the ridge where many of the poorest households live. Day by day, more poor women appear at the Nambudiri wells at the edges of the brown and dusty rice fields. In March goats graze the stubble of the mundakan rice harvest. Landowners who can see their fields from their cool verandahs call out to children playing soccer or cricket on the fields "Adu, Adu—goat, goat." They are supposed to chase them to another field, but usually they are chattering and running and pay no attention to the calls. By April the goats can find no more stubble to graze. Still there are no clouds in the sky. Temperatures rise at 4:00 p.m. to 105 degrees Fahrenheit, dropping only into the 80s at night. Sleep is difficult. Work is hard to find. Without the sufficient supplies at government-controlled prices at the ration shop, many poor families would fail to eat on many days during this time. As we shall see in Chapters 8 and 10, even with the shop, some households do not get enough.

The long dry season at Nadur provides good reasons for Kerala's attachment to the coconut: this crop comes in during the very portion of the year when rice is most difficult to obtain. In Thrissur District, 50% of all coconuts are harvested during the months of February through May (GOI 1966:27). Since a coconut tree can yield 10 nuts per month during this period, even a poor household with only a single tree derives substantial nutritional benefits from it. The leaves can be used to repair the house. Some families are able to sell the harvest. At 4 rupees per nut, 3 trees can provide 120 rupees per month, enough money to supply the annual food needs of 1 adult member of the household.

Eighty-one per cent of Nadur sample households owned at least 1 coconut tree in 1987. One household had 75 trees; the average number was 7. Most poor households owned 1 or 2: the 32 households (19%) having no trees suffer during the long midlands dry season.

## *A Dry Season Wedding*

The early dry season is a time for weddings. The cool, dry air combines with the nearness of the January harvest to offer a time for public ceremonies of this kind.

Nadur marriage ceremonies are greatly influenced by the wealth of the families involved. Rich Brahmins hold ceremonies lasting several days with lavish feasts and prolonged and expensive religious rituals. Poor low caste farm laborers hold brief, simple events. For those with even a bit of money, at least some crowd of friends and relatives will be invited, musicians and fancy dress employed, and some food offered.

Nadur marriages are mostly arranged. A very small percentage of "love marriages" occur, but these are usually without parental consent and do not receive public celebration. The average age of marriage in Nadur is 27 for men and 19 for women. The male average is higher than the 1981 Indian average of 23, but Nadur women equal the all-India average and are below the Kerala state average of 21 years (Franke and Chasin 1989:88; see also Tables 11.7 and 11.8).

Astrologers are consulted to determine whether a proposed union is auspicious. A latent function of the use of astrologers is that either family can back out of the marriage for almost any reason including displeasure by either partner after they meet. The astrologer discovers inauspicious elements in the horoscopes: the marriage is canceled.

When the wedding takes place, a canopy covers part of the house compound courtyard of the bride's family. Floral designs on the ground reminiscent of the Onam decorations designate an altar. Small piles of limes, incense sticks, flowers, and fancy cloth surround a 2-liter cooking oil can filled with rice stalks. The foods are fertility symbols. Nearby stand several *vilaku*, or coconut oil lamps to be lit during the brief formal ceremony.

The groom's party arrives down the road, accompanied by 1 or more drummers and Indian oboes, the *nagaswara*, or "snake voice." The groom and his followers enter the canopied area where the bride's party greets them. They are seated on the fancy cloths. After a few short prayers, the groom places a string or necklace around the bride's neck. This *tali*, or thread tying, is the traditional act of marriage among many Kerala castes, although it is said to have originated among the Nairs. It was previously part of a child marriage ceremony which betrothed a 10-year-old girl to 1 of her uncles for ritual purposes. When older, she had great sexual freedom, including the opportunity to select lovers from among Nair and Nambudiri Brahmin men. Because the traditional Nair kinship system was matrilineal and women lived together and held property in common in their lineage, it was not necessary to know the identity of the biological father. We shall describe Nair marriages and household structure in more detail in Chapter 4.

Today's marriages are greatly modified by a series of British and Indian laws pushing the system towards a patrilocal nuclear or extended family. The bride and groom most likely move to his parents' house until the new family accumulates enough wealth to construct a new house on the parental compound. The wife thus moves in with her husband's parents and other relatives where she becomes part of a crowded environment of strangers. If she is from Nadur, she can visit her own family fairly easily, but many marriages are arranged from other villages and she may face a period of adjustment in her new house without much social support from her existing friendship and family networks. In the village, she will probably not work outside the house unless the family are mostly agricultural laborers or unless they are from professional groups such as teachers where the woman's income-earning potential may have played a role in the match. Among 164 marriages over the past 30 years for which we collected data, 37 (23%) included payment of a dowry. Money, gold, jewelry, or a plot of land have been used as dowries in Nadur.

Following the tali-tying, bride and groom may also exchange rings after which people lightly knock together the newlyweds' heads and join them in smearing sandlewood paste on each others' foreheads. The entire formal ceremony of arrival, tali-tying, head-knocking, and sandlewood paste smearing takes only 15 minutes.

Now it is time to eat. Guests are seated on the ground in rows with banana leaf plates and rented plastic cups before them. Water or tea may be served along with rice and several curries and pickles dished out of aluminum buckets by passing "waiters" from the bride's family who move along the guest rows with giant ladles. Food is eaten with the right hand.

After the main course, a moderate to wealthy wedding will include Nadur Nambudiri *payasam*, a sweet rice pudding made with jaggery, a sugar produced from coconut sap turned to toddy and then cooked down to a thick molasses. If possible, milk will be added to make the payasam rich and delicious. Nambudiri men specialize in festival and wedding cooking for a fee. This work helps them compensate for their losses in the land reform. Foods are prepared in enormous vats brought to the site for the occasion and cooked over wooden or charcoal fires. Several castes may eat together, breaking older traditions prohibiting the interdining of castes.

After the meal, guests line up at buckets where waiters pour water over their outstretched hands for cleaning. Guests leave behind small contributions of money. These are auspicious if in uneven amounts. Better to give 59 rupees rather than 60. Better yet to give 61!

### Puuyam: Subramanian's Birthday

In mid-February, just before the dry season begins to pinch incomes and create water problems, Nadur celebrates *puuyam*. This festival honors the birthday of Subramanian, the son of Siva and Parvathy, 2 important Hindu deities. Subramanian rides a peacock, a bird which eats snakes. His father Siva is often symbolized by the snake.

In Nadur in 1987, the puuyam committee was headed by one of the village goldsmiths, who arranged the first stage of the festival at his house late on the night of 11 February. Men gathered in front of the house while women and children huddled together on the sidelines. Inside, Nambudiri priests chanted vedic prayers while making offerings to fires burning in coconut oil lamps. They smeared their foreheads with sandlewood paste. Following this, men began shouting and twirling furiously in the front courtyard.

The men's enormous headdresses were made of flowers. Many were higher than the dancers. They came in beautifully colored combinations, shaped like tops, and made a spectacular sight. With 10 such whirling dancers and several drums beating and nagaswaras blowing, a state of ecstasy and excitement was quickly reached. The dancing went on for hours.

The next morning, the dancing continued, followed by a procession of musicians and onlookers who paraded through the village lanes, across the rice fields, and past each of the major temples where they stopped for several minutes to twirl as on the previous night. They were joined by a *panchavaadyam*, or 5-piece musical group consisting of drums, trumpets, nagaswaras, and string instruments. The festivities moved on to the village center on the north ridge between the post office and panchayat office where a crowd of several hundred watched the music, the twirling, and each other. A few enterprising snack sellers appeared with fried goods and drinks. The ceremony finally died out in the afternoon at one of the other temples.

### March-April: The Dry Season Turns Hot and Difficult

In March and April, clouds begin forming as the searing heat over the Indian Ocean sucks huge amounts of moisture upwards. Slowly the monsoon drifts north and east towards the Indian subcontinent. As the monsoon gathers, heat and humidity turn Nadur into an oven of unpleasant days and oppressive nights. Laborers find no work. Farmers tap their harvest supplies. Those with government salaries or private sector employment in tea stalls or other establishments are best off since they have regular cash incomes during this trying time.

Each day brings more women to the few wells that still have water. Morning and evening they come, lining up behind others who arrived before them.

### Puram: Birthday of Ayyappan

Times may be difficult for many, but *Puram* must be celebrated. It is the birthday of Ayyappan, the god of the local temple. A village committee has been working for weeks to prepare the day's events. Rice and flower designs are laid out before gates in a fashion similar to that of Onam. Contributions are collected: 51 rupees is the recommended amount, but many of the poorest villagers contribute less or even nothing.

April 12 was the day for Nadur Puram in 1987. The celebration began at the Siva kavu above Nadur City. Members of all castes were present. A hired troupe of panchavaadyam musicians played. Three elephants stood facing the shrine, "caparisoned," with gold coverings draped over their backs and heads and running down their trunks. Their front feet were chained at a distance allowing them to walk but not run. On their backs sat men with ornate umbrellas. When the trumpets called out over the drums, the riders stood, lifted the umbrellas, and held up ceremonial spears and shields, the latter beautifully designed with animal skins and bird feathers of different colors.

Suddenly a deafening blast pierced the festive atmosphere. Rocket fireworks exploded 20 meters in the air, spreading smoke over the crowd.

Just after noon, the musicians, elephants, and riders led a procession down the grazing field in front of the shrine. They passed quickly through Nadur City and turned north towards the rice fields, passing the bank, the electrical transformer, the Ayurvedic pharmacy, the village office. Slowly, noisily, they made their way to each of the main temples, ending at the one farthest from the center of Nadur where 2 large fields flank the temple. Here fruit sellers had set up watermelon stands, nut confectioners wrapped a handful of peanuts in a small piece of newspaper for 1 rupee, lime drinks were available, and cheap plastic toys and other small shop goods were on sale. For this one time in the year, even ice cream could be purchased in Nadur.

The fireworks continued at this *maidan*, or temple ground, for hours. Five hundred people took part. Finally the elephants and the musicians departed. Darkness fell, but kerosene and gas pressure lanterns appeared, making this a night for staying out at Nadur. As the evening wore on, many went inside the temple walls where they sat, prayed, talked, laughed, but did not sleep for the rest of the night. Ayyappan's birthday had its cost. Rental for each elephant was 700 rupees, with a few hundred more for the musicians and the fireworks. Altogether the formal costs of the festival must be equal to the average annual per capita income of 2 Nadur households. Puram creates much excitement and joy, however. Perhaps it is a necessary diversion to prepare for the April heat and time of work shortage. For some villagers, the loud rocket blasts help open the skies for the monsoon, telling the storm gods where to bring their rains.

### May-June: The Big Planting

The heat becomes more oppressive. For the poor, water is a major daily task. Women walk up to 2 kilometers in the morning to reach a functioning well, then carry their containers of precious liquid back to the house. In the late afternoon they repeat the ordeal. As the water situation becomes more desperate, a rich high-caste household arranges privately for a deep bore to be dug into the rock behind their house. For 2 days the motorized drill goes down, finally hitting the water table 50 meters below the surface. The family's own diesel motor pump is hooked up to the long tube. The starter is tugged, and suddenly water flows copiously from the spigot. Every day a government truck comes to the house to collect thousands of liters of water to be driven to various locations in Nadur at specified times. For a while, the women's walk for water has been shortened while the high-caste household has made a contribution to the welfare of the poorer groups. The son in this high-caste household is a local leader of the Communist Party-Marxist. As leaders of the newly-elected state government, they have pinpointed the

provision of water as a major short-term goal. Meanwhile, the
Panchayat officer eagerly awaits a drill-rig that is to put in more permanent and public water access such as a tube well right in the Panchayat
office garden centrally located in Nadur. The officer wants another well
dug from the highest point of the village so that the piping system, in-
stalled a few years ago, can be used to bring water to the main road at
intervals of a few hundred meters where faucets already are in place.
The lowest caste households, far from the main road, will then have to
walk only 1/2 kilometer for their water. If the drill rig comes, much of
Nadur's suffering can be removed; but this season it does not arrive.

As the rain clouds gather in late May, the humidity rises and life
becomes ever more lethargic. With temperatures over 100 degrees
Fahrenheit and humidity nearing 100%, the great monsoon is clearly
approaching. Late afternoon is sunny and bright and even a bit cool.

Landowners call their workers. Workers come to the owners' homes
looking for work. The tractor or animal plowing was done in early May.
Now it is time to hoe and seed.

A late May planting operation may include additional plowing. The
animals drag the plow diagonally across the previously plowed and
furrowed fields. The soil is remixed so that different layers contribute
their unique minerals and bacteria to the top levels. The soil absorbs
oxygen. Fertilizer is laid down.

On one field an old man appears. His 2 oxen tug slowly at the plow.
He moves across the half-acre field of the landowner at 4:00 p.m., taking
45 minutes to replow. Shade from the coconut trees make the work less
exhausting.

Then he moves out with a coir basket filled with seed saved from the
previous harvest. He is well over 60 years old, but the muscles on his
body look strong and sturdy. He wears no shirt and ties up his Malayalam *lungi* or sarong so he can hunch down close to the earth. He flings
out the seeds in semicircular patterns with his hands.

The shadows lengthen, the afternoon turns cool, the planter finishes
his work and begins whipping his oxen forward towards the road from
which he will turn them homeward for feeding and bedding down.
Once he did many such fields for several days in May; now the tractor
has replaced him and his oxen on most fields.

### The Monsoon Arrives

In early June thick black clouds move across the village. The rains
are late this year. The air is so heavy it seems hard to breath. Without
warning lightening flashes crackle almost to the ground; the peal of
thunder seems right next to one's ears. Water pours from the sky; it falls

so hard that some power above the clouds seems to be pushing it down with a force to send it through to the underworld where Maveli lives. Is Vishnu the god of the monsoon's water?

The rains stop. Sometimes for an hour or two the foggy denseness lifts a bit. Other times the earth just steams. Then the rains come again; sometimes with sharp bolts of lightening followed by incredible thunder blasts; sometimes quietly with nothing but the sound of water dripping and pounding, splashing, running, and gurgling.

For 2 months and more the rains pour down on Nadur. The lanes become so slushy that walking requires constant energy to pull up one's feet from the sucking mud. The coconut trees bend and sway in the winds and rains that batter their top leaves. The rice fields fill with water to a depth of 15 centimeters. The overflow runs down the valley. Everything seems to be covered with fungus; villagers report the cobras are coming out of their holes along with numerous other dangerous reptiles and stinging insects. It is hard believe that this is the season for which people had yearned.

On the paddy fields, green shoots appear. Each day they seem to grow to almost twice their previous size. Still the waters pound down.

The rice reaches a height of 1 meter. Men and women appear on the fields, sometimes adjusting the height of the dikes so that water will flow more or less, other times pulling the weeds that might compete with the precious food stalks, planted 25 centimeters apart.

Gradually the rains diminish. In August blue sky appears in the afternoon, stars are visible at night. The rice flowers and then the grains appear at the end of the stalks. The rice plants start to lodge or fall; the fields are drained by cutting into the dikes next to the *thodu*.

The rice browns and suddenly rows of women appear in the fields, cutting the stalks with sickles. While the harvesters bend gracefully over the landowners' produce, Kerala's magnificent green parrots sit plaintively on coconut tree crowns, on the branches of banyan trees, on the electric power lines, awaiting their share. Another Malayalam year has passed; it is *Onam*.

Now food is abundant; the ration shop has special offers of cooking oil and cloth. Flowers bloom everywhere in tropical abundance in bright orange and red and purple. Maveli's great sacrifice is recalled. Reverence combines with dancing and games and feasting in an atmosphere of life and vibrancy that is a fitting memory to the great ancient mythical king—and also to the hard-working farmers and farm laborers—the ones who make the land fertile and yielding as no king has ever done. They now celebrate briefly the material rewards of their hard work this season. Perhaps they reflect too on their decades-long political struggles for justice and a greater share of Kerala's substantial bounty.

# 4

# The Castes

## Caste in India

Caste is an Indian-wide system of traditional social inequality. The castes of India constitute a giant classification system in which all people were traditionally placed. Each person is born into the caste of his/her parents. In the past and to a certain extent still, your caste determines whom you can marry, what kinds of work you do, which religious rituals you perform, which gods you worship, to which people you owe special duties, how others treat you and think of you, even how your body will be dealt after you die. The caste system penetrates all aspects of Indian life.

A major function of the caste system was to sort people into categories of wealth and status in a highly *un*equal way and then to provide social and religious justification for that inequality. One way of doing this was through the concepts of "purity" and "pollution." The highest castes were the richest, most powerful, and *pure*. The lowest castes were impoverished, powerless, and so dirty or polluted that higher castes considered them literally "untouchable" or even unapproachable within certain distances.

## Analytical Importance of Caste

Knowing the castes in Nadur is important for analyzing redistribution. Castes are legal, religious, kinship-, and status-based units. They can also be considered as emblems of the particular expected life style of their members (Béteille 1969:46, 190-191).[1] Castes are *emic*, known and understood by their members. Castes are related to classes, but are fundamentally different analytical units. Castes are *closed* groups.

## Table 4.1
## Caste in India and Kerala

| All-India Caste Categories | Typical Occupations | Main Kerala Names |
|---|---|---|
| Brahmins | Priests, Landlords | Nambudiris, Tamil Brahmins |
| Kshatriyas | Warriors, Administrators | Kiriyattil Nairs |
| Vaisyas | Artisans, Traders | Kammalans; for traders, no precise equivalent; the functions are filled by Christians and Muslims |
| Sudras | Cultivators, Servants | Nair Sudras (Lower Nairs) |
| "Unclean" Castes: | | |
| [No apparent All-India term] | Tenants, Servants | Ezhavas (Iravas) Tiyyas |
| Untouchables | Farm and Menial Workers | Pulayas, Cherumas |
| | Tribal Peoples | Live separately from Larger Society |

*Note: According to the 1981 census, as many as 105 million Indians belong to formerly untouchable or related groups (Joshi 1986:3).*

Although castes may attempt as whole units to change their ritual position, individuals only rarely move into or out of castes.

A simplified picture of India's caste system is given in Table 4.1. The highest caste is the Brahmins. They hold the most sacred place in Hindu rituals. In many rural areas, the Brahmins also were and continue to be the main landowners. They were thus generally the wealthiest and most powerful group, though only a tiny portion of the population.

Below the Brahmins, people were grouped in descending order of Hindu "purity"—and wealth and status approximately—until the bottom group was reached. These were the untouchables. In addition to the ritual and religious connotations, untouchables were so named also from the dirty and demeaning work they did. This included agricultural field labor, handling corpses of animals or humans, washing menstrual garments of high-caste women, and cleaning feces from the latrines of higher caste households.

Untouchables lived in extreme poverty in outlying "colonies." They had no political rights and were considered disgusting and immoral in their behavior by the higher castes.[2] The untouchables, however, did much of traditional India's basic labor and thus produced much of the wealth others enjoyed. From the privileged Brahmins at the top to the underfed untouchables at the bottom, the caste system enforced and perpetuated rigid control.

## Caste in Kerala

Of all the regions of India, Kerala had the most rigid and elaborate caste structure. The 19th Century Indian reformer Swami Vivekananda called Kerala "a madhouse of caste." In Kerala, enforcement of caste privileges went further than anywhere else. The requirements of the system to demean and degrade those at the bottom can be seen in the following partial list of behavior demanded of the lowest castes:

1.   They were tied or bonded to particular high caste households for whom they were always on call as laborers or servants.
2.   They lived on land owned by the master households and could be evicted at will if they displeased them.
3.   They were forbidden entry into the main Hindu temples.
4.   They were not allowed to bathe in the temple ponds.
5.   They were not allowed in the public markets.
6.   They were not allowed to put gate houses at the entrance to their garden plots.
7.   They were not allowed to have tile roofs on their houses.
8.   They were not allowed to wear shirts, blouses, or a covering cloth above the waist.
9.   They were forbidden to come physically within prescribed distances of higher caste members and could be punished by death

for violating this taboo. This "distance pollution" was more developed in Kerala than in any other part of India. Mukkuvan fishing caste members and Kammalan or craftspeople, for example, could approach up to 24 feet of a Nambudiri, Ezhavas only to 32 feet, Pulayas to 64 feet, and the very low caste Nayadis only 72 feet (Mencher 1965:167; Fuller 1976:35).

10. They had to use extremely self-debasing forms of speech when talking to members of castes above them.
11. They could not take water from wells belonging to other castes...

(Fuller 1976, Iyer 1981, Mathew 1986, Mencher 1980a, and Unni 1959).

These restrictions were deeply humiliating. But, as with modern racism, the caste system entailed grinding poverty and exploitation.

Despite decades of sustained struggle against caste discrimination, Kerala, like the rest of India, still suffers consequences of the traditional caste system. Analytically, *caste is still a relevant variable because it measures the effects of the accumulated privileges and disabilities of the past*. At the highest and lowest levels in particular, caste correlates with class and with income. In the intermediate castes, things are less clear.

To gain insight into the caste effects of Kerala's reforms in Nadur village, we shall describe the major castes in Nadur. Then we shall compare their percentages in Nadur with the all-Kerala population for the two most recent dates—1931 and 1968—for which all-Kerala caste breakdowns are available. This will help us to know what the caste names imply traditionally and to see how representative Nadur Village is of Kerala State.

## Castes in Kerala and Nadur

No Kerala village contains a precise microcosm of the castes found in the state. Nadur village contains a representative sample of the castes in fairly similar percentages as found more generally.

The last Indian Census to include data on caste membership was in 1931. The most recent caste breakdown for Kerala was done in the late 1960s and published in 1970 as the *Report of the Backward Classes Reservation Commission*, on appointment of the Government of Kerala. It is also known as the "Nettoor Commission Report" (Nair 1976:3 and 33). The castes are comparable to those in Nadur.

Table 4.2 summarizes the percentages of the various castes in Kerala and Nadur. Overall caste percentages are fairly constant from 1931 to 1968 in Kerala as a whole. It is reasonable to assume that caste ratios in Nadur have also remained stable.

From Table 4.2 we can see that Nadur has more Nambudiris and Nairs than the Kerala average. It has fewer Muslims and Ezhavas. None of Nadur's three Christian households in 1971 were included in our 1987 sample. Representation of other castes is pretty close to the all-Kerala figures. Except for Christians, Nadur has a representative sample of Kerala's main castes.

We present the major castes in Nadur throughout this study from highest to lowest in the traditional ritual hierarchy. Middle caste groups such as Ezhuthasan, Craft, Ezhava, Chetty, and Muslim offer no clear-cut ritual order (cf Radhakrishnan 1989:31-41), but the position of Nambudiris, Ambalavasis, Nairs, Ezhavas, Mannans, and Pulayas are well established historically (Fuller 1976:33-38; Gough 1961:306-314; Jeffrey 1976:11-26).

## Nambudiri

These are the Brahmin priests and traditional landlords. Nambudiris are one of the best studied castes of Kerala. Their name is thought to derive from the word *nambuka*, meaning "trust" and *tiri*, meaning "sacred" (Iyer 1981:170). They may have come to Kerala as early as the 4th century B.C. and were almost certainly present by the 8th century A.D. (Mencher 1966:185). Nambudiris constituted a landed aristocracy that controlled vast wealth until the land reform undercut their control of the rice fields and house compounds of their lower caste tenants. When being addressed by lower castes, Nambudiris were given special linguistic honors. A Nair, for example, addressing a Nambudiri, would call himself *atiyaan*, or "foot servant." He would call his loin cloth "an old cloth" while referring to the Nambudiri cloth as *vastram*, or "white or superior cloth." (Iyer 1981, vol 2:279) Unlike Brahmins in other parts of India, Nambudiris did not officiate at life cycle ceremonies for lower castes (Mencher 1966a:187), but kept to themselves in their manor-like estates (*illams*) or in the temples where they were served by special temple caste assistants, the *Ambalavasis* (see below). The Nambudiri routine included prayers and other rituals for much of the day and evening. Because only the oldest son could marry and inherit the family property, land was kept unpartitioned for centuries. Kerala in the early 20th century had an almost intact feudal aristocracy. Unmarried men lived in bachelors' houses, or *pathayapura*, engaging in sexual liaisons

Table 4.2
Castes in Kerala and Nadur
Percent by Caste in Kerala, 1931 and 1968
and the Nadur Sample, 1971 and 1987

| Caste | Kerala 1931 | Kerala 1968 | Nadur Sample 1971/1987 |
|---|---|---|---|
| Brahmin (Nambudiri) | 1.7 | 1.8 | 7.6 |
| Ambalavasi (Variar) | 0.4 | n.a. | 1.2 |
| Kiriyattil Nair | 2.5 | n.a. | 3.5 |
| Nair Sudras | 13.4 | 16.7 [a] | 44.1 |
| Craft | 3.7 | 3.8 | 6.5 |
| Chetty | 0.5 | 0.4 | 3.5 |
| Ezhuthasan | n.a. | 1.3 | 4.1 |
| Muslim | 16.3 | 19.1 | 12.9 |
| Ezhava (Thandan) | 20.8 | 22.2 | 7.6 |
| Mannan | 0.9 | 0.4 | 2.4 |
| Pulaya (Cheruma) | 8.6 | 7.9 | 6.5 |
| Christian | 20.4 | 21.1 | 0.0 |
| Tribal Peoples | n.a. | 1.3 | 0.0 |
| Totals | 89.2 [b] | 96.0 [b] | 99.9 [c] |

Sources: for 1931, Fuller 1976:37; for 1968, Nair 1976:3
*Notes*
a. *The 1968 number is for all Nairs without regard to subcaste.*
b. *Totals for 1931 and 1968 do not add to 100% because of castes and Scheduled Tribes which cannot be identified or placed with larger caste groups and because of changes in ways of naming castes over the time periods.*
c. *Totals for Nadur for 1971/1987 do not add to 100% due to rounding errors.*
d. *We derived the Kerala percent of Kiriyattil and Sudra Nairs for 1931 from Fuller 1976:37.*

with women of the Nair caste two levels below them. Nambudiri women were married off to older men as secondary wives or kept secluded on the manors of their parents, except for those few who became first wife of the eldest son in each illam. So secluded were Nambudiri women that most took the name *antharjanam,* or "inside person" to symbolize their status and role within the household.

## Nambudiri Reform Movements

At the turn of the century some younger Nambudiris, influenced by changing marriage practices among the Nairs, agitated for reforms. A crisis occurred in 1917 at the Thrissur Vedic School near Nadur when young men demanded that English be taught and the marriage laws changed. Some burned their "sacred threads," worn diagonally across the chest, and criticized the older teachers in public. These agitations resulted in the Nambudiri Marriage Act of 1933, allowing partition of the household property and marriage by the younger brothers of the family.

Despite their privileged position, many Nambudiris supported radical movements including the Communist Party and even helped to propel the land reform struggles that eventually eroded their own economic privileges in the villages. One of Kerala's main Communist leaders, E. M. S. Namboodiripad (1976; 1984), is a descendent of one of the wealthiest and highest status Nambudiri illams of Kerala. Upon receiving a massive property inheritance in 1940, he sold it off for the then phenomenal sum of 70,000 rupees which he donated to establishing a publishing company for the workers' movement. He has since led an economically austere life. Namboodiripad was the Chief Minister in the first elected Communist government of Kerala in 1957-59 which promulgated the land reform. He later became the all-India leader of the Communist Party Marxist (CPI-M or CPM).

The Thrissur District is an ancient center of Nambudiri residence and their numbers throughout the area are greater than in either Malabar or Travancore.

### Variar

Variars are the temple assistants and maintenance workers. Their larger caste grouping is called *Ambalavasi*. The true Variars make temple garlands for use in prayer services. Others, called *Marars*, are primarily responsible for drumming at the temple (Iyer 1981 vol 2:17). Variars are not separately listed for Kerala as a whole, but represent less than 1% of the population. As can be seen on Table 4.2, all Ambalavasi combined represented 0.4% of Kerala's population in 1931. In the past, Variars had marital relations with the Nair caste just below them ritually similar to those of the Nambudiri Brahmins. They could engage in sexual liaisons with Nair women, but kept their own property rights intact by marrying other Variars (Iyer 1981:139). Variars traditionally held *kanam*, or "superior" tenancy rights to some of the temple lands which they then subleased as *verumpattam*, or "inferior" tenancies to castes below them (Iyer 1981 vol 2:157). Some were rich landlords. Others practiced astrology or became knowledgeable in Sanskrit, but many were fairly poor (Iyer 1981 vol 2:141). While below the Nambudiris in wealth, they derived most of their income from these subleases, and thus experienced loss from the land reform. Many have gone into professional jobs, but others have become owner-operators of rice land that they once let out to others.

### Nair

Nairs served the Nambudiri Brahmins as soldiers, officers, court personnel, and political administrators. They were first mentioned by Pliny in his *Natural History*, in 77 A.D. and were frequently referred to by Arab, Portuguese, Dutch, and British travelers, traders, and conquerors from the 14th century on (Fuller 1976:1). Like the Nambudiris, Nairs are a well-studied caste. Their unusual marriage practices and family structure have been subjects of an extensive literature.

Two features of Nair life intrigued foreigners: (1) their military training and skill and (2) their matrilineal kinship combined with great sexual freedom for the women. Nairs provided a permanent, specialized militia for Kerala's rulers. From the age of seven, high subcaste Nair boys would train in gymnastics and use of weapons—mostly swords—at the village *kalari*, or gymnasium. After puberty, they received weapons for use in police control of lower castes or fighting their Raja's wars (Gough 1952:76).

The need for mobility of the troops along with the unique relation between Nair and Nambudiri marriage and sexual practices may explain the origin of the Nair "visiting husband." Nair society was built on the *taravad*, a matrilineal, matrilocal household. Nair taravads might contain from 20 to 75 members, led by a senior male but related to each other through mothers and sisters. Women were formally married twice and in practice many times after that. The first marriage, called *tali*-tying, occurred before the girl reached puberty. It lasted for four days, and was symbolic. This marriage was followed by a marriage called *sambandham*. It included sexual relations, but was not limited to one man, even though the marriage ceremony was.

After the sambandham, Nair women took lovers for the night at their taravads. The presence of the man's sword on the verandah warned others that he was there (Gough 1952:73). Some Nair women engaged in polyandry with sets of brothers. When this occurred, each male might have a prescribed time of day or week for sexual access to his shared wife. Some advantages of this system for a specialized military caste were (1) that the men were not responsible for the upbringing of their children, (2) that men did not know which children were theirs, and (3) that men were not tied sexually or emotionally to a particular woman in a particular location. Men had no legal responsibilities for their children; inheritance passed through the female taravad. The descent system is known as *marumakkattayam*, from *marumakan*, meaning "sister's son" and *tayam*, meaning "share" or "inheritance" (Fuller 1976:54).

Another adaptive feature of the system was that Nair female sexual freedom offered Nambudiri younger sons a pool of women in the village with whom they could cohabit without economic encumbrances (Panikkar 1983:35-37). This was important to them since—as we noted above—only the first sons had hopes of attaining economic independence and marriage. Many Nambudiri women were left no outlet for their sexual needs.

### Decline of the Nair Matrilineage

Following the British conquest of Kerala in 1792, Nair armies were disbanded and the kalari fell into disuse. With the military basis of their marriage system undermined, Nairs became more monogamous, but the taravads continued to function into the late 19th century when colonialism further undermined them. The opening of roads and railroads, the beginnings of job mobility, and the partition of lands created by the colonial economy weakened the taravads. Tali-tying declined in importance and the sambandham developed into the only marriage. Men spent more time in the houses of their wives and began to participate in bringing up their children (Gough 1952:78-79).

With powerful forces dismantling them, taravads declined in size. An intermediate unit called the *tavari* emerged, with three to four adults. Nuclear families began to replace the tavari. The Malabar *Marumakkatthayam* Act of 1933 legalized the right of Nair men to claim individual parts of the land of their taravad (Gough 1952:81). In the early 20th century, Nair marriages came to be thought of as *kalyanam*, the general Kerala Hindu (Sanskrit) word for marriage. Polyandry, which had substantially died out anyway, was legally abolished with the 1955 Hindu Law Code (Mencher 1965:179-180). The Kerala land reform may have furthered the process of taravad decline along with its consequent loss of sexual freedom for Nair women by further breaking up the property of the matrilineal kinship unit (Mencher 1962). By 1960, Joan

Mencher recorded in a village in south Malabar that about 50% of Nair households were "small matrilineal tavaris" with an average of 3.5 adults per household while 15% were nuclear units and the rest groupings with various assortments of relatives (Mencher 1965:177; cf. Mencher 1962:238). In 1971-72, Fuller (1976:63) found in a central Kerala village south of Nadur that 90% of Nair households were matrilineal nuclear while 9% were joint families of various types—that is, including two or more siblings and offspring with parents, etc. Only one household was "collateral joint," either a traditional taravad or transitional tavari. In Nadur, we found in 1987 that 40% of Nair households were nuclear, 4% had only one member, 35% were extended, and 10% were "complex," a term we use for joint and joint-extended. These complex households resemble the tavaris of recent studies. Another 11% of Nair households were "matrifocal," a category not used in the other studies. In matrifocal households women provide most of the income and control the decision-making process. Matrifocal households are not smaller versions of the ancient Nair taravad, but responses to modern conditions such as abandonment by the husband or his prolonged absence for work outside Nadur. In Nadur, Nair matrifocal households average 4.2 members (N=9) while Nair nuclear households average 5.1 members (N=33). Complex households have 6.8 members (N=8), extended 8.0 (N=29). The average size for the entire combined sample of 170 households is 6.1. These data show that remnants of the taravad or tavari do not appear as a major type of modern household. This confirms the studies by Mencher and Fuller.

Nair households in Nadur in 1987 retain certain features of the old system, however. Many men continue to spend part of the week in their maternal houses where they retain influence and also contribute part of the support.

### Nair Subcastes

Perhaps because of the wide variety of their service roles to the Brahmin elite, Nairs came to include a number of subcastes. Researchers have identified up to 20 of these subcastes, but only four or five have large and important populations (Fuller 1975:298-299). The highest Nairs were the Kiriyattils who derived from taravads who had royal appointments as village leaders (Gough 1961:306-308). In 20th century Cochin, Kiriyattil Nairs may have shared kanam tenancy rights with ambalavasis. In areas where Nambudiris or other Brahmins were not present, Kiriyattil and some other high subcaste Nairs took on the role of landlords, holding vast tracts of rice and house compound land.

The lowest subcaste Nairs included *Vettekadus,* or coconut oil press-ers, and *Athikurussi* who were funeral priests for the Nambudiris. The Vettekadus may have added the designation "Nair" to their caste in an attempt to raise its status. Of all Kerala's higher castes, Nairs, because of their own heterogeneity, were the most accessible for groups seeking upward mobility within the caste system.

*Sudras* (also *Illattu*) form the largest group of lower Nairs. They were traditionally house servants, tenants, and farm laborers on the Nambudiri estates (Gough 1961:309; Iyer 1981 vol 2:15). In Nadur Nair-Sudras held verumpattam rice land tenancies and were *kudiyirippu* house compound tenants (we explain these terms more fully in Chapter 7) along with the lowest castes.

Nadur's sample population includes six Kiriyattil, three Vettekadu, and one Athikurussi Nair subcaste households along with 71 Sudras. Because the Vettekadu and Athikurussi are low-ranked, we included them with the Sudras. The Kiriyattil Nairs shared with the Variar caste kanam tenancy rights as well as matrilineal descent. Because the Nair subcastes include such a broad range, we examined whether the group Kiriyattil/Variar differed significantly from the group Sudra/Vetteka-du/Athikurussi. We considered income, pre-land reform holdings, household size and structure, and several other variables. The differenc-es were small, so we concluded that the entire Nair/Variar group in Nadur is homogeneous within the overall caste distribution. For the analysis of inequality that begins in Chapter 6, therefore, we present only a single Nair caste category which includes the 4 Nair subcastes along with the 2 Variar households in the sample.


## Craft


These castes include goldsmiths (*Thattan*), blacksmiths (*Karuvan*), and carpenters (*Aasari*) in Nadur. We also included the stone masons (*Kallasari*). In other parts of Kerala there are also bell-metal workers and leather workers along with a few highly specialized small castes such as carpenters who make only wooden idols for the temples (*Silpi Asaris*). Overall, the craft castes are called *Kammalans.* Inscriptions from around 1,000 A.D. indicate that they once lived outside the villages in separate colonies like the untouchables (Iyer 1981 vol 1:342-343). In the 1987 Nadur sample, we kept the individual craft castes as close as possible to their particular group number in the Census Block in 1971. The overall craft representation is 6.5%. Goldsmiths are better off economically than are blacksmiths with carpenters and stone masons falling in between.

The craft castes are considered "Backward Castes," referring to their low traditional social status.

The Kammalans have adopted many of the customs of the Nairs, such as *tali*-tying marriages and certain religious practices. These may be part of an attempt to elevate the status of their caste. At the beginning of the 20th century, they were still required to address Nairs with all the forms of self-deprecation that we noted above for the Nairs vis à vis the Nambudiris (Iyer 1981, vol 1:353). They are currently being pulled in contradictory ways economically by the spread of cheap factory goods that reduce their incomes, but also by their ability to perform skilled labor which is becoming more valued in some ways at the same time.

### Chetty

The Chetties are descendants of itinerant merchants from Tamil Nadu and Karnataka. Most sell clothes or supply *pappadams*, the Indian fried gram chips eaten daily in Nadur. Chetties are part of a larger caste grouping of immigrant weavers, oil pressers, and bamboo workers. Together many of these subcastes are known as *Devangas* (Iyer 1981 vol 3:369-374).

### Ezhuthasan

They were traditionally writing teachers to higher caste children. Ezhuthasan means "father of writing." In Nadur they are road contractors, forest wood choppers and field laborers. Iyer (1981 vol 2:104) lists the Ezhuthasans as a subcaste of Nairs who achieved the title of "teacher" through somehow gaining access to education, but in Nadur they consider themselves to be a separate caste.

### Muslim

Kerala's Muslims are primarily followers of the *Sunni* tradition, meaning that they do not require Islam's modern leaders to show descent from the prophet Mohammed. Like other Kerala castes, they are broken into subcastes, with some, apparently deriving from Nair converts, carrying Nair marriage customs and matrilineal inheritance, while others are patrilineal (Gough 1961:415).

Islam may have reached Kerala in the seventh century at the trading port of Muziris, the present-day Cranganore or Kodungallur at the southern edge of Thrissur District. The community can be firmly dated from at least 782 A.D. through a gravestone inscription (Miller 1976:42-43; cf Iyer 1981 vol 3:460-461).

Kerala Muslims are called *Mappilas*, or *Moplahs*, a term most likely from the Malayalam words *maha*, meaning "great" and *pilla*, meaning "child." This term is one of honor given traditionally to foreign guests and reflects the wealth and high status of Muslims during their first several centuries in Kerala (Miller 1976:30-31).

Fishing communities and many other low caste Hindus converted to Islam (Gough 1961:415), possibly as a way of breaking out of their caste-imposed poverty and low status. This created large Muslim populations in rural Malabar and Cochin.

Muslim prosperity received a death blow from the Portuguese in 1498. With superior firepower and a consuming hatred of every Muslim in whom they saw a Moor, the Portuguese blockaded the Malabar coast, wrecking the thriving Muslim-controlled commerce that had grown up over 800 years (Miller 1976:60-76). Kerala's Muslims were reduced to being mostly petty traders, tenant farmers, and field laborers (Gough 1961:417).

Shifting political and military alliances combined with Dutch and then British control to further undermine Mappila fortunes. British rule from 1792 to 1947 was based largely on alliances with Hindu rajas. In Malabar, British rule was built on the interests of Hindu landlords whose rents combined with colonial taxation to bring Muslim tenant farmers and farm laborers to a state of near ruin.

So harsh were the British financial exactions that Malabar Muslims rebelled throughout much of the 19th and early 20th centuries. From 1821 to 1921, 51 outbreaks were recorded, many of them including violent actions against high caste (usually Nair) Hindu landlords and British officials (Miller 1976:109). Severe government repression bottled up the resistance without removing its causes.

The Moplah rebellion of 1921 followed a brief attempt by Gandhi and Muslim supporters of the Indian National Congress to built a united Hindu-Muslim organization in Malabar. A British raid on the house of a Muslim leader triggered rioting and pitched battles in which over 600 Muslims were killed. Attacks took place against Hindu property, inflaming religious passions on both sides. The final death toll of the Moplah rebellion may have reached 10,000, with 252 executions and many hundreds of deaths in police confinement along with losses in armed skirmishes (Miller 1976:135-148).

Since Indian independence, Kerala Muslims have remained poorer and less educated than most other castes. In 1894, the British colonial government had recognized some Mappilas as a "backward caste," but they did not apparently benefit from the educational grants supposedly available by this designation. In Malabar where most Mappilas live, their literacy rate was only 5% in 1931, a figure comparable to the lowest caste Pulayas (Miller 1976:205).

Today Mappilas have political expression through religious parties such as the Muslim League. They have had shifting alliances with secular parties such as the Congress and Kerala's two major Communist Parties. Despite Islam's hostility to communism, many Mappilas vote communist because of communist support for land reform and worker rights (Miller 1976:196-204).

Kerala's Muslim population in 1968 was 19.1%; in the Nadur census block it is 12.9%. This figure is representative of the southern border of the main Mappila area in which Nadur is located. Like their fellow Mappilas, most Nadur Muslims are poor traders, farmers, or field workers. They are beginning to respond to Nadur's educational opportunities, as we shall see in Chapter 11, but they remain behind other groups.

## Christians

Fewer than 10 Christian households are in the Nadur census block, but Christians are 21.1% of Kerala's population. They are most heavily concentrated in Travancore, where they make up 40% of the population in some areas. Like the Muslims, their earliest communities developed in and around the port of Muziris. According to Kerala tradition, the Apostle Thomas came to Muziris in 52 A.D. where he founded a series of churches by converting several Brahmin households (Menon 1984:84). Solid evidence of Christian communities in Kerala is available from the 5th or 6th centuries. The community grew slowly, with Syrian rite services under leadership of Eastern Nestorian and Jacobite Bishops (Iyer 1981 vol 3:438).

The arrival of the Portuguese in 1498 ushered in a period of conflict and fragmentation among Kerala Christians. The Portuguese were shocked to find non-Roman Christians in India and attempted to suppress the alien Eastern Rites. They destroyed ancient documents concerning the early history of Christianity in Kerala (Iyer 1981 vol 3:440). Eventually the Latin Rite church came to compete with the Syrians. In the 19th century, the Church Missionary Society and the London Missionary Society added the Protestant version of Christianity, translating the liturgy into Malayalam. Many low caste people converted to Christianity in Travancore and Cochin (Fuller 1976a:55), much as their counterparts had done for Islam in Malabar. The former untouchable population of Kerala was reduced from about 25-30% to 8.3%.

Unlike the Muslims, Christians were never subjected to extreme political repression. Christians were the first community in Kerala to take full advantage of education under the colonial system. They now control a number of banks and other financial establishments (Iyer 1981 vol 3:456). In parts of central Kerala, Syrian Christians became large landowners, supplanting the Nambudiri or high caste Nairs. Christians have provided support for the right wing in Kerala politics, helping to organize militant opposition to the elected Communist Ministry of 1957 that contributed to its downfall in 1960. Today Christians are split between wealthy right-wing business leaders and followers of Liberation Theology who tend to support the left.

### Ezhava

This is the largest caste in Kerala with 22.2% of the population in 1968. The name Ezhava (Irava) is thought to come from Izham, an ancient name for Sri Lanka (Ceylon). The north Kerala name for this caste is Tiyyan, which may be a cognate for *dweepan*, or "islander." These terms suggest that Ezhavas were immigrants from Sri Lanka (Iyer 1981 vol 1:277). Although some may have fought as soldiers along with the Nairs in Travancore, the majority probably have worked as field laborers for the last few centuries (Iyer 1981 vol 1:278,327). Ezhavas can be thought of as a low-middle caste, just above the untouchables in status.

Although most may have been verumpattam (inferior) tenants and field laborers (Gough 1961:405), the Ezhavas are traditionally thought of as coconut tappers and coconut fiber workers. The tappers climb the tall trees up to four times daily. Highly skilled and careful treatment is required to tease out the sap without injuring the delicate coconut or palmyra palm.

After tapping the sap of many trees, the Ezhava climber will save or market the drink, a self-fermenting liquid rich in minerals and of low alcoholic content, called "toddy." It can be distilled into *arrack*, a far more inebriating palm wine, or cooked down to jaggery, coconut palm sugar (GOI 1967:45-49). All these products are available in Nadur.

Coir (coconut fiber) production takes place mostly in the coastal areas where the coconut trees are plentiful. Here largely Ezhava tappers place hundreds of coconut husks in large mud-covered beds under about two meters of salt backwater. These *retting* piles are left for nine months after which the rotted husks are dug up and transported in canoes to the shore for threshing. Women and young girls beat the husks, chop at them with machetes, and finally pull out the husk fibers into piles of threads from which spinners—also female—turn out a heavy, strong cord that can be made into ropes or woven into mats. For many decades, Kerala coir rope was used to hold ships at anchor around the world and coir mats found their way to the markets of Europe and the U.S. (Sankaranarayanan and Karunakaran 1985:191-221; Isaac 1984).

## The Ezhava Reform Movement

At the beginning of the 20th century, Ezhavas became politically active. Educated Ezhavas agitated against caste discrimination. Dr. Palpu, an Ezhava doctor from a wealthy lineage near Thiruvananthapuram, influenced a young Ezhava student who became one of Kerala's most important reform leaders. He was Sri Narayana Guru, who established the *Sri Narayana Dharma Paripalana Yogam*, (Association for the Propagation of Sri Narayana's Principles) or S.N.D.P. Yogam in 1903. This religious organization encouraged education and economic advancement among Ezhavas, but also took a broader social outlook, eventually coming to oppose all caste discrimination. Its slogan was:

> One Caste, One Religion, One God for Man
> Progress of Man, Irrespective of Religion
> Power Through Organization
> Freedom Through Education
> (cited in Kannan 1988:92)

The Ezhava caste improvement movement drew radical reformers to it. Among them was one of Kerala's greatest poets, Kumaran Asan, an Ezhava who had met Narayana Guru in 1891, and became General Secretary of the S.N.D.P. from its founding in 1903 until 1919 (George 1972:55-56; Sanoo 1978:66).

Asan was impressed with Narayana Guru's support not only for their own caste's entry to the high caste temples, but also for the lowest untouchables such as Pulayas, who were then also beginning to demand greater rights. When Pulayas were attacked by Nairs in southern Kerala in 1915 for attempting to get their girls admitted to a local school, Narayana Guru worked to convince local Ezhavas to support the Pulayas rather than attempt to raise their own caste status alone by ingratiating themselves with the Nairs (Sanoo 1978:106-107).

Although much of Asan's poetry was religious or erotic, his attachment to the anti-caste struggle led him to write social and political poems. One of the most famous of these is called *Duravastha*. It is set in the aftermath of the Moplah rebellion of 1921. A Nambudiri woman named Savitri takes refuge in the hut of Chathan, a Pulaya untouchable. He gives her protection and she lives with him. Their friendship turns to love and they decide to marry, uniting the lowest with the highest caste. At first torn with doubt, Savitri reflects on her new love:

> Why should I mourn?
> Lo! The doves fly about with no concern.
> They do not brood and bruise the heart.
> They do not weep and inflame the eyelids,
> They do not grieve because of caste,
> A distinction never seen nor known.

The poet goes on to warn in a famous passage of Malayalam verse:

> Change you the laws yourselves, or else,
> The laws will change you indeed.
> (George 1972:66)

Another influential Ezhava of this period was T. K. Madhavan, who founded the newspaper *Deshabhimani* and became a major leader of the Vaikom Temple Entry Movement in 1924. This movement united progressives from the highest castes with their low caste comrades. Madhavan was also an early organizer of the Indian National Congress and the first Gandhian *satyagrahas*, or truth struggles, in Kerala (Jeffrey 1978:156-159). As Kerala's caste associations gave way to class-based politics in the 1930s, Ezhava toddy tappers and coir workers became a major force in the trade unions and Communist Party (Nossiter 1982:78, 134).

Ezhavas have gained much in education and have benefited from their alliance with the left, obtaining government jobs and political influence. Still, most remain poor coconut tree workers or field laborers.

### Mannan

The members of this former untouchable caste are also called *Velans* in other parts of Kerala (Iyer 1981 vol 1:155). Originally, they were washers of clothes and funeral garments for the higher castes as well as cloths to cover idols in high caste temples. This was done by beating the dirty clothes in water mixed with cow dung, then submerging them in water mixed with wood ashes, steaming, then beating again on a stone, drying in the sun, then moistening them with starch and indigo before drying and folding. Some Mannans climbed coconut trees. Others made umbrellas. A few practiced magic and sorcery for healing which eventually brought them into medical work (Iyer 1981 vol 1:169). The Mannans have recently specialized in traditional Indian Ayurvedic pharmacies and medical practice. This has brought them a great deal of income. As we shall see in Chapter 12, they have benefited greatly from scholarships and "affirmative action" hiring programs designed to help them overcome their untouchable heritage.

## Pulaya

Besides Mannans, Kerala's untouchable castes include *Pulayas*, *Vettuvans*, *Koodans*, *Kanakkans*, *Pulluvans*, and a number of other small groups such as *Parayans*. They have the lowest status and the dirtiest jobs. Some remove animal carcasses or take care of the dirty clothes of the upper castes. Most are agricultural field laborers.

The *Pulayas* represent about 45% of Kerala's untouchable population. Some scholars derive their name from the word *pula*, meaning "pollution" (Iyer 1981 vol 1:87). Others contend that Pulayas were once land owners in Kerala and that Pulaya comes from *pulam* or field (Saradamoni 1980:51). In Malabar Pulayas are known as *Cherumas*. Until the 19th century, Pulayas—along with most other untouchables—were slaves, owned by their landlord masters. They could be sold or rented. Children could be separated from their parents. These *agrestic* or agricultural slaves were considered similar to pieces of land. When full property rights were sold, the transaction was known as *jenm*, when mortgaged, *kanam*, when rented out for short-term work, *pattam*. (Iyer 1981 vol 1:92-93). These terms are identical to the forms of land ownership and leasing prevalent in pre-land reform Kerala which we shall describe further in Chapter 7.

Although the British officially abolished slavery with their conquest in 1792, enforcement was delayed until the late 19th century. Strict punishments for slave holding and sale or rent were contained in a law of 1862 (Iyer 1981 vol 1:95).

A grim account of daily life for Kerala's untouchable farm laborers was recorded by Krishna Iyer in 1909 (1981 vol 1:122):

In rural parts, very early in the morning, they may be seen going with a pot or leaf-basket to their masters' houses for the remains of food and instructions for the day's work. They are kept toiling all day manuring, planting, weeding, and transplanting with the sun or rain beating upon their naked heads and often with their feet in the mire or water several feet deep. In the evening after their hard work, when they return to their huts hungry or fatigued, they have to prepare their food which consists of rice with some pepper and salt or perhaps some curry, and before their meal is prepared, it is about ten o'clock or sometimes even later.

Because of their poverty and social oppression, many Pulayas responded positively first to Muslim and then to Christian missionaries. We noted above how Islam attracted a number of poor farm laborers from the lower castes during its time of prosperity from 800 to 1498 A.D. In the 19th century, especially in Travancore, many Pulayas converted to Christianity.

## Pulaya Reform Struggles

One of the earliest Pulaya protests for civil rights was a ride taken in a bullock cart by activist and social reformer Ayyankali in 1893 (Mathew 1986:121). His simple act constituted a major public protest against caste indignities. He should have walked. He should have called out his presence to any higher caste persons so they could avoid coming into contact with him or even close to him. He should have been prepared to get off the road altogether in the presence of Nair men, who might otherwise have killed him on the spot.

In 1898 Ayyankali led a group of untouchables along a public road and into a public market. This act stirred the passions of high-caste Hindus, some of whom attacked the group. Over the next 30 years, he helped organize school entry actions and even some strikes by farm laborers (Saradamoni 1980:147-148). The strikes were generally unsuccessful and many of the schools were burned down by upper caste opponents to change (Mathew 1986:102-103). The inspiration of Ezhava struggles led Ayyankali to contact Sri Narayana Guru. Pulayas came to take part in the Temple Entry Movement, including the great Vaikom struggle of 1924-25 (Mathew 1986:104).

## The Temple Entry Movement

Among the many temple *satyagrahas* were the Chengannoor struggle of 1917, the Vaikom Temple Entry Satyagraha of 1924, the struggle at Kerala's most famous temple at Guruvayoor in 1932, and the fight for the eventual Travancore Temple Entry Act of 1936 (Mathew 1986:104).

The most dramatic was the campaign to open the great Siva Temple at Vaikom in north Travancore, launched in 1924. As with other temples, Vaikom's approach roads were closed to low-caste people, including Ezhavas, Mannans, and Pulayas. It was near the subdistrict of Shertallai, where an incipient leftist movement had begun among Ezhava coir workers. The first act was an attempt to use one of the roads by three leaders, a Nair, an Ezhava, and a Pulaya (Jeffrey 1978:152; Saradamoni 1980:166). The three nonviolent disobeyers of the law were arrested before thousands of assembled onlookers. Similar arrests occurred for eleven days. Then the government set up barricades before which thousands of people sat, fasted, and sang patriotic songs. Eleven months later the regional legislature failed by a single vote to pass a law opening the roads.

The following year the Indian nationalist leader Gandhi visited the protest, but was able only to negotiate a temporary standoff agreement that left the demonstrators unsatisfied. Finally in November 1925, twenty months after it began, the Vaikom Temple Entry Satyagraha ended when the government completed a series of alternative roads so that low-caste people could approach the temple while high-caste people still had a vestige of their old privileges. In 1936 the temple was finally and fully opened to all castes (Jeffrey 1978:152-153).

Although the Vaikom struggle ended in somewhat of a mixed outcome, it stimulated great excitement and political ferment throughout Kerala. The spectacle of the police barricading the roads to the temple and facing off against crowds in the thousands fostered greater passions and more radical ideas among Pulayas and Ezhavas, along with some of their Nair and Nambudiri allies.

## The Workers' Movement and Anti-Caste Struggles

In the aftermath of the temple entry struggles, untouchables became more and more united with Kerala's growing trade union and communist movements. It was then that some of the caste system's ugliest features were frontally attacked. One feature of this process was the role of high-caste radicals in helping to organize unions among the poorest and lowest caste people. This meant going to their houses, sitting next to them at meetings, and—when police repression struck, as it often did—hiding with them, working at close quarters with them, and breaking the dining segregation that was a major symbol holding pollution in place.

Anthropologist Kathleen Gough notes that although all the major political groups in Kerala officially preach an end to untouchability, "it is the Communists who eat in the homes and tea shops of Harijans [former untouchables], organize drama clubs among them, file suits on their behalf, and agitate for fixed tenures, higher wages, and a share in the land" (Gough 1970:149).

Joan Mencher quotes a former untouchable in 1971 who remembered:

> Twenty years ago, the influence of Communism brought a new shape to the life of my village. Some of the high-caste Nairs became the spokesmen of this new ideology. My father and uncles also joined them. They, the leaders of all castes, conducted meetings in Pulaya houses, slept in Paraya houses, etc. This phenomenon actually swept away the caste feeling in my village, especially untouchability. I have gone to the homes of many high-caste friends, and they come to my house also and accept food. We have many Nair friends who come to my family house, take food and sleep overnight (Mencher 1980a:280).

Along with the real and important role of union and communist organizers in helping to win economic benefits such as land reform and higher wages, people attached great importance to simple acts such as breaking the eating taboos and crossing the thresholds of each others' houses. These acts cemented the anti-discrimination struggle by making its principles real in people's immediate lives.

As agricultural laborers as well as an oppressed caste, Pulayas came to support radical leaders and in particular the Communist Party. They also have their own caste organizations, dating from 1907 when Ayyankali formed the *Sadhu Jana Paripalana Sangham* (Mathew 1986:109).

### Results of the Anti-Caste Struggles

Kerala's Pulayas are more literate than former untouchables in the rest of India. They are also nearer to the higher castes in educational levels than low-caste people in any other state. This can be seen from Table 1.2.

Although they have gained much educationally, Pulayas have a mixed record in occupations and income. For Kerala as a whole, in 1988 they held 10.4% of higher (*Gazetted*) government jobs and 11.2% of lower level positions (GOK 1989:99). Just how recent has been their entry into top government jobs is indicated by the fact that in 1950 there were no Pulayas among the 75 gazetted positions (Mathew 1986:141). The Communist and Communist-led Left Front governments of 1957 and 1967 respectively each had 4 Pulaya cabinet ministers (Mathew 1986:106). In 1971, the first Pulaya became a District Collector, one of the highest appointed offices in Kerala (Mathew 1986:140).

Pulayas lag behind other castes economically and in many areas of employment (Sivanandan 1976; 1979). Figures for the private sector in Kerala do not appear to be available. But in government positions, we see a serious lack of Pulaya representation in education and education administration. Only 2% of the staff at the University of Calicut was Pulaya or related Scheduled Castes in the late 1970s. At the University of Kerala, the figure was 1% and at Kerala Agricultural University 2%. Only 1% of lower level teachers and 2% of principals were Pulayas (Mathew 1986:146).

## Caste and Class

We noted at the beginning of this chapter that caste and class sometimes overlap and sometimes remain distinct. In order to appreciate their complex relationships in the context of reform, we need to set up operational class categories. We take up this task in Chapter 5.

## Notes

1. Hurst (1992:41-43), Harris (1988:418-421), and Cohn (1971:121-141) are among the many sources providing succinct general introductions to caste in India.

2. The English word *pariah* comes from the Tamil name for one of the former untouchable castes in the Madras region. North Americans also sometimes use caste terms to refer to elite groups such as *Boston Brahmins*.

# 5

## The Classes

Class is the most important form of inequality in modern societies. In India, class intersects caste in complex ways. In this chapter we shall describe Nadur's social classes as we have derived them from our data, and explain how caste and class relate to each other. We shall also consider how representative of Kerala are Nadur's classes.

### Definition and Characteristics of Class

"If a large group of families are approximately equal in rank to each other and clearly differentiated from other families, we call them a *social class*" (Gilbert and Kahl 1987:16). For more precision in our analysis of classes in Nadur, we can consider 9 aspects of class (Gilbert and Kahl 1987:12-16): (1) occupation, (2) income, (3) wealth, (4) personal prestige, (5) association, (6) socialization, (7) power, (8) class consciousness, and (9) mobility.

### Class as Occupation

Occupation defines the "major work that a person does to earn a living" (Gilbert and Kahl 1987:12). As we shall see later in this chapter, Nadur's occupational structure is quite complex owing to the several jobs held by many earners.

### Class as Income

Income refers to monetary gain received in a certain period of time. Because it is a dependent variable in this study, we shall not use it as a class marker. "Upper," "Middle," and "Lower" class will not appear in this analysis: they are vague and inconsistent terms of emic significance in the U.S. but of little etic analytical value. Instead, we shall group households by income quintiles in order to compute inequality measures such as the Gini index. We shall then compare these quintiles with certain caste and class units created by Kerala society and history.

## Class as Wealth

This includes savings, property, land, equipment, all things combined that can be called assets. In agrarian societies such as rural Kerala, land is an important source of wealth. In our analysis of the land reform, we will consider the degree of redistribution of wealth as indicated by its effects: income in particular years.

Despite its apparently agrarian character, Nadur, like many other third world villages, is becoming increasingly dependent on wages: skilled labor, service sector, and even professional. As De Janvry (1981:246) has noted for Latin America, "for the bulk of the rural poor, employment availability and wage levels are more important determinants of welfare than is agricultural productivity" (quoted in Bernal 1991:82). For Nadur, we shall see in Chapter 6 (Table 6.3), that salaries far outweigh land-derived income. For many households, land has become an investment for insurance against food price inflation; for many others it remains a primary source of income. The pattern of dependence on the land is complex. We will try to set it forth accurately in later chapters.

## Class as Prestige, Association, and Socialization

Prestige refers to respect from neighbors and can be determined by questionnaires regarding attitudes (emic) or deferential behavior (etic) observed by the researcher. Association indicates patterns of contact, including marriage. It can be measured by observations of frequency and quality of interaction among individuals and groups. Socialization tells us how skills, attitudes, and customs are transmitted to individuals and groups telling them how to speak and act towards other individuals or groups (Gilbert and Kahl 1987:12-13). In narrative portions of this study, we shall indicate according to our available data, whether and how much prestige, association, and socialization have changed. In Kerala, prestige, association, and socialization are largely governed by the caste system.

## Class as Power

Power is the capacity to carry out one's will or to make choices even against the opposition of others. Classes can exert their power with violence, with strikes, marches, and demonstrations, or with electoral politics.

An important and often neglected feature of class power is that the highest classes exercise much of their power through the day-to-day operations of the government—its courts, bureaucrats, police, etc.—and other powerful institutions such as banks, corporations, factories, schools, the media, etc. The class power of the ruling or most powerful classes thus appears as the norm for the society, even though its consequences may be harsh and brutal for those at the bottom.

Class power refers primarily to broad economic and political areas (Gilbert and Kahl 1987:13). In Kerala it means determining priorities for land ownership and use, government subsidies, and other applications of state resources. Class power in Kerala is closely connected to class consciousness.

## Class Consciousness

How aware are people that they are a group with shared political and economic interests? To what extent are they able to translate this awareness into political action and to what extent is this political action successful in advancing the interests of the class? Class consciousness is crucial in Kerala where it has played an important role in pushing forward the demands of the most oppressed groups. Class consciousness is not easily measured quantitatively and is not a formal part of our Nadur village analysis. Instead, we argue that class consciousness in Kerala generally has contributed to political and economic changes in Nadur. Our argument consists mainly of historical synopses of the struggles of Kerala's tenants, workers, and low caste people generally to win greater power and wealth either by increased production or by redistribution. In Chapters 7, through 11, we show how these struggles have brought enactment of the redistribution that constitutes our main independent variable.

## Class Succession and Mobility

Do people move up, drop down or stay the same relative to the class position of their parents or of their own household at an earlier time? If they change classes, how does this affect their incomes and lifestyles? Our comparison of households at 2 points in time approximately 1 generation apart is ideal for considering mobility. In Chapter 12 we establish techniques for determining whether mobility has occurred. We also examine what structural and individual factors have produced the mobility or lack of it.

### Instability of Class Membership

One reason for class mobility is that households can move in and out of classes. This does not happen with castes, as we explained in Chapter 4. The number of households in a class can change. Or, class numbers can remain the same while containing a different mix of castes. Comparative class analysis at 2 points in time requires a breakdown of the classes at each survey period. We can see this breakdown on Table 5.1.

Table 5.1
Numbers and Percents of Households in Each
Class in Nadur Village Kerala 1971 and 1987

| Class | 1971 | | 1987 | |
| --- | --- | --- | --- | --- |
| | N | Percent | N | Percent |
| Landlord | 2 | 1.3 | Redistributed | |
| Professional | 11 | 6.9 | 11 | 6.5 |
| Service | 7 | 4.4 | 9 | 5.3 |
| Craft | 10 | 6.3 | 14 | 8.2 |
| Farmer | 10 | 6.2 | 23 | 13.5 |
| Petty Trade | 24 | 15.0 | 18 | 10.6 |
| Recipient | 25 | 15.6 | 30 | 17.6 |
| Tenant Farmer | 21 | 13.1 | Redistributed | |
| Laborer | 43 | 26.9 | 57 | 33.5 |
| Agricultural Laborer | 7 | 4.4 | 8 | 4.7 |
| TOTALS | 160 | 100.2 | 170 | 99.9 |

*Note: Totals do not add exactly to 100% in this and on any other tables owing to rounding errors, unless otherwise explained.*

## Class Definition for Nadur Households

We define class for this study as **the main source of wealth of the household.** This definition captures both occupational and resource-based income. Households depending mainly on rent from land are landlords. Households with the main source of income from owning and operating a farm are farmers. Those deriving the largest single source of income from wage labor are wage earners. We divide the wage earners into classes by the educational levels demanded of their jobs, amount of income they get, and the prestige associated with the work.

Rural households depend on multiple sources of income. In order to assign Nadur sample households to classes, we chose the primary source of income, no matter which household member earns it and no matter how many other sources of income the household utilizes to make up the total income. This approach has the shortcoming of oversimplifying the data, but has the advantage of allowing us to use households rather than individuals as units of analysis. It also keeps the occupational class structure simple enough to make sense of the data. In the household case studies in Chapters 9 and 12, we detail the multiple income sources.

## Occupational Class Breakdown

Table 5.1 gives the occupational class breakdown of the Nadur sample for the years of the 2 surveys. We list them from top to bottom in their approximate order of income-generating potential and status. As with the castes, the order of the middle groups can be disputed, but the top and bottom groups would be widely agreed upon.

## Class Descriptions

We now briefly describe each of the occupational classes to which we have assigned the sample households.

### Landlord

Two households in 1971 received most of their income from tenants' rental payments on rice land and house compound land. Five others garnered a portion of their income from rent in 1971 but did not depend on it primarily. In the years up to 1971 landlords in Nadur were receiving about 1/3 of the total harvest from their tenants. At 1971 prices this meant about Rs 201 per acre of rice land. In the 1950s and before, at least 3 sample households had held more than 60 acres and had received greater shares of the harvest, making rent alone sufficient for substantial incomes. The landlord class was abolished legally by the Kerala Land Reforms Act (Amendment) of 1969, which we analyze in Chapter 7.

## Professional

Professionals are highly educated persons employed in positions requiring advanced technical knowledge, teaching in accredited schools, and/or supervising the labor of others. Most professionals in Nadur have college-level education. Professionals are the highest income earners in Nadur. Teachers in Nadur's government school could earn Rs 2,000 per month, or Rs 67 per day in 1987. This compares with Rs 20 per day for male agricultural field laborers and Rs 10-12 for female farm workers, the 2 groups at the bottom of Nadur's wage scale. School teachers also have regular work weeks and a guaranteed number of paydays per year. Farm laborers, as we shall see Chapter 8, have difficulty in getting even 100 days of paid labor in a year. In 1971 the professional class included 6 teachers, a school headmaster, a midwife, a rubber estate supervisor, an ayurvedic physician and an ayurvedic researcher. One professional earner resided in each of 11 households. In 1987 the class was defined by the occupations of 3 school teachers, 1 Vedic school teacher, the village postmaster, a government auditor, 2 corporate executives, a midwife, 2 rubber estate supervisors, a government development block office supervisor, a government medical supervisor, and 3 ayurvedic physicians, 16 individuals combined within 11 households.

## Service

Below the professionals are skilled or educated office workers such as middle level government employees whose salaries and benefits are greater than those of other villagers but less than what professionals can obtain. Several other trained workers earn similar salaries. In 1987 the service class had an educational level above all classes except professionals (Table 11.7). The 1971 service class contained 2 bus drivers, a postal clerk, a mail carrier, and a veterinary attendant. Bus drivers in 1987 earned Rs 800 per month or Rs 27 per day, with work throughout the year. In 1987 there were 6 bus drivers, the mail carrier, a police officer, and a court clerk.

*Craft*

The craft class overlaps almost precisely with the craft caste. Workers and tradespeople with specialized skills make up this class. Formal education is not a requirement for craft class membership since craft work is passed from father to son within the household. Income varies with the type of craft. A goldsmith may take in as much as Rs 1,000 per month while blacksmiths earn about Rs 200 per working craftsman. Carpenters in Nadur can earn Rs 800 per month for 7 months of the year. During the heaviest rainy periods, carpenters may depend on other income sources such as agricultural labor. The craft castes were traditionally of low status. Between 1971 and 1987 tailoring entered Nadur as a new craft. The skills and technology required by tailoring make it comparable to other crafts, but since no traditional caste exists, members of various castes are trying to put their children into tailoring. By 1987, 1 household was living primarily off the income of a tailor member, and several other households had children studying the skill. The 1971 craft class was composed of 2 goldsmiths, 7 blacksmiths, 2 carpenters, and 2 masons. In 1987 the class contained 2 goldsmiths, 5 blacksmiths, 1 carpenter, 3 masons, and 3 tailors.

*Farmer*

In 1971, 10 households (6.2%) were farmers. Only 3 of these were owner-operators of rice fields for their main income. The other 7 received more from sale of coconuts from their house compounds. In 1987 the farmer class had 23 households (13.5%), comprised of the 2 former landlords, 5 former tenant farmers, and other households. As can be seen from Table 5.2, the 1971 farmer class had 8 self-identified working farmers while in 1987 there were 10. Why were their fewer individual farmers than farming households? The emic perceptions of respondents did not coincide with the etic class definition we are using in our analysis. For 1971, 1 household listing the occupation of the household head as tenant derived most of the income from sale of coconuts for which no particular household member took responsibility. The other household head described his occupation as plower with his bullock team, but the largest single source of household income was sale of coconuts and other house compound crops.[1]

For 1987 the discrepancies are similar. In 23 households, only 10 self-identified working farmers appear. One household listed all 3 adult wage earners as unemployed, but they all lived mostly off the sales of coconuts. Low-caste workers did the farming. The household as a unit of analysis thus belongs to the farmer class though none of its members see themselves that way. The other 9 households listed their members as engaged in various wage earning activities while also living off garden products. In many of these households, several members may actually engage in the work of cultivating or at least harvesting and selling the garden produce, but they do not count this activity among their income-earning tasks because they spend little time at it. Most of the work is done by hired labor.

## Petty Trade

Households in this class in 1971 included 9 deriving most income from small stationery, food, tea, and general provision shops. One owned an ayurvedic pharmacy. Three others depended on their bullock carts to transport materials or goods for other households or the stores, 2 contained clothes peddlers, and 9 more had members engaged in buying and selling vegetables, wood, cattle, or manure. Two maids, 2 tenant farmers, 2 ayurvedic physicians, 1 nursing assistant, 1 clothes washer, and 4 agricultural laborers also identified themselves within the petty trade households in 1971.

The 1987 petty trade class was 29% smaller and quite a bit more homogeneous. Along with 1 food store, 1 bottled soda business, 1 tea and 1 postal savings agent, there were 5 clothes peddlers (all Chetty caste members) and 1 bullock cart owner. The heart of the petty trade class is made up of 9 combination tea and food shop owners with their family assistants. Of Nadur's 9 tea shops in 1987, 4 are considered large, 3 medium, and 2 are small by local standards. One of the smallest shops has no newspaper subscription and carries only tea, coffee, beedis (cigarettes) dosai (pancakes) and iddily (steam cakes). The other 8 have a selection of up to 3 different newspapers, along with various breads and cakes. The largest shops also carry flashlight batteries, pens, pencils, envelopes, local vegetables, and open market rice. Many items, such as cooking oil and plastic containers, require a trip to nearby towns.

The remaining 4 petty traders include 1 road contractor, 1 wood seller, 1 dealer in cotton seed oil and other goods, and 1 bullock cart owner. The 7 individuals working outside the class of their household included a nursery school cook, a spinner in the local factory of the Kerala State spinning and weaving corporation, a farmer, 2 house compound laborers, a rail repair worker, and an agricultural laborer.

## Recipient

This class includes households receiving their main incomes from remittances from absent workers who send money from the overseas Gulf states where many Kerala workers went in the 1970s and 1980s, or from office or tea shop work in Bombay, Madras, or stone cutting in northern Kerala. Some households also live off pensions.

For secondary occupations, the 25 recipient households in 1971 included 10 agricultural laborers, 4 servants, 2 shop owners, 5 tenant farmers, 3 general laborers, and 1 farmer. These local occupations were all secondary since, by definition, the main source of income was from outside Nadur. The precise number of individual absent workers is difficult to determine from the 1971 census sheets.

In 1987, 30 recipient households contained 46 absent workers (see Table 8.2). These absent workers provided the main incomes in 26 of the households. One household was living off bank interest, while 3 others had pensions as their main economic support. The 30 households included 6 individual pensioners and 28 other members who brought in secondary income through agricultural labor (9), masonry (2), pappadam making (2), general labor (4) and 1 each lottery agent, servant, buffalo milk seller, farmer, cook, village watchman, social worker, temple servant, estate supervisor, and camera repairman.

Recipient class households have to have some resources to start with to be able to send an able-bodied worker to live outside Nadur. This class also contains many households in the process of mobility. If the absent worker makes a large sum, the next generation will have rice land or post-secondary educational opportunities. On the other hand, recipient households may also fail to progress if the absent worker earns only enough to keep the household afloat or dies or disappears while away. Recipients of pensions are generally households on the decline since they have lost a primary wage earner who now receives as pensioner less than 50% of former income.

## Tenant Farmer

Although 38 households (24%) in 1971 held some rice land as tenants, only 20 derived their major income from their tenancies. Within these 20 households, 41 individuals listed themselves as tenant farmers. The other 18 households with rice land tenancies contained tenant farmers who derived larger incomes from other activities such as agricultural labor, house compound labor, and plowing, using the tenanted farms as supplementary income or security. As can be seen from Table

5.2, only 12 individuals (23%) in the tenant class were working in major occupations outside their own tenanted farms. Using average figures, we estimate that a tenant household in 1971 took in an after-rent, after-cost rice harvest surplus of Rs 165 per acre. Since the average tenancy was 1.2 acres, the average income to the tenants would only have been Rs 198. Rice land tenancy did not provide large incomes to tenants whose small holdings could not be gathered into large sums like the rent of their landlords. These figures support the view of land reform proponents that tenancy was holding its members in poverty despite their hard work and their essential contribution to the general food supply and economy. In 1987 the average net return after costs on fully owned rice land in Nadur was Rs 1,273 per acre, an increase of 772%. The economic value of rice land was increased in part by the land reform that transferred rent to the cultivator. In Nadur, the average holding, however, had declined to 0.7 acres, making the average net income from rice land Rs 891 for the 61 rice land owning households, an increase of 450% over the annual value of an average tenancy in 1971. In Chapter 7, we shall see that former tenants gained slightly in income compared to other groups while the few landlords lost amounts large enough to make a clear statistical impression. Like landlords, tenants as a class were made illegal by the 1969 land reform act.

## Laborer

The 1971 labor class contained 43 households with 70 self-identified employed individuals. Of these, 49 (70%) met the criteria for labor class activity used here. Class occupations included servants (4), pappadam makers (5) forest guard (1), village sweeper (1), and elephant mahoot (1) along with 36 general rural laborers, mostly working the coconut trees or other crops in house compounds of others, or on pineapple or rubber estates. The estates are essentially large house compounds. All 18 individuals not working as general laborers identified themselves as agricultural laborers. The labor class contained no professionals, no service workers, no shop owners, no farmers.

The 1987 labor class of 57 households was similar in composition. Of 130 identified occupations, 92 (71%) were in the class. House compound laborers numbered 53, estate laborers 11, servants 2, pappadam makers 5, spinners 5, wood cutters 2, along with 1 nurse trainee, 1 mason, 1 fitter, 1 loader/unloader (a unionized job), 2 bicycle repairmen, and 8 cooks at local or nearby tea shops or restaurants.

House compound laborers earn Rs 20 to Rs 30 per day. Some can find work for up to 4 months. Estate workers may earn Rs 25-30 and can sometimes work 9 months of the year. Servants earn only about Rs 5 per day in 1987, but get 1 or 2 meals, and may also receive other irregular benefits such as clothing, help with medical expenses, or other payments in times of need. The decline of servant work in Nadur suggests that workers prefer the less personalized market wage system when possible. Servant conditions include long hours, constant demands by employers, and potential humiliation (Schenk-Sandbergen 1988).

Individuals outside the class were 29 agricultural laborers, 5 pension recipients, 1 lottery agent, 1 small shop owner, and 2 farmers. Some people had more than 1 occupation, making the total number of occupations greater than the number of individuals. The 1987 laborer class thus included a slightly more varied list of occupations than did its 1971 counterpart.

### Agricultural Laborer

Households in this class garner the largest portion of their income from plowing, planting, transplanting, weeding, applying fertilizer, harvesting, threshing, and pounding the rice of others. Agricultural field labor pays less than other labor in Nadur. Male agricultural laborers earn Rs 20 per day, but in 1987 more than 50% of agricultural work was done by women who earn only Rs 10-12.

Work opportunities in agriculture are also more limited than other rural labor in Nadur: they are tied to the rice farming seasons. The low wages and limited work days mean that households mostly dependent on agricultural labor have lower incomes and lower status than those able to get other rural labor jobs.

In 1971, 7 households gaining most of their income from agricultural labor had 14 self-identified field laborers, 1 of whom was also a tenant farmer, and 1 who also worked as a maid as well as part-time garden laborer. The purely agricultural laborers thus numbered 12. The 1987 class of 8 households contained 23 field laborers of whom 1 was also a farm owner-operator, 3 engaged in plowing, and 1 who worked partly as a maid. This leaves a total of 17 individuals working only as agricultural laborers.

### Internal Class Composition

Classes are not as homogeneous as castes. Some individual variation occurs within classes when grouped by households. Table 5.2 tabulates the numbers and percents of individuals engaged in the occu-

Table 5.2
Numbers and Percents of
Individuals Engaged in the Occupation of the Household Class

| | Number and Percent of Individual Earners | | | | | |
| | 1971 (N=255) | | | 1987 (N=312) | | |
| Class | In the Class | Out of the Class | Percent In | In the Class | Out of the Class | % In |
|---|---|---|---|---|---|---|
| Landlord | 2 | 0 | 100 | 0 | 0 | 0 |
| Professional | 12 | 12 | 50 | 12 | 9 | 57 |
| Service | 5 | 5 | 50 | 8 | 7 | 53 |
| Craft | 13 | 4 | 76 | 26 | 8 | 76 |
| Farmer | 7 | 3 | 70 | 8 | 16 | 33 |
| Petty Trade | 20 | 12 | 62 | 24 | 12 | 67 |
| Recipient | 0 | 25 | 0 | 5 | 27 | 16 |
| Tenant Farmer | 41 | 4 | 91 | 0 | 0 | 0 |
| Laborer | 49 | 21 | 70 | 92 | 34 | 73 |
| Agricultural Laborer | 12 | 8 | 60 | 17 | 7 | 71 |
| | | | | | | |
| TOTALS | 161 | 94 | 63 | 192 | 120 | 62 |
| Without Recipients | 161 | 76 | 70 | 187 | 93 | 67 |

pation of the class to which the individual's household is assigned. For 1971, data is incomplete for individuals not contributing major portions of the household income.

From Table 5.2 we can see that average occupational composition of the classes was similar over the period between surveys, but some variation occurred among particular classes. Among landlords in 1971, no other occupations were recorded. Professionals and service class households both had half the members engaged in occupations within and half in occupations outside the main source of income. The other classes maintained averages between 60% for agricultural laborers and 91% for tenants. The recipient class appears on Table 5.2 as an anomaly because the main earners are absent workers engaged away from the household.

In 1987 internal class structures were similar to 1971. Among farmers the 1971 figure of 70% was replaced by 33% in 1987. This reflects the declining income from agriculture and the corresponding need of farming households to supplement their incomes with earnings from other

Table 5.3
Individual Agricultural Laborers by Class
Nadur Village Kerala 1971 and 1987

| | Agricultural Laborers | | | |
| | 1971 | | 1987 | |
| Class | Number | Percent | Number | Percent |
|---|---|---|---|---|
| Landlord | 0 | 0 | (0) | (0) |
| Professional | 1 | 4 | 0 | 0 |
| Service | 0 | 0 | 1 | 7 |
| Craft | 2 | 12 | 4 | 12 |
| Farmer | 1 | 10 | 3 | 10 |
| Petty Trade | 3 | 9 | 1 | 3 |
| Recipient | 12 | 48 | 9 | 28 |
| Tenant Farmer | 3 | 7 | (8) | (27) |
| Laborer | 21 | 30 | 29 | 23 |
| Agricultural Laborer | 12 | 52 | 17 | 71 |
| TOTALS | 55 | 22 | 64 | 21 |

*Note: Percents on this table differ from Table 8.2 because here unemployed, household tenders, and students are not counted.*

sectors of the economy. At the bottom of Nadur's class structure are households with only agricultural labor to support themselves. At the top, landlords in 1971 and professionals in 1987 could avoid low-paying, menial work. We can see the nature of the class hierarchy by counting the numbers of individuals in each class who resort at any time of the year to agricultural labor. These data appear in Table 5.3. Table 5.3 shows that the lower the household class the greater the degree agricultural labor supplements the household income.

Landlords in 1971 and service and professional class households at both survey periods did not have to resort to agricultural labor by their members. Laborer and recipient class households sent 23% and 28% of their able-bodied workers to the rice fields, however. Craft and farmer households also made some use of field labor, usually a wife or adult daughter to provide small supplements to the main income.

## Class and Caste

Some class inequality is already contained in the description of caste inequality. This is the case particularly at the very top and bottom of the caste hierarchy where ritual status (part of caste identity), relation to the means to production (part of caste and class identity), and income (related to both) coincide.

As we noted in Chapter 4, castes are closed, emic, marked ritually, and (previously) marked legally. Classes have different characteristics:

1. They are more open (Berreman 1981:15). A person is born into the social class of the parents, but can leave it by acquiring the income, position, or occupation that determines membership in a different class.
2. Class membership need not be recognized by respondents. Classes are etic constructions, defined by the researcher in order to analyze the data.
3. Class identifying badges such as clothing, speech, and life style rituals, are more flexible and varied than those of castes.
4. Demarcation lines between classes are less rigid than between castes. Classes tend to shade into each other at the boundaries (Kerbo 1991:19).
5. Modern classes do not usually confer formal legal rights or disabilities. The workings of the class structure are subtle, behind-the-scenes, and often contrary to official ideologies of equality of opportunity and mobility.

Caste limits class access both traditionally and now. In Chapter 12 (Table 12.3) we shall consider how much class mobility occurred between 1971 and 1987 and how much lingering influence caste maintains on class and income possibilities.

## Classes in Kerala and Nadur

How representative are the Nadur class categories and percentages of those in Kerala generally? The classes have been differently defined in various Indian censuses. Nonetheless, some general indications can be given that will help place Nadur's occupational and ownership class structure in an all-Kerala perspective. We shall consider 4 comparative sources.

Table 5.4
Rural Ownership and Occupational Classes
in Cochin State 1911 and 1951 and Nadur Village 1971 and 1987

|  | Cochin Percent of Persons | | Nadur Percent of Households | |
| --- | --- | --- | --- | --- |
| Class | 1911 | 1951 | 1971 | 1987 |
| Landlords | 1.9 | 1.7 | 1.3 | 0.0 [a] |
| Cultivating Landowners | 7.8 | 8.5 | 6.9 | 13.5 |
| Cultivating Tenants | 22.5 | 12.6 | 12.5 | 0.0 [a] |
| Agricultural Laborers | 18.2 | 21.9 | 4.4 | 4.7 |
| Other Rural Laborers | n.a. | n.a. | 26.9 | 33.5 |
| Farming Subtotals | 50.4 | 44.7 | 52.0 | 51.7 |
| Nonagricultural Commodity Production | 23.2 | 21.6 | 6.3 | 8.2 |
| Commerce/Transport | 13.5 | 13.6 | 19.4 | 15.9 |
| Others | 12.9 | 20.1 | 22.5 | 24.1 |
| Totals | 100 | 100 | 100.2 | 99.9 |

Sources: adapted from Varghese 1970:129. The category "cultivating landowners" in 1911 includes those cultivating "special products" (2.7%). See also Herring 1983:160-161 and Kannan 1988:46.
a. *Classes abolished by the land reform.*

## The Cochin Censuses of 1911 and 1951

The Cochin Princely State censuses of 1911 and 1951 can be compared with our Nadur class categories as shown on Table 5.4. From Table 5.4 we can see that the Nadur samples are generally close to the all-Cochin figures. The apparently smaller percent of agricultural laborers in Nadur as compared with Cochin State probably results from different methods of classification. Many of those we have labeled laborers would be in the agricultural labor category according to the Indian census from which the statewide data were gathered.

Turning to the ownership categories, we see that landlords were about the same in 1911 and 1951 in Cochin as in 1971 in Nadur and that "cultivating tenants" in 1911 (22.5%) were about the same as in Nadur in 1971 (23.8%). The decline to 12.6% in 1951 in Cochin results from "land-transfers and family partitions" (Varghese 1970:130). These data suggest changes in land ownership in the region prior to the land reform. We will discuss these in Chapter 7.

### Rural Households in Kerala 1983-84

Using households as the unit of measurement, the Kerala Department of Economics and Statistics surveyed agricultural and other rural laborers in Kerala for 1983-84. They sampled 30 rural labor households in each of 336 villages throughout Kerala that had also been chosen for the 38th round of the National Sample Survey. Their definitions do not correspond precisely to those we used for Nadur. Households living off garden produce and those transporting farm goods to market were counted as agricultural labor households. Using those criteria, the study estimated the agricultural labor households in 1974-75 (the closest year to the Nadur 1971 survey) at 27% and other rural labor households at 15% of the state's population for a total of 42% (GOK 1985b:8). In Nadur in 1971 the combined agricultural and other rural labor total was 31%.

The all-Kerala study found that in 1983 agricultural labor households remained at 27% while other rural labor households increased from 15% to 22% for a total of 49% (GOK 1985b:10). In Nadur in 1987, agricultural labor households by our definition were only 4.7%, but other rural labor households had risen to 33.5% with the total for Nadur at 38.2% (see Table 5.1).

### Economic Census of 1931 and Nettoor Commission Report of 1968

Other data come from the Economic Census of 1931 (Jayadevadas 1983:76) and the "Nettoor Commission" report of the *Sample Survey on Socioeconomic Conditions of Castes/Communities in Kerala, 1968* (Nair 1976). Comparing the breakdown of occupations from the 1931 census and the Nettoor survey of 1968, with the 2 Nadur surveys, we get the comparative data shown in Table 5.5.

From Table 5.5 we can see that Nadur is representative in a general way of total laborers, of trade, and of the professions. Nadur does differ from the cities and some rural areas such as Allapuzha's (Alleppey's) coir production belt where rural industry is more highly developed.

Table 5.5
Classes in Kerala 1931 and 1968 and
Nadur 1971 and 1987

| | Kerala Percent of Persons | | Nadur Percent of Households | |
|---|---|---|---|---|
| Class | 1931 | 1968 | 1971 | 1987 |
| Professions | 8.5 | 6.9 | 6.9 | 6.5 |
| Service | n.a. | 8.1 | 4.4 | 5.3 |
| Craft and Industry | 23.0 | 16.0 | 6.3 | 8.2 |
| Trade | 15.4 | 8.1 | 15.0 | 10.6 |
| Farming | n.a. | 19.8 | 19.4 | 13.5 |
| Other | 7.8 | 0 | 16.9 | 17.6 |
| Subtotals | 54.7 | 58.9 | 68.9 | 61.7 |
| Other (Rural) Laborer | 15.2 | 4.4 | 26.9 | 33.5 |
| Agricultural Laborer | 30.1 | 36.7 | 4.4 | 4.7 |
| Labor Subtotal | 45.3 | 41.1 | 31.3 | 38.2 |
| Grand Totals | 100 | 100 | 100.2 | 99.9 |

Sources:  for 1931 data, Jayadevadas 1983:76; for 1968 data, Sivanandan 1976:11 and 1979:478.

The 1968 all-Kerala breakdown indicates that Nadur was very similar in 1971 in total labor, agricultural labor, professions, and farming; and pretty close on craft and service occupations.  The 16.9% "Other" on the table for Nadur in 1971 includes remittances (15.6%) which are similar to labor except they come from outside the village, and 1.3% landlords who may have been included in farming on the 1968 all-Kerala survey.  With these qualifications in mind, we can conclude that the occupational and ownership class distribution in Nadur in 1971 was generally representative of the Kerala class distribution of 1968.

With Nadur Village described, and with the castes and classes defined, we can now start the main analysis in our study.  Our first topic will be to measure the income inequality among the sample households in 1971 and in 1987.  We do this in Chapter 6.

## Notes

1.  Because the house compound land for these crops was held by a landlord in 1971, we might consider these households tenants. Two reasons make it more logical to put them in the farmer class. First, the rent for house compound land seems not to have been tied to output as was the case with rice land tenancies and the total rent of Rs 50 per acre was only 1/4 that of rice land. Second, the entire literature on land tenancy in Kerala considers tenants as a class to be holders of leases on rice land. For us to add in house compound tenancies would make our data hard to compare with other studies.

# 6

# Redistribution Versus Inequality

We are ready now to consider the main independent variable: redistribution. Has it really occurred? Can we measure it? Does it correlate with Kerala's reform programs? How has it affected different groups in Nadur?

## Economic Change in India and Kerala

During the period 1971 to 1987 both India's and Kerala's economies changed substantially. Table 6.1 indicates the sector changes.

From Table 6.1 we see that Kerala's economy differs from the Indian national average in important ways. Agriculture remained slightly above the all-India average in both 1971 and 1987. In both all-India and Kerala, the percent of income generated by agriculture dropped significantly. Kerala's industrial share was below the all-India average in 1971 and fell relatively farther below by 1987, producing only 18% of income versus the national average of 25%. By contrast, services in Kerala stayed 3 percentage points ahead of the all-India figure by increasing at the same rate.

## Income Levels in India, Kerala, and Nadur

How does Nadur Village fit into the all-India and all-Kerala income picture? Table 6.2 gives the data. As can be seen from Table 6.2, average per capita income in Nadur—the only statistic directly comparable to state and national figures—was 294 rupees below, or was 51% of the Kerala average, which was 39 rupees below, or 94% of the all-India average in 1971. In 1987 Nadur's per capita was 1,254 rupees below, or

Table 6.1
Economic Change in India and Kerala
1971 to 1987

| | Percent of Income Generated | | | |
| | India | | Kerala | |
| Sector | 1971 | 1987 | 1971 | 1987 |
| --- | --- | --- | --- | --- |
| Agriculture | 48 | 36 | 49 | 39 |
| Industry | 21 | 25 | 16 | 18 |
| Services | 31 | 40 | 34 | 43 |

Source:  GOK 1988:cover

47% of Kerala's average which was 604 rupees below or 80% of the all-India average.  Nadur thus slipped 4 percentage points in its relationship to the Kerala average—probably an insignificant amount.  But Kerala dropped 14 percentage points vis à vis all-India, a much larger amount.

What do these figures mean?  They reflect the often-noted greater rate of economic growth in many parts of India outside Kerala.  But they do not necessarily tell us that Kerala's people are losing relative to the rest of India, because much of the all-India gain could be concentrated in the hands of a few rich families while Kerala's wealth is more evenly distributed.

Table 6.2
Per Capita Incomes in India, Kerala, and Nadur
1971 and 1987

| Per Capita Income in Rupees | 1971 | 1987 |
| --- | --- | --- |
| Nadur | 300 | 1,117 |
| Kerala State | 594 | 2,371 |
| All India | 633 | 2,975 |

Source:  GOK 1988:9

## Economic Change in Nadur

What have these general economic shifts meant to Nadur villagers? Nadur has also undergone substantial economic change in the 16 years between the 2 village surveys. These changes are evident from the data in Table 6.3. Sources are listed in descending order of importance for 1987.

As can be seen, salaries, already the most important source in 1971 with 22%, increased their share to 29% of total income in 1987. House compound labor remained far above agricultural labor and increased its share as well.

Remittances, mostly from labor outside the village, also declined from 11% to 9%. Labor by those living in the village increased. These were mostly cases of villagers getting jobs in tea shops in nearby towns or in the village spinning coop. House compound crop sales declined slightly and craft income also declined as a percent of total income.

One of the most important income sources, rice production and its associated agricultural labor, declined. If added together, these 2 rice economy sources dropped from 13% to only 9%.

Rents and interest fell from 7% in 1971 to 1% in 1987. As we shall see in Chapter 7, this is a consequence of the land reform. The decline in rice land income undercuts the intentions of the land reform movement, however. While tenants on both house compound and paddy land have received security against the threat of eviction, they have not gained as much income as might have been hoped. A major cause of this short-coming is that rice production in Kerala has declined in recent years.

The decline in rice production may have many causes. First, Kerala's green revolution was introduced in the late 1960s and most output gains had already been achieved by 1971. Without improvements in irrigation and other infrastructure supports, rice production may have reached a plateau. Higher prices for rubber and other plantation crops have stimulated investment in house compound land rather than rice (Kannan and Pushpangadan 1988). Furthermore, flooding and drought frequently affect the harvest. In the 1986 main monsoon season, sample farmers claimed losses of 849 paras of paddy (6,113 kilograms), or 12% of the total sample harvest for that season. In Chapter 14 we briefly de-scribe the People's Resource Mapping Programme, an initiative of the Left Democratic Front (LDF) government of 1987-1991, which attempts to mobilize farmers to find their own local solutions to these problems.

In sum, we can say that changes in Kerala's economy are reflected in Nadur. The declines in rents and interest suggest declining inequality. These are offset by a large increase in the salary sector, much for high-

Table 6.3
Income Sources by Category
Nadur Village Kerala 1971 and 1987

| | Percent of Sample Total | |
| --- | --- | --- |
| Source | 1971 | 1987 |
| Salaries | 22 | 29 |
| Garden Labor | 10 | 14 |
| Petty Trade | 10 | 9 |
| Remittances | 11 | 9 |
| Other Labor | 5 | 8 |
| Garden Crops | 8 | 8 |
| Craft | 12 | 8 |
| Rice | 9 | 6 |
| Agricultural Labor | 4 | 4 |
| Welfare/Pensions | 0 [a] | 4 |
| Interest/Rent | 7 | 1 |
| Totals | 98 | 100 |
| Rupees Totals | 274,678 | 1,168,059 |

*a. Less than 0.2% in 1971*

income professional employment, however, which might lead to increased levels of inequality. What has been the overall trend?

### Nadur's Income Quintiles: 1971 and 1987

As we explained in Chapter 2, we have organized inequality data according to a standard economists' format of population and income quintiles. Table 6.4 gives the general characteristics of the household income quintiles for Nadur Village in 1971 and 1987.

From Table 6.4 we can see that the lowest quintile in 1971 earned only 189 rupees, or about US$25. One US dollar in 1971 equaled 7.5 rupees (Westley 1986:327), while in 1987 the average was about 13 rupees. The highest quintile earned 15,422 rupees or US$2,056. In 1971 the highest income household took in 82 times that of the lowest. In

Table 6.4
Minimum, Maximum, and Average Incomes in Rupees
For Household Income Quintiles
Nadur Village Kerala 1971 and 1987

| | Household Income in Rupees | | |
| | Minimum | Maximum | Average |
|---|---|---|---|
| **1971 Quintiles** | | | |
| Top | 2,449 | 15,422 | 4,516 |
| 2nd | 1,401 | 2,448 | 1,821 |
| 3rd | 900 | 1,400 | 1,085 |
| 4th | 620 | 899 | 743 |
| Bottom | 189 | 619 | 419 |
| | | | |
| Entire sample | 189 | 15,422 | 1,717 |
| **1987 Quintiles** | | | |
| Top | 9,200 | 54,000 | 1,6588 |
| 2nd | 6,000 | 9,199 | 7,323 |
| 3rd | 3,920 | 5,999 | 4,794 |
| 4th | 2,900 | 3,919 | 3,466 |
| Bottom | 840 | 2,899 | 2,184 |
| | | | |
| Entire sample | 840 | 54,000 | 6,871 |

*Note: Rupees levels are not controlled for inflation.*

1987 the difference was 840 rupees ($65) versus 54,000 rupees ($4,154), a larger absolute amount, but a reduction of 22% in relative terms to 64 times. The average for the lowest quintile in 1971 was 419 rupees ($56). For the highest it was 4,516 ($602), a difference of 11 times. In 1987 the range for the averages went from 2,184 rupees ($168) to 16,588 ($1,276), differing by a factor of 8. The rate of inflation in India during the years 1971 (1970=100)[1] to 1987 was about 368% (GOK 1988:119). This compares to an increase in average sample income of about 395%, meaning that Nadur villagers did a little better than inflation, or, that they raised their actual incomes on the average slightly.

Table 6.5
Distribution of Household Income by Quintiles
Nadur Village Kerala 1971 and 1987

|  | 1971 Income Percent* | 1987 Income Percent | | | | |
|---|---|---|---|---|---|---|
|  |  | With Land Reform and Workers Act | With Welfare* | With Lunches | With Ration Shop | Points Change |
| **Quintile** | | | | | | |
| Top | 52.6 | 48.8 | 48.3 | 48.1 | 46.3 | -6.3 |
| 2nd | 21.2 | 21.5 | 21.3 | 21.4 | 21.5 | +0.3 |
| 3rd | 12.6 | 13.6 | 14.0 | 14.0 | 14.6 | +2.0 |
| 4th | 8.7 | 10.1 | 10.1 | 10.2 | 10.7 | +2.0 |
| Bottom | 4.9 | 6.1 | 6.4 | 6.4 | 6.9 | +2.0 |
| | | | | | | |
| Total | 100.0 | 100.1 | 100.1 | 100.1 | 100.0 | |
| | | | | | | |
| **Gini Indices** | 50.7* | 45.4 | 44.8* | 44.6 | 42.2 | -8.5 |
| | | | | | | |
| **Details in Chapters** | | 7,8 | 9 | 10 | 10 | 6 |

\* *The actually observed samples.*

### Income Inequality: 1971 and 1987

What happened to income inequality by household in Nadur between 1971 and 1987? The data are shown on Table 6.5

Table 6.5 shows that the Gini coefficient dropped by 8.5 points, or 16.8% between 1971 and 1987. It also shows that the decline in inequality proceeds with each added reform as the columns are read from left to right. Looking first at the top quintile, we see that in 1971 it had 52.6% of the income. In 1987, its share had dropped to 48.8%. This drop follows the implementation of the land reform and the Kerala Agricultural Workers Act of 1974.

## Inequality and Redistribution Programs

To get the most informative picture of the effect of each reform, we added or subtracted certain data. The second column marked "With Land Reform and Workers Acts," consists of the 1987 sample household data with all welfare income subtracted. It shows the changes in the inequality level attributable to those 2 programs which we discuss in Chapters 7 and 8. The starred column "With Welfare" is the actual sample as observed in which welfare payments such as unemployment compensation, aid to households with disabled members, and the like were included since they were reported on the questionnaires. We discuss these programs in Chapter 9. As can be seen, the welfare payments resulted in a very slight drop in the level of income for the top quintile, from 48.8% to 48.3%.

Moving now to the column marked "With lunches," we see the income distribution after we added the rupees value of school lunches for those households that reported making use of them. As we will see in Chapter 10, these lunches went more to lower income households than to those at the top. For now we can see that they also slightly reduced the relative share of income for the top quintile from 48.3% to 48.1%

In the column marked "With Ration Shop," we see the effects of the public distribution of food through subsidized prices at the ration shop. Here the share of income is calculated as the opportunity cost or difference between the open market price and the subsidized price of the rice purchased at the shop. As with welfare and the school lunches, the distribution by the ration shop purchases favors households with lower incomes. Counting in the effects of the ration shop, which are explained in greater detail in Chapter 10, we can see the most reduced level of inequality in the sample data. Here the top quintile has dropped to a 46.3% share of sample income.

The final column on the right shows the points change for each quintile from 1971 through the various redistribution programs to the most reduced level including the ration shop. We see that the top quintile has lost 6.4 percentage points but still has substantially more than a 20% share of the income that would be required by perfect equality. Losing Gini points does not mean it lost income—only that other groups gained relative to it. We can also see that the points redistributed from the top quintile went almost entirely to quintiles 3, 4, and 5, each of which raised its share by about 2 percentage points. The actual

Table 6.6
Effects of Different Programs on Income Inequality
Nadur Village Kerala 1971 and 1987

| Measurement Unit | Gini Index | Points Decline | Percent Decline |
|---|---|---|---|
| 1971 Sample* | 50.7 | | |
| 1987 With Land Reform and Workers' Act | 45.4 | 5.3 | 10.5 |
| 1987 With Welfare* | 44.8 | 0.6 | 1.3 |
| 1987 With Lunches | 44.6 | 0.2 | 0.4 |
| 1987 With Lunches and Ration | 42.2 | 2.4 | 5.4 |
| 1971 vs 1987 With Lunches/Ration | | 8.5 | 16.8 |

* *Observed samples*

shares for each of the quintiles 2 through 5 (the bottom quintile) can also be read from Table 6.5.

Looking now at the bottom line of Table 6.5, we can see what happened to the Gini coefficient. In 1971 the Gini was 50.7, but dropped to 45.4 after implementation of the land reform and workers acts. It dropped further to 44.8 in the observed sample with welfare payments. When school lunches were added, it dropped to 44.6, and further to 42.2 when effects of the ration shop were factored in. A summary of the declining Ginis is presented in Table 6.6.

The points and percent declines are in each case from the Gini immediately above except for the bottom row which summarizes the overall income inequality decline from 1971 to the most egalitarian form of the 1987 data. Table 6.6 can be read as follows: The land reform and agricultural wage improvements resulted in a decline in income inequality of 5.3 Gini points or 10.5%; a further 0.6 points or 1.3% was effected by pensions and welfare payments; another 0.2 points or 0.4% by the school and nursery feeding programs; and yet another 2.4 points or 5.4% by the public distribution of rice through the ration shop. Computing the highest versus the lowest Gini, we observe a decline in income inequality of 8.5 Gini points or 16.8% in the village of Nadur between 1971 and 1987. The decline by per capita and adult equivalent income units closely parallels that of household income.

## Income Inequality by Caste

Income inequality by caste presents a slightly more complex problem. As noted in Chapter 2, we cannot compute an accurate Gini coefficient by caste. Since the caste distribution was kept constant in the 1971 and 1987 samples, we can, however, make direct comparisons between comparable units. These data are shown on Table 6.7. In order to measure changing caste income inequality, we list the Nadur castes from top to bottom from highest to lowest in traditional Hindu ritual status along with the average income of each caste. Next we list the percent of total household income in 1971 and 1987. This is followed by the 1971 average rupees income and the ratio of the average income of the caste to that of the sample average. The next 2 columns provide the same information for the caste in 1987.

Finally, we present the actual rupees gain in the average for 1987 over that of 1971 and the rate of gain or index to 1971. For 1987 data, we use the most egalitarian form of the income distribution, with land reform, the workers act, welfare, lunches, and the ration shop—equal to the column marked "With Ration Shop" on Table 6.5. These data are shown on Table 6.7.

From the first 4 columns of Table 6.7 we can see important changes in the patterns of income inequality by caste. The Nambudiris were 8% of the sample but had 20% of income in 1971. By 1987 this had dropped to 12%. Because they were the primary landlord group, the Nambudiri decline is likely related closely to the land reform as will be shown in detail in Chapter 7. The Nair, Craft, Ezhuthasan, Chetty, and Muslim castes were unaffected overall in their percents of income. Both former untouchable castes made small gains: the Mannans went from 4% to 6% of income while the most dispossessed Pulayas went from 4% to 5%.

The gains reflect the pattern indicated by the changing shares of income, but this can be more clearly seen in the Index column. Here we see that Nambudiris gained at a rate far below that of the sample average, 248 versus 425[2]. Craft castes and Ezhavas also lagged behind the average as did the Muslims, but the Muslims were at least ahead of the inflation rate of 368%. The Nairs also gained substantially relative to inflation as did the Pulayas, whose 571% ratio was second only to the Mannans, the most successful of the castes.

Comparing the columns on caste income to sample average for 1971 and 1987, we see the same pattern. Nambudiris went from a ratio of 2.7 in 1971 to 1.6 in 1987, leaving them still quite far above average, but not so privileged as in 1971.

The middle castes stayed about the same, but the Mannans regis-

Table 6.7

Caste and Income Inequality
Nadur Village Kerala 1971 to 1987

| Caste | N | Percent of Sample | Percent of Income | | 1971 Avg | 1971 Ratio to Avg | 1987 Avg | 1987 Ratio to Avg | 1971 to 1987 Gain in Rupees | Index |
|---|---|---|---|---|---|---|---|---|---|---|
| | | | 1971 | 1987 | | | | | | |
| Nambudiri | 13 | 8 | 20 | 12 | 4,699 | 2.7 | 11,671 | 1.6 | 6,972 | 248 |
| Nair/Variar | 83 | 49 | 41 | 48 | 1,379 | 0.8 | 7,119 | 1.0 | 5,740 | 516 |
| Craft | 11 | 6 | 10 | 7 | 2,664 | 1.2 | 8,349 | 1.1 | 5,685 | 313 |
| Ezhuthasan/ | | | | | | | | | | |
| Chetty | 13 | 8 | 6 | 7 | 1,496 | 0.9 | 6,683 | 0.9 | 5,187 | 447 |
| Muslim | 22 | 13 | 10 | 10 | 1,457 | 0.8 | 5,792 | 0.8 | 4,335 | 398 |
| Ezhava | 13 | 8 | 6 | 5 | 1,352 | 0.8 | 4,977 | 0.7 | 3,625 | 368 |
| Mannan* | 4 | 2 | 4 | 6 | 2,435 | 1.4 | 17,545 | 2.4 | 15,110 | 721 |
| Pulaya* | 11 | 6 | 4 | 5 | 896 | 0.5 | 5,067 | 0.7 | 4,171 | 566 |
| Totals and Averages | 170 | 100 | 101 | 100 | 1,717 | 1.0 | 7,290 | 1.0 | 5,573 | 425 |

* Former untouchables

tered a dramatic increase on this indicator, going from 1.4 times average in 1971—already a good figure for a formerly untouchable group—to 2.4 times average in 1987, making them the highest average income caste for that year. The Pulayas raised their ratio from 0.5 to 0.7 of average, a 40% increase in their relative share. In later chapters we shall see how land reform, the workers acts, pensions, school lunches, and the ration shop have combined with special programs to provide employment and other benefits to former untouchables to help produce this result. The Nairs went from 0.8 in 1971 to 1.0 in 1987, coming thus to equal the sample average. Their increase in ratio to average was 25%.

In sum, we can say that caste inequality has declined measurably with the highest Nambudiri caste losing much relative income and the 2 lowest, former untouchable castes, gaining the most.

## Income Inequality by Class

In measuring class inequality, we face greater complexity. As we noted in Chapter 5, class membership does not remain constant as does that of castes. Because of this factor, we must compare the percent of sample with the percent of income at each sample survey period separately. This means more numbers to read and interpret. The data appear on Table 6.8.

From Table 6.8, we see that the landlord class in 1971 contained only 1% of the sample (2 households) but held 8% of the income. The 1971 average income of the class was 11,135 rupees ($1,485), or 6.5 times the average for the sample as a whole.[3] In 1987 this class had disappeared because of the land reform. We can trace these 2 households, however. Both households have merged into the farmer class. We calculate that they have 2% of the 1987 income, and 1.4 times the average for the sample in 1987. The numbers in parentheses on Table 6.7 indicate for both former landlords and former tenants how they are doing now. The former landlords are the only group to register a negative absolute change in average income, reporting only 91% of the income in 1987 that they took in during the 1971 survey period. As we shall see in Chapter 7, these figures indicate that the land reform took a substantial amount of income-generating resources away from the highest groups. But because it is distributed widely across several other classes, we cannot see its effects there as clearly.

Looking at the tenants, we see that they were 13% of the sample in 1971 and had 6% of income. If we follow the same 20 households to 1987, we find they are 12% of the sample, but are spread across several classes

Table 6.8
Class and Income Inequality
Nadur Village Kerala 1971 to 1987

| Class | Percent of Sample | | Percent of Income | | 1971 Avg | 1971 Ratio to Avg | 1987 Avg | 1987 Ratio to Avg | 1971 to 1987 Gain in Rupees | Index |
|---|---|---|---|---|---|---|---|---|---|---|
| | 1971 | 1987 | 1971 | 1987 | | | | | | |
| Landlord | 1.3 | (0.0) | 8.1 | (1.8) | 11,135 | 6.5 | (9,850) | (1.5) | (-1,285) | (88) |
| Professional | 6.9 | 6.5 | 16.3 | 23.3 | 4,067 | 2.4 | 24,983 | 3.7 | 20,624 | 610 |
| Service | 4.4 | 5.3 | 8.1 | 9.2 | 3,187 | 1.9 | 12,268 | 1.8 | 10,723 | 375 |
| Craft | 6.3 | 8.2 | 9.7 | 8.6 | 2,664 | 1.6 | 7,699 | 1.1 | 5,467 | 268 |
| Farmer | 6.9 | 13.5 | 4.3 | 12.1 | 1,069 | 0.6 | 6,353 | 0.9 | 3,372 | 574 |
| Petty Trade | 15.0 | 10.6 | 13.9 | 10.5 | 1,596 | 0.9 | 7,284 | 1.0 | 6,088 | 423 |
| Recipient | 15.6 | 17.6 | 13.9 | 11.7 | 1,530 | 0.9 | 5,014 | 0.7 | 3,442 | 290 |
| Laborer | 26.9 | 33.5 | 17.1 | 21.4 | 1,092 | 0.6 | 4,886 | 0.6 | 3,894 | 392 |
| Tenant | 12.5 | (0.0) | 6.4 | (7.3) | 883 | 0.5 | (3,949) | (0.6) | (3,066) | (447) |
| Agricultural Laborer | 4.4 | 4.7 | 2.1 | 3.1 | 824 | 0.5 | 5,024 | 0.6 | 4,325 | 521 |
| Totals and Averages | 100.2 | 99.9 | 99.9 | 99.9 | 1,717 | 1.0 | 7,290 | 1.0 | 5,573 | 425 |

Note: Numbers in parentheses refer back to former categories; that is, how much of 1987 income is held by the 1971 landlord and tenant class households.

in that year. In 1987 they had 7% of income. These data suggest that the land reform alone provided small but measurable benefits to rice land tenants.

The other class registering a big change is the craft class, which experienced a relative decline from 1.6 times average in 1971 to 1.1 in 1987. Craft incomes may be suffering from competition with factory-made products.

One important finding on Table 6.8 is the reduction in the range of inequality from the richest to the poorest classes. In 1971, landlords garnered 13.5 times the average incomes of agricultural laborers. In 1987 the wealthiest class was the professionals with 4.9 times the average income of agricultural laborers.

## Summary and Conclusions

The several Gini numbers and income averages in this chapter all indicate that substantial redistribution of wealth occurred in Nadur Village between 1971 and 1987. Although the rich are still rich, those in the 3 lowest quintiles, the most oppressed castes, and lowest classes have gained income faster. Furthermore, changes in the degree of inequality can be associated with the introduction of specific programs.

How did each program contribute to the reduction in inequality? We shall now attempt to assess the impact of specific Kerala reforms. Chapter 7 begins this assessment with the Kerala land reform.

## Notes

1. Indian government statistical sources use the year 1970 as a baseline for inflation computations. Since it is only one year earlier than the year of the Mencher survey, we take it as our baseline when 1971 statistics are not available.

2. The average increase is 425 here rather than the 395 reported earlier in the chapter because here we have added the indirect rupees benefits of the school lunches and the ration shop that are explained in Chapter 10.

3. We computed the ratios with sample percents unrounded. The sample percent for landlords is actually 1.25%, so that the share of income computes to 6.5 times rather than the 8 times that would result from using the rounded figures.

# 7

# The Land Reform

The centerpiece of Kerala's redistribution program was the land reform of 1969. This reform abolished tenancy on both farm land and house compound sites, attempted to redistribute land through a ceiling provision, and attempted to redistribute wealth through a progressive tax. In this chapter we shall consider the historical background, legal components, and income inequality effects of Kerala's land reform in Nadur.

## The Historical Context

Kerala's land reform attempted to abolish a complex system. Land reform historian Ronald Herring (1983:157) aptly called it "the most bewildering...maze of intermediary rights, esoteric usufructuary mortgage tenures, [and] complex subinfeudation." For rice land there was at the top a class of landlords (*jenmies*) mostly of the Nambudiri caste who owned the land but did not cultivate it. Below them was a class of "superior" tenants (*kanamdar*) who leased the land from the jenmies and subleased part to all of it to a third class of "inferior" tenants (*verumpattamdar*) who were the actual cultivators. *Kanam* leases were generally in writing and usually had a 12-year term that the jenmies were somewhat obliged to renew if asked. *Verumpattam* leases were usually verbal and could be easily terminated by the landlord or the superior tenant.[1] Even if written, the lease was under effective control of the landlord caste-class in the villages. The cultivators often employed Pulaya untouchables to do the hard field labor. A great deal of land was officially owned by Hindu temples in some villages, but this was rented at a nominal fee to Nambudiri landlords who effectively added it to their already large estates.

In addition to the tenancies for rice fields, the same landlords owned

the sites on which other villagers built their houses. Those renting rice
land from a particular landlord also lived on house compound land held
by that landlord. The landlords' threats of eviction from either type of
land constituted a powerful lever to pry high rents and cheap labor from
the other type. One is reminded of a US company town.

The three regions of Kerala had different versions of this tenure
system and different land histories (Sathyamurthy 1985:174-88). In
Travancore, or southern Kerala, land reforms introduced by 19th century
royal reformers mostly eliminated tenancy, creating a fairly large class of
small owners.[2] By contrast, Malabar, or northern Kerala, witnessed the
ossification of the superior-inferior tenant relationship. One feature of
this ossification was the steady increase in evictions throughout the late
19th century which resulted in greater landlord power and greater
landlord extraction of rent from tenants (Panikkar 1989:42-43).[3]

In Cochin, an intermediate development took place. Here *kanam*
tenancies were to be given permanent use rights under influence of the
Travancore reforms, but landlords bypassed the law by turning many
*kanam* leases into *verumpattam*, or inferior leases. As one Nadur elderly
former landlord explained:

> My grandfather was manager of a temple in Travancore in 1914, and he
> warned us about the new law. Any *kanam* tenant with 30 years tenancy
> would no longer be subject to eviction. So, before they heard about the
> law, we returned the fixed deposits of all our *kanam* tenants and rewrote
> their contracts as *verumpattam*. Because so many people wanted to
> become tenants [so many were landless that those who were tenants
> could ill afford to turn down a landlord's offer], it was easy to get our
> tenants to go along with the changes. At that time our family held land
> worth 7,000 paras in annual rent.

The 7,000 paras equaled 50,400 kilograms of unhusked rice, an
incredible fortune in those days. In this way, Cochin landlords managed
to evade most of the provisions of the moderate "Cochin Tenancy Bill" of
1914 (Slater 1918:128-129). Additional Cochin Tenancy Acts were passed
in 1938, 1943, and 1944 along with three proclamations on the rights of
house compound tenants (1937, 1947, and 1949), all attempting to provide security of tenure (Sankaranarayanan and Karunakaran 1985:85-86;
Varghese 1970:134-136). They were ineffective. It was only the complete
legal abolition of tenancy and the legal prohibition against reclaiming of
both types of land in 1969 that granted real security of tenure.

To get an idea of the level of exploitation involved in these complex
relationships, we refer to a study from Cochin in the 1940s in which it
was found that cultivator households were paying at least 60% and

sometimes even above 80% of the *gross* returns to the classes above them. The split between *jenmies* and the *kanamdars* is not given (cited in United Nations 1975:58; Herring 1983:161).[4]

Statistics gathered on the eve of the 1969 land reform act indicate that owners of more than 5 acres constituted only 8.1% of land owning households, but controlled 44.4% of all leased land and 61.8% of leased wet-rice lands (Herring 1980:A67). When only the 8,000 households for whom rent could have been the main source of income were considered, economists estimated they held nearly 30% of the total area and 80% of area leased out (United Nations 1975:68). Landholding inequality among cultivating households in Kerala in 1971 was expressed by a Gini index of 68 making it the third most unequal state in India at that time (Mukherjee 1979:6-9; Sundrum 1987:189), but the study probably greatly underestimated actual land inequality.

## Popular Struggles for Land Reform

Kerala's land reform law was the outcome of more than a century of spontaneous rebellion, organizing, petition signing, marching, meetings, strikes, battles with police and landlord goon squads, election campaigns, and parliamentary debates. Except for armed revolution, virtually every form of political activity took place in Kerala's land reform struggles.

Of the three major regions that made up Kerala State at its formation in 1956—Travancore, Cochin, and Malabar—Malabar had the most intense struggles over land rights. In the 19th century, British-imposed legal concepts had caused vast deterioration in traditional tenancy conditions for the poorest groups. Frequent rebellions broke out against this deterioration. From 1836 to 1853, more than 20 uprisings are recorded in Malabar, in which mostly Muslim tenants attacked mostly high-caste Hindu landlords. Despite the obvious class elements in these uprisings, many British officials chose to see them only in caste and religious terms.

For the next 80 years until the 1930s, these struggles resulted in government commissions, studies, reports, recommendations, and laws, all of which appear to have strengthened the owners rather than the tenants or workers (Sathyamurthy 1985:146-150). In 1921 a major violent outbreak occurred, the *Moplah*, or Muslim, rebellion (see Chapter 4) in which up to 10,000 people were killed and others imprisoned, but the 1930 law that resulted from this rebellion still achieved nothing for the poorest tenants (Sathyamurthy 1985:151-152; Miller 1976:147).

In 1915 militants formed the Malabar Tenancy Association. By 1933 it had been transformed into the Kerala Karshaka Sangham (KKS), or Kerala Farmers' Association, which allied itself with the increasingly radical elements in the Kerala branch of the Indian National Congress, the umbrella nationalist movement that was struggling for independence. By 1940 the KKS had 30,000 members. In 1938, with the Great Depression ravaging already-impoverished living conditions, KKS units launched a massive series of rallies and *jathas*, or processions, all over Malabar. These *jathas* coincided with worker strikes in southern Kerala. Landlords hired thugs and frequently called the police to break up the disturbances, which continued throughout the area into the 1940s. The KKS was banned, but in 1942 militants reorganized it under a new name, the Kerala Kisan Sangham, or Kerala Peasants' Union (cleverly keeping the same initials). Much of the leadership had to operate from underground, and many organizers had by this time joined the newly formed Kerala branch of the Communist Party of India (CPI). In 1946 the CPI led an unsuccessful worker uprising just to the south of Malabar in central Kerala. This uprising is known as the Punnapra-Vayalur rebellion after two villages where it reached its climax (Kannan 1988:119; Isaac 1983). Many workers were killed in police and military attacks on their camps and the party was outlawed. Many peasants and organizers were killed in prison. (Sathyamurthy 1985:152-158,166,176). Despite the repression, organizing and protests continued.

The turning point came in 1957, when voters of the new state of Kerala elected a Communist Party of India (CPI) majority to power in the State Legislative Assembly. By this time, the KKS claimed nearly 190,000 members.

The CPI government included for the first time in Kerala cabinet members who were themselves seasoned militants of the peasant and worker movements. Their electoral charge clearly included radical land reform, and they set out to meet this charge with a series of four major land reform laws.[5] Landlords were quick to respond, organizing right-wing demonstrations and appealing to the Indian central government to dismiss the Communist state government. In 1959 the Communist government passed the Kerala Agrarian Relations Bill which provided major economic relief to tenants. Just three weeks later, the state government was indeed dismissed, and Kerala entered a period of political instability with recurrent presidential rule from New Delhi. The Kerala High Court declared the Communist land reform law unconstitutional. In 1964 a Congress Party ministry passed a greatly watered-down land reform act which one socialist legislator ridiculed as "the Kerala Landlords' Protection Bill" (Sathyamurthy 1985:225; Varghese 1970:147-148).

Tenants and their allies continued to agitate. In 1967 the United Left Front was voted into power. In 1969 this coalition of Communist and other leftist parties finally enacted the law that has come to be considered Kerala's radical land reform. By this time tenants had become disillusioned with parliamentary processes, and in many areas they took matters into their own hands, planting red flags on their tenancies and claiming the right to farm the land without paying rents to the landlords. Further clashes occurred, but by this point popular pressure had become so great that most political parties supported the land reform. A constitutional device was worked out with the central government in New Delhi allowing the law to circumvent the ever-hostile Kerala courts which ruled against land reform at every opportunity. Land reform in a compromised form less radical than that of 1959 but more radical than that of 1964, finally became a law in 1969.[6]

From the 1940s on, and particularly in the 1960s, many tenants refused to pay rents. Where radical organizations were most powerful, they were often able to prevent eviction despite landlords' goon squads and court actions.

What were the results of all this struggle? We turn now to the main features of the Kerala land reform and their effects in Nadur village.

## The Land Reform

Kerala's 1969 land reform contained three major components:

1. A ceiling on absolute size of holdings, with excess to be redistributed to the landless.[7]
2. The abolition of rice land tenancy and thus the abolition of rental payments from actual operators to non-cultivating landlords. Stays of eviction prevented landlords from using this provision in a reactionary way to simply throw tenants off the land.
3. The abolition of tenancy in house compound land, and thus the abolition of rents to the landlords who held title to them. As with provision 3, eviction stays put tenants in the superior political position so they could not be thrown off the land.

Observers agree that the ceiling provision was not extensively applied (United Nation 1975:49-51 and 60-64; Herring 1980:A65-66). Statewide, only 85,000 households received rice land averaging 0.59 acres under the ceiling provision (Radhakrishnan 1989:176). We found no evidence in Nadur of its implementation. Provisions two and three, however, have resulted in massive redistribution of land rights. Across Kerala, 1,290,000 tenant households gained titles to 1,967,593 acres (1.5 acres each) of rice land. The abolition of house compound tenancy transferred rights to 21,522 acres to 269,028 hutment dwellers (0.08 acres each). Several thousand hutment dwellers seized their house compounds without filing official transfer papers, making the house compound beneficiaries total about 340,000 (Radhakrishnan 1989:174-76; United Nations 1975:65).[8]

### Redistribution of Rice Land

The 1971 survey of all 356 Nadur households indicates that Nambudiri caste landlords totaling 7.6% of the population directly controlled 50% of agricultural land, while the local temple board—controlled traditionally by the same Nambudiri households—held title to another 37% of the rice fields. Another 7% of the land was owned by Nambudiri households living outside the village, leaving only 6% of the rice land owned by members of other castes.

How much land was redistributed? The sources of information create a problem. Landlords in 1971 were reporting much smaller holdings than were their tenants. One landlord, for example, told the researcher that he held no agricultural land as a jenmy, but tenants' reports indicated that he owned more than 7 acres. With house compound land even larger discrepancies occurred. In addition, landlords were not reporting their access to temple lands but tenants were doing so. For these various reasons, we used the tenants' figures for the analysis.

Among the 160 households in the 1971 sample, 7 jenmies (4.4%) lost an average of 7.5 acres each, while 47 households (29%) gained title to an average of 0.74 acres each. The losses do not equal the gains because land was passing both within and out of the sample. As they held no tenancy rights, 103 households (64%) were not directly affected by the rice land redistribution. The largest jenmy loss was 19.42 acres by a single landlord. At 1971 production and price levels, this land would have been worth 3,903 rupees in rent, a figure 6.6 times the per capita income of Kerala of 594 rupees in that year. If all 36.70 sample acres of jenmied land were receiving rent, a total of 7,377 rupees were being generated, equal to 3% of the total income generated by the entire sample of 160 households, 14% of the entire value generated by the rice fields in that year, and 91% of the income earned by all the agricultural laborers in the sample during the two seasons of that year. These comparisons give some idea of the burden which rents represented in the local economy. In decades prior to 1971 the holdings were far larger and rent levels higher. They once must have produced far more income than was received by the laborers who did virtually all the work.

The same large landlord also lost 12 of 13 rice land acres to which he claimed owner-operator rights in 1971. Some of the latter land may have been passed to offspring in partitions—in part to bypass the land reform. The largest total single rice field holding in the sample was thus 32.42 acres in 1971. In 1987 the largest rice land holding in the sample was 2.8 acres, held by a non-Brahmin household that was never a landlord. The upper limit of ownership size has thus been vastly reduced.

How did the land reform affect land inequality? To measure this, we employed both unit distribution data and the Gini index of inequality. In 1971 the top decile of owners controlled virtually all the rice land. Comparing the types of rice land tenure in 1971 with the one direct form of ownership in 1987, we get the results shown in Table 7.1.

In 1971, of 160 households, 48 or 30% held rice land in some form. This included 7 jenmies, 10 owner-operators, and 39 tenants, a few of them overlapping with more than one form of ownership. The average holding was 1.4 acres, close to the all-Kerala average for that year of 1.2 acres (George 1979:15). The total sample acreage for each category is given at the bottom of the table. The column labeled "Combined" is the sum of land held under jenmy and that under owner. The tenancy total (44.30 acres) does not equal that of the land under jenmy control (36.70 acres) because some jenmies had tenants outside the sample while tenants likewise had landlords outside the sample. Similarly, the total for the combined ownership category in 1971—64.65 acres—does not equal the total simple ownership sum in 1987—52.14 acres—because land was redistributed to tenants in and out of the sample. Household partitions and other processes such as market purchases have redistributed land in ways that confound the precise measurement of the effects of the land reform. The cross-section represented by the data is not a closed system.

The 48 owners in 1971 (30% of the sample households) divide into 4 equal quartiles of 12 households each. The 61 owners in 1987 (36%) break down into four equal quartiles of 15 households each (one small holder was dropped to simplify the calculations). These 61 owners held a total of 52.15 acres, or 0.85 acres on average, a large decline from the 1.4 acres average in 1971. The overwhelming concentration of land ownership is indicated by the Gini coefficients ranging from 94.5 to 99.4, approaching perfect inequality. Tenancies were more evenly distributed with a Gini of 54.4. If landless households are included, the Gini for tenancies was 91.6.

Table 7.1
Percentage of Rice Land Held by Landholding Quartiles
Nadur Village Kerala 1971 and 1987

| | 1971 Tenures (N=48) | | | | 1987 |
|---|---|---|---|---|---|
| | Jenmy | Owner Operator | Combined | Tenant | (N=60) Owner |
| **Landholding Quartiles** | | | | | |
| Top | 100 | 100 | 98.2 [a] | 57.0 | 50.7 |
| 2nd | 0 | 0 | 1.7 | 26.9 | 26.1 |
| 3rd | 0 | 0 | 0 | 14.5 | 15.5 |
| 4th | 0 | 0 | 0 | 1.7 | 7.6 |
| **Gini Indices** [b] | | | | | |
| Land Holders | 99.4 | 95.7 | 94.5 | 54.4 | 41.4[9] |
| Landless Included | 100 | 100 | 100 | 91.6 | 85.0 |
| Total Acres | 36.70 | 27.95 | 64.65 | 44.30 | 52.15 |

a. *The two figures of 100% in the top decile for 1971 produce a combined figure of 98.2% because membership in the top quartile varies slightly by type of ownership.*
b. *Ginis on this table are computed with 1/8 units rather than quartiles.*

By 1987, ownership had changed substantially. Sixty-one owners (35%) held land in a single ownership category. The top quartile accounted for 50.7%. Using the 1971 Jenmy, Owner, or Combined columns for comparison, we find the Gini index dropped from 100 or 98 to 41.4, a 50% decline. Using the tenancy column, we observe a 13 point or 24% decline. If the rice land landless are included in the calculation, the Gini changes from 91.6 to 85.0, down 6.6 points or 7.2% from 1971. The concentration of rice land ownership has been substantially reduced.[10]

From Table 7.1 it can also be seen that the households in the top ownership quartile were the major losers of land; these were the high-caste landlords. The table hides a number of important things, however. The top 20% of holders in rice land are now no longer pure renters, but must at least manage the land to which they hold title. They may hire a foreman and thus avoid actual field labor or even supervisory work, but they can no longer simply retain paper holdings and receive rent. The household described earlier which held 60 acres in 1954 now has 1.65 acres which they manage directly and in which even the younger Nambudiri men sometimes work during the peak labor demand periods such as harvest time.

The redistribution of rice land appears to have benefited mainly those in the 2nd to 4th ownership quartiles. The 4th quartile still has only a tiny share of the available rice land (7.6%). Ten new land owning households have been created in the sample. The percentage of households not paying rent increased from 7.6% of the sample households to 35.9% in the 16 year period.[11]

### Redistribution of House Compound Land

An important component of Kerala's land reform was the abolition of a second kind of tenancy. In addition to the rice fields, the same landlords owned the compounds on which tenants and agricultural laborers built their houses. These houses, or "huts" (*kudi*) produced the *kudikidappukaran* and *kudiyirippu* tenants who paid rent for the space on which the huts were built.

House compound land in Kerala is often of great agricultural and economic value. Bananas, coconuts, cashews, arecanuts, mangoes, cassava, and other crops are grown there. The threat of eviction from these lands was a powerful weapon in the hands of landlords in getting exorbitant rents for the rice fields. Thus part of the rice land rent was derived indirectly from house compound tenancy relations. Up to the 1930s at least, jenmies also levied additional charges such as wages for the harvest measurer, payments to the jenmy at birth and death ceremonies, and payments just prior to harvest. Recalcitrant tenants could be disciplined with the threat of eviction supplemented by denial of services from other castes such as barbers, washers, and priests. Jenmies could also limit their low-caste tenants' use of village pathways and could hire agents to beat tenants, rob their house compound, steal their livestock, set fire to their hay supplies, and the like (Radhakrishnan 1989:92). Our survey indicates that *kudiyirippu* tenants—the type found in Cochin— paid large amounts of the produce from their gardens to their landlords. Interviews with former tenants yielded examples such as "50 strings of bananas", "several bunches of vegetables", and so forth. Written landlord records referred to earlier gave money figures. These indicated that house compound rent averaged 50 rupees per acre or 1/2 rupee for each

Table 7.2
Percentage of House Compound Land Held by Landholding Quintiles
Nadur Village Kerala 1971 and 1987

| | 1971 Tenures (N=48) | | | | 1987 |
|---|---|---|---|---|---|
| | Jenmy | Owner Operator | Combined | Tenant | (N=60) Owner |
| **Landholding Quintiles** | | | | | |
| Top | 100 | 100 | 100 | 50.3 | 61.4 |
| 2nd | 0 | 0 | 0 | 25.9 | 18.3 |
| 3rd | 0 | 0 | 0 | 14.2 | 10.7 |
| 4th | 0 | 0 | 0 | 8.0 | 6.7 |
| 5th | 0 | 0 | 0 | 1.6 | 3.0 |
| **Gini Indices** | 100 | 100 | 100 | 53.4 | 61.0 |
| **Total Acres** | 47.84 | 27.37 | 75.21 | 72.75 | 92.64 |

cent of land in 1969. With full ownership rights, the tenant has a more direct stake in maintaining and improving the house garden site *and* the house itself. The removal of the threat of eviction rendered more effective Kerala's large-scale house construction subsidy for hut dwellers (Franke and Chasin 1989:37-38).

Prior to the land reform, all households had either tenancy or ownership rights to their house compound land. Following the land reform, all households have title to their house compound land. It is thus not necessary to divide the Ginis into landless versus landed only. In 1971 the Gini coefficient was 100; by 1987 it had dropped to 61.0, a 39% reduction in inequality. This can be seen in Table 7.2.

The land reform's effects on distribution of house compound land are different from those on rice fields. The Gini has declined more in *relative* terms than for rice land, but the coefficient is still quite high at 61.0. The reason for the continuing high inequality in house compound land is that house compound land not officially tenanted was exempt from land reform; only lands on which people had built huts and which they could thus claim as *their* house compound lands were redistributed. In Nadur some large tracts of forest and coconut groves remained in the hands of the wealthiest former landlords. Rubber, areca, and cashew groves are common recent investments on these lands. The transfer of small tenancies from jenmy to former tenant combined with the continued ownership of the large forest and coconut groves produces the higher Gini coefficient of ownership in 1987 (61.0) as compared with the tenancy column for 1971 (53.4).

How much house compound land was redistributed? In 1971, 7 jenmies owned 47.84 acres as landlords, averaging 6.83 acres; 15 households held direct ownership of 27.37 acres, to average 1.82 acres each; and 142 households were tenants on 72.75 acres, for an average tenancy of 0.51 acres. The largest single holding was by one jenmy who held 27.15 acres as landlord and 12 acres in simple ownership. This jenmy—the same as the largest rice land jenmy—lost the greatest single amount in the sample: 31.35 acres of which 27.15 at least were directly from the land reform.

By 1987, 170 households held title to a total of 92.64 acres, for an average of 0.54 acres. Unlike rice land, for which the sample as a whole showed an overall loss, the sample households gained 13.94 acres, owing again to the particular configuration of relationships with jenmies within and outside the sample. In 1987 the largest single holding was 7.8 acres, land remaining to the former largest jenmy from 1971. Overall, during the 16 year period, 12 households lost an average of 4.72 acres while 147 households gained an average of 0.48 acres each. The largest single gainer added 5.5 acres, resulting from a family partition while the second largest gainer received 2.45 acres in the land reform.

In all, 91.9% of Nadur households received title to some house compound land. As can be seen by comparing the Combined column for 1971 with the Owner column for 1987 on Table 7.2, the 2nd-5th ownership quintiles received all of what was distributed, including even agricultural laborers and members of the lowest, (former) untouchable castes. The lowest quintile, however, received very little. Households in that category were mostly agricultural laborers living in the outcaste or untouchable colonies on the edges of the village on small hillside plots. These plots became theirs, but few coconut, mango, or other trees will grow there (cf. Mencher 1980a:267). The statistics on the land reform do not fully reflect the continuing poverty of the resources of the very poorest group.[12]

Combining both rice field and house compound land, we can summarize the Kerala land reform in the Nadur sample as follows: 14 households lost land totaling 105.83 acres to their former tenants while 145 households gained 102.14 acres averaging 0.70 acres each. One household neither lost nor gained land and ten households in the 1987 sample derived their holdings from partitions from the households in the 1971 sample.

## Land Reform and Income Inequality

How much income effect did the land reform have? One problem is to estimate rent intake by the landlords. Although the act was passed in 1969 and went into effect in 1971, both transfer of title from landlord to tenant *and* ending of rental payments for many households took place either earlier or later. Because of the many decades of militant tenant and farm worker struggles starting in the 1930s and the election victory of the Communist Party in 1957, some tenants stopped paying part or all of their rent long before the official enactment date. Similarly, some landlords—sensing the inevitability of some kind of reform—sold title to the tenancies to some or all of their tenants prior to enactment. Others filed jointly with their tenants on 1 January 1970 to avoid court costs and improve the chances of getting compensation. At the other end, many households did not actually receive title to their land until the late 1970s, and might have been coerced into paying rent beyond the reform enactment date to jenmies who had powerful local political connections.[13] There is no completely satisfactory solution to this problem for the analysis, but the fact that two of our three major research assistants were local residents of Nadur made it possible to cross-check much of the household survey information. In the tables below, it will be seen that some land in both paddy fields and house compound areas was already described as owned outside the landlord-tenant system. Thus the 1971 survey captures the situation as it was unfolding and is probably fairly accurate. In any case, since some land had already been transferred by 1971, the comparison of this survey date with 1987, when all transactions had been completed, therefore indicates the *minimum* effects of the reform and could not exaggerate the degree of redistribution.

Another problem is that none of the many land reform studies provide information on rental rates or payments. One family allowed us access to their holdings and rental listings for 1954. These showed the family owning nearly 60 acres of rice land and 28 acres of house compound land. In 1966 only 2.5% of Kerala households owned more than 10 acres of land (United Nations 1975:71). Although records for that time period are difficult to evaluate precisely because of price differences etc., this sample landlord took in 1969 a rent of 33% of the gross, amounting to about half the surplus value produced by the tenant farmer at the time. Using these figures along with 1970-71 price and production figures, we can calculate that each acre of rice land was theoretically worth 201 rupees in rental value to the landlord.

Rent and harvest data were not collected in the 1971 Nadur survey. To get the most meaningful estimate of the income effects of the reform, we made the following assumptions for 1971:

1. All farmers in the sample were producing the Kerala State average rice output per unit of land.[14]
2. Tenants were paying the last locally recorded rental rates (1969) in Nadur: 33% of the gross.
3. Rents on one-crop land were for one harvest only, while for two-crop land, they were for both harvests. The amounts have been adjusted in the income figures. One-crop and two-crop land categories are not shown on Table 1.
4. Tenants were paying the last locally recorded rental rates (1969) for house compound land of Rs 0.50 for each cent (.01 acres).

To limit extraneous variables as much as possible, we employed a number of techniques. In comparing incomes of 1987 with those of 1971, we subtracted all post-1971 welfare programs such as agricultural labor pensions. This makes the 1987 income inequality patterns as unequal as possible, or, in other words, indicates the likely *minimum* effect of the land reform. In addition, as we will see in Chapter 12, changes in the job market have tended to *increase* levels of inequality. Thus, outside forces can be thought of as having counteracted the land reform, again making our statistical findings reflective of the minimum effects of the reform on income inequality. We are not able to separate out the possible consequences of wage increases for agricultural laborers won by Kerala's militant trade unions. Increases did occur during the period between the two household surveys, especially as a consequence of the 1974 Kerala Agricultural Workers Act. Many small landowners work as farm laborers. Since some of the income inequality data are affected by that act, we cannot be certain of how much it contributed compared to the land reform. In Chapter 8 we will consider wage increases and in Chapter 9 we will measure the income effects of welfare and pension programs.

We also concluded that the parity index did not shift significantly in favor of farmers. The parity index expresses the ratio of prices received by farmers to prices paid by them. If the index is above 100, farmers are profiting; below 100 they are losing in so far as they must purchase things with money earned from their farms. In 1971, the index was 93. In 1987 it was 96. Over the 16 year period between surveys it averaged 96 ranging from a low of 83 in 1983 to a high of 109 in 1974. It was over

Table 7.3
Distribution of Household Income by Income Quintile
With Land Reform and Workers Act
Nadur Village Kerala 1971 Versus 1987

|                                         | 1971 Income Percent (N=160) | 1987 Income Percent (N=170) |
| --------------------------------------- | --------------------------- | --------------------------- |
| **Income Percentage by Income Quintile** |                             |                             |
| Top                                     | 52.6                        | 48.8                        |
| 2nd                                     | 21.2                        | 21.5                        |
| 3rd                                     | 12.6                        | 13.6                        |
| 4th                                     | 8.7                         | 10.1                        |
| 5th                                     | 4.9                         | 6.1                         |
| Total                                   | 100.0                       | 100.1                       |
| Gini indices                            | 50.7                        | 45.4                        |

100 in only 6 of the 16 years (computed from George 1982:149; Herring 1989:108; GOK 1989:14; GOK 1990:16). These numbers would not raise the incomes of the former tenants in a way to influence the Gini independently.

We distinguish two forms of change in the patterns of inequality. One form is the general degree of inequality which can be expressed by comparing units such as quintiles and computing the Gini index. The other form is *mobility among individual households or groups*. In this chapter, we survey the decline in inequality, using quintiles of household income, then caste and class. In Chapter 12 we consider mobility in relation to the land reform, after we have described other forces that interact with it.

Table 7.3 shows the quintile distribution of household income for both surveys. This table repeats the 1971 data from the first column of Table 6.5. The 1987 data have welfare payments and agricultural labor pensions removed. They correspond to the second column of Table 6.5. The Gini coefficient was reduced by 5.3 points, or by 10.4%.

From Table 7.3, we see that the inequality declined mostly where advocates of land reform wanted: the middle to poorest Nadur households. Quintiles 3 and 4 got most of their increases from the land re-

Table 7.4: Income Quartiles and Gini Index
Rice Land Owning Households Only
Nadur Village Kerala 1971 and 1987

|  | Percent of Household Income | |
|---|---|---|
|  | 1971 (N=48) | 1987 (N=60) [a] |
| **Income quartiles** |  |  |
| Top | 70.3 | 57.6 |
| 2nd | 16.1 | 21.8 |
| 3rd | 8.3 | 12.5 |
| 4th | 5.2 | 8.1 |
| Gini Indices | 65.3 | 48.3 |

*a. Welfare and pensions have been subracted from 1987 incomes.*

form. But those in the bottom quintile benefited only by receiving title to their garden lands, which, as noted above, are not always the most productive. Much of the redistribution in the bottom quintile probably came from wage increases.

If we consider rice land owners only, the change in inequality becomes more distinct. These data appear in Table 7.4. The Gini drops 17 points or 26% among rice land owners only. The greater change in the Gini among owners supports the view that the abolition of tenancy caused a redistribution of income among land owning households.

## Land Reform and Caste Inequality

Has the relationship between land and caste been altered by the land reform? In Table 7.5 are presented the comparisons of caste percents in the village population with percent of types of rice land owned in each survey period.

From Table 7.5 it is apparent that major changes in ownership by caste have taken place. In 1971 the Nambudiri landlords held 100% of all landlord rice land, 85% of that in direct owner-operator ownership, and 3% of the recorded tenancies. By 1987 this caste had lost 52.25 acres of rice land and owned 18% of the sample rice land against its 8% of the population. The concentrated holdings of the Nambudiri landlords were

Table 7.5
Percent of Rice Land Owned by Caste
Nadur Village Kerala 1971 and 1987

| | Percent of Sample | 1971 Land Tenure Percents | | | 1987 Ownership | |
| | | Jenmy | Owner Operator | Tenant | Percent Owned | Gain/Loss Acres |
|---|---|---|---|---|---|---|
| **Caste** | | | | | | |
| Nambudiri | 8 | 100 | 85 | 3 | 18 | -52.25 |
| Nair/Variar | 49 | 0 | 15 | 79 | 53 | 23.30 |
| Craft | 6 | 0 | 0 | 0 | 1 | .20 |
| Ezhuthasan/ | | | | | | |
| Chetty | 8 | 0 | 0 | 14 | 12 | 4.31 |
| Muslim | 13 | 0 | 0 | 2 | 12 | 4.35 |
| Ezhava | 8 | 0 | 0 | 1 | 1 | .70 |
| Mannan* | 2 | 0 | 0 | 2 | 2 | .76 |
| Pulaya* | 6 | 0 | 0 | 0 | 2 | 1.00 |
| **Total Acres** | | 36.70 | 27.95 | 44.30 | 52.15 | -17.63 |

* *Former Untouchables*

redistributed across several other castes, in particular the Nairs who were the main tenant group in Nadur. One of the major rice land gaining castes was the Muslims who held only 2% of tenancies in 1971, but had increased this to 12% of land owned in 1987. Of the former untouchable castes, Mannans turned their tenancies into equal amounts of owned rice land. Because all Nadur Pulayas in 1971 were agricultural laborers, they did not qualify for direct rice land transfers in the land reform. During the 16 year period between surveys, however, one Pulaya household saved enough money from the work of members outside the village to purchase land from a household of another caste. The land reform created the land market to make possible this change, but the financial resources came from processes outside the reform.

With house compound land, the situation is similar. The data appear in Table 7.6. As with rice land, Table 7.6 shows that house compound land was highly concentrated within the Nambudiri Brahmin caste. This small elite held 100% of the land in 125 landlord parcels, and 82% of the owner-operator acreage as well. The tenancies were fairly

Table 7.6
Percent of House Compound Land Owned by Caste
Nadur Village Kerala 1971 and 1987

| | Percent of Sample | 1971 Land Tenure Percents | | | 1987 Ownership | |
| | | Jenmy | Owner Operator | Tenant | Percent Owned | Gain/Loss Acres |
|---|---|---|---|---|---|---|
| **Caste** | | | | | | |
| Nambudiri | 8 | 100 | 82 | 6 | 25 | -47.87 |
| Nair | 49 | 0 | 6 | 59 | 41 | 35.38 |
| Craft | 6 | 0 | 0 | 3 | 3 | 2.27 |
| Ezhuthasan/ | | | | | | |
| Chetty | 8 | 0 | 0 | 8 | 8 | 6.72 |
| Muslim | 13 | 0 | 10 | 12 | 13 | 8.43 |
| Ezhava | 8 | 0 | 2 | 7 | 7 | 5.66 |
| Mannan* | 2 | 0 | 0 | 2 | 1 | 1.31 |
| Pulaya* | 6 | 0 | 0 | 3 | 2 | 2.02 |
| **Total Acres** | | 47.84 | 27.37 | 72.75 | 92.64 | 13.94 |

*\* Former Untouchables*

evenly distributed among the other castes, except that the Nairs had somewhat more than their population percentage while the Pulayas were distinctly under-represented.

Following the land reform, Nambudiris still retain an enormous advantage over the other castes, owning 25% of the land while constituting only 8% of the sample population. The Nairs now have slightly under their "fair" share, holding 41% of the land with 49% of the population. Other groups have remained almost exactly even with their tenancies becoming private holdings on which they no longer must pay rent. Rent income to Nambudiris was removed from 47.87 acres, almost exactly the prior jenmied house compound land of 47.84 acres. As with rice land, some Nambudiri households lost land to tenants outside the sample, while some tenants gained land from jenmies outside the sample. The sample as a whole received 13.94 acres more than were lost by its landlords. As with rice land, the discrepancies reflect transfers into and out of the sample population as well as some post-reform buying and selling of land.[15]

## Land Reform, Caste, and Income Inequality

How has the land reform influenced the relationship between caste and income? The data are presented in Table 7.7.

From Table 7.7 we see that the Nambudiris saw their share of the sample income drop from 20% in 1971 to 13% in 1987. By contrast, Nairs increased their share from 41% to 48%, almost exactly their proportion of the population. Muslims and Pulayas held even while the Mannans raised their level from 4% to 6%.

Looking at the columns on the right of the table, we can see that Nambudiris gained on average 245% (1987 income divided by 1971 income times 100) while Nairs increased at the much faster rate of 479%.[16]

Because the data by caste do not lend themselves well to Gini calculations, we have computed instead the ratio of the average income for each caste to the sample average for the appropriate survey year. This technique shows a reduction in inequality. The 1971 ratios range from 2.7 for the Nambudiris to 0.5 for the Pulayas. In 1987 the range was 1.7 for Nambudiris to 0.6 for Pulayas. While there was some movement by other castes such as Nairs who went from 0.8 in 1971 to the (rounded) average of 1.0 in 1987, the most dramatic change is the rise of the Mannans to the top position with 2.5 times the sample average for 1987.

Correlation coefficients confirm these land and income relationships. For 12 Nambudiri households in 1971, the Pearson coefficient for household income with rice land jenmied or owned was 0.86**, and for house compound land jenmied or owned 0.89**. By contrast, coefficients for the other castes were very low while those for tenancies were all below 0.20.

In 1987 these coefficients had changed substantially. The 13 Nambudiri household incomes correlated with rice land owned only -0.09 and with house compound land only -0.19. For all 61 rice land owning households income correlated at 0.36*, but only the Nair caste, the former main tenants, had significant correlations with 0.29* for household income and rice land and 0.36** for house compound land with household income.

These correlations indicate that for the Nambudiri caste in 1971, land was the main determinant of income; by 1987 this was no longer the case. A more precise test would be the correlation between the income changes and the land holding changes. Producing such a correlation is fraught with many imprecisions, however. Which income change is more informative, the rupees increase or the ratio of that increase to the 1971 baseline? With land changes, should house compound be grouped

## Table 7.7
## Land Reform, Caste, and Income Inequality
## Welfare, Lunches, and Ration Shop Not Included
## Nadur Village Kerala 1971 to 1987

| Caste | N | Percent of Sample | Percent of Income | | 1971 Avg | 1971 Ratio to Avg | 1987 Avg | 1987 Ratio to Avg | 1971 to 1987 Gain in Rupees | Index |
|---|---|---|---|---|---|---|---|---|---|---|
| | | | 1971 | 1987 | | | | | | |
| Nambudiri | 13 | 8 | 20 | 13 | 4,699 | 2.7 | 11,527 | 1.7 | 4,855 | 245 |
| Nair/Variar | 83 | 49 | 41 | 48 | 1,379 | 0.8 | 6,606 | 1.0 | 5,259 | 479 |
| Craft Ezhuthasan/ | 11 | 6 | 10 | 7 | 2,664 | 1.6 | 7,840 | 1.2 | 5,480 | 294 |
| Chetty | 13 | 8 | 6 | 7 | 1,496 | 0.9 | 6,177 | 0.9 | 4,926 | 413 |
| Muslim | 22 | 13 | 10 | 10 | 1,457 | 0.8 | 5,254 | 0.8 | 3,895 | 361 |
| Ezhava | 13 | 8 | 6 | 5 | 1,352 | 0.8 | 4,477 | 0.7 | 3,181 | 331 |
| Mannan* | 4 | 2 | 4 | 6 | 2,435 | 1.4 | 17,284 | 2.5 | 14,850 | 710 |
| Pulaya* | 11 | 6 | 4 | 4 | 896 | 0.5 | 4,235 | 0.6 | 3,339 | 473 |
| Totals and Averages | 170 | 100 | 101 | 100 | 1,717 | 1.0 | 6,789 | 1.0 | 5,016 | 395 |

* Former Untouchables

with rice land or not? And how do we factor in the effect of pre-reform tenancies, the fact that land went to households that were to some extent already benefiting from it?

After examining the data in several ways, we found that correlating the rupee increase with each type of land separately gave the most information. For Nambudiris the rupees change in household income correlates 0.50 with the change in rice land ownership and 0.55 with the change in house compound ownership.[17] Nair caste household income changes correlate 0.23 with rice land changes and 0.38** with house compound changes. Among the other castes, only the Ezhuthasans had a significant relationship, owing to a few large transfers to a small number of households including one that is now the largest rice land owner in the sample with 2.8 acres. The highly concentrated land-based wealth of the Nambudiris was distributed across a sufficiently wide spectrum of other castes so that we can measure statistically the income associations only for the former landlord elite and somewhat less clearly for the Nairs who include most of the former tenants.

### Land Reform and Class Inequality

How did the patterns of land ownership by occupational class change in Nadur between 1971 and 1987? On Table 7.8, we show the ownership patterns by occupational/ownership class in 1971. As can be seen from this table, those living off landlordism controlled 72% of landlord rice lands, and 46% of owner-operated rice lands, although they were but 1% of the sample population. Five other households with some jenmy lands were deriving their main incomes from other sources, mostly professional employment. The 12% of the sample (N=20) who were living mostly off tenancy held no jenmy lands and no owner-operated lands, but accounted for 66% of the tenancies, similar to that of the landlord jenmy holdings (72%).

If we now follow out the progress of these households in the two right hand columns, we see that the former landlords now hold simple—owner-operator—title to a mere 2% of the rice land owned by members of the sample. This figure is shown in parentheses to indicate that it refers back to a former category. The landlord class did not exist in 1987. The two former landlord households lost 38.48 acres of rice land to their tenants. The former tenants now hold 25% of the rice land. They gained 0.64 acres each on average. Other classes gained smaller average amounts of land.

Reversing the numbers, we can look backwards from the 1987

Table 7.8
Percent of Rice Land Owned by 1971 Class
Nadur Village Kerala 1971 and 1987

| | | 1971 Land Tenure Percents | | | 1987 Ownership | |
| | Percent of Sample | Jenmy | Owner Operator | Tenant | Percent Owned | Gain/Loss Acres |
|---|---|---|---|---|---|---|
| **1971 Class** | | | | | | |
| Landlord | 1 | 72 | 46 | 0 | (2) | -38.48 |
| Professional | 7 | 17 | 26 | 9 | (14) | -6.28 |
| Service | 4 | 0 | 5 | 3 | (4) | .60 |
| Craft | 6 | 0 | 0 | 0 | (1) | .20 |
| Farmer | 7 | 8 | 12 | 5 | (16) | 2.17 |
| Petty Trade | 15 | 0 | 5 | 5 | (12) | 4.62 |
| Tenant | 13 | 0 | 0 | 66 | (25) | 12.80 |
| Recipient | 16 | 2 | 3 | 11 | (9) | 2.98 |
| Laborer | 27 | 0 | 0 | 0 | (6) | 3.20 |
| Agricultural Laborer | 4 | 0 | 0 | 0 | (2) | .56 |
| Partitions | (6) | 0 | 0 | 0 | (9) | 0 |
| **Total Acres** | | 36.70 | 27.95 | 44.30 | 52.15 | -17.63 |

*Note: Numbers in parentheses refer back to former categories, ie. land owned in 1987 by members of the 1971 class.*

occupational classes as shown on Table 7.9. Here a remarkably altered picture emerges. Those who were former major jenmies have become farmers with 14% of the sample, holding 34% of the rice land but having lost 34.44 acres. All other classes except recipients gained at least some land on average, but the craft and agricultural laborer classes gained hardly any. Significant inequality remains with laborers owning only 9% of rice land for their 34% of the population and agricultural laborers holding 2% with 5% of households. By contrast, the richer classes own more than their mathematical fair share with professionals holding 11% of rice land against their 7% of the sample population while service workers have 10% with only 5% of the population. These data indicate that privileged workers such as managers, doctors, teachers, bus drivers, police, and office clerks are investing at least some of their stable in-

Table 7.9
Percent of Rice Land Owned by 1987 Class
Nadur Village Kerala 1971 and 1987

| | | 1971 Land Tenure Percents | | | 1987 Ownership | |
|---|---|---|---|---|---|---|
| **1987 Class** | Percent of Sample | Jenmy | Owner Operator | Tenant | Percent Gain/Loss Owned | Acres |
| Professional | 7 | (2) | (5) | (12) | 11 | 2.13 |
| Service | 5 | (0) | (3) | (12) | 10 | 4.09 |
| Craft | 8 | (0) | (0) | (1) | 2 | .90 |
| Farmer | 14 | (85) | (68) | (21) | 34 | -34.44 |
| Petty Trade | 11 | (0) | (0) | (11) | 16 | 6.61 |
| Recipient | 18 | (13) | (22) | (14) | 17 | -2.36 |
| Laborer | 34 | (0) | (1) | (26) | 9 | 4.24 |
| Agricultural Laborer | 5 | (0) | (0) | (4) | 2 | 1.20 |
| **Total Acres** | | 36.70 | 27.95 | 44.30 | 52.15 | -17.63 |

*Note: Numbers in parentheses refer back to former categories, ie. land owned in 1971 by members of the 1987 classes.*

comes in rice land. Some petty traders may be doing the same, as their 11% of the population holds 16% of the rice land. Land is a valuable investment in Nadur and in rural Kerala generally. Despite high farming costs and low farm prices, rice land means security against inflation, and is probably a safer investment than the savings bank, or the investment pools (*chitties*) which a few Nadur households also try as ways to get a good return on the money they earn on the job.

But what of the house compound land? Table 7.10 indicates what happened to the 1971 occupational/ownership classes. As with rice land, we see a high concentration among the 2 landlords who controlled 70% of the jenmy holdings along with 47% of that owner operated. Tenancies are far more dispersed. Looking forward from 1971 on Table 7.10, we see that by 1987 the former landlords held 9% of the house compounds after having lost 37.63 acres through the land reform. All other groups except the professionals gained land in this category.

Table 7.10
Percent of House Compound Land Owned by 1971 Class
Nadur Village Kerala 1971 and 1987

| | | 1971 Land Tenure Percents | | | 1987 Ownership | |
| --- | --- | --- | --- | --- | --- | --- |
| | Percent of Sample | Jenmy | Owner Operator | Tenant | Percent Gain/Loss | |
| | | | | | Owned | Acres |
| **1971 Class** | | | | | | |
| Landlord | 1 | 70 | 47 | 0 | (9) | -37.63 |
| Professional | 7 | 27 | 33 | 7 | (17) | -6.02 |
| Service | 4 | 0 | 4 | 3 | (4) | 2.79 |
| Craft | 6 | 0 | 0 | 3 | (2) | 2.27 |
| Farmer | 7 | 4 | 2 | 6 | (7) | 4.40 |
| Petty Trade | 15 | 0 | 4 | 17 | (13) | 10.66 |
| Tenant | 13 | 0 | 2 | 15 | (12) | 10.81 |
| Recipient | 16 | 0 | 1 | 25 | (13) | 11.74 |
| Laborer | 27 | 0 | 7 | 21 | (16) | 12.87 |
| Agricultural Laborer | 4 | 0 | 0 | 3 | (2) | 2.05 |
| Partitions | (6) | 0 | 0 | 0 | (5) | 0 |
| **Total Acres** | | 47.84 | 27.37 | 72.75 | 92.64 | 13.94 |

Note: *Numbers in parentheses refer back to former categories, ie. land owned in 1987 by members of the 1971 classes.*

Now looking backwards from the 1987 classes on Table 7.11, we see similar developments. The former landlords—indicated by jenmy numbers in parentheses showing what they formerly held—have become part of the farmer class. Former house compound jenmies are now cultivating their house compounds which are still large estates, planting coconuts, arecanuts, mangoes, or rubber. But the table hides the concentration of house compound land in 1987 where just the two former landlord households had 26% of the land of all farmers. Laborers and agricultural laborers do not have house compound commensurate with their population percentages. When we consider further the fact that the farmers hold land of substantially higher quality than do the laborers or agricultural laborers, we can say that the Kerala land reform transferred only minimum house compound benefits to the poorest groups.

Table 7.11
Percent of House Compound Land Owned by 1987 Class
Nadur Village Kerala 1971 and 1987

| | | 1971 Land Tenure Percents | | | 1987 Ownership | |
| | Percent of Sample | Jenmy | Owner Operator | Tenant | Percent Owned | Gain/Loss Acres |
| --- | --- | --- | --- | --- | --- | --- |
| **1987 Class** | | | | | | |
| Professional | 7 | (6) | (0) | (8) | 8 | 7.06 |
| Service | 5 | (0) | (0) | (9) | 9 | 8.37 |
| Craft | 8 | (0) | (4) | (6) | 5 | 3.33 |
| Farmer | 14 | (95) | (78) | (18) | 34 | -36.34 |
| Petty Trade | 11 | (0) | (0) | (12) | 11 | 9.12 |
| Recipient | 18 | (5) | (8) | (20) | 12 | 6.53 |
| Laborer | 34 | (0) | (8) | (27) | 19 | 15.10 |
| Agricultural Laborer | 5 | (0) | (2) | (1) | 1 | .77 |
| Total Acres | | 47.84 | 27.37 | 72.75 | 92.64 | 13.94 |

Note: *Numbers in parentheses refer back to former categories, ie. land owned in 1971 by members of the 1987 classes.*

## Land Reform and Income Inequality by Class

Has the land reform reduced income inequality among the occupational/ownership classes? Data in Table 7.12 provide the answer. Landlords in 1971 were just 1.3% of the sample population but had 8.1% of the income, 6.5 times the sample average. Tenants had 12.5% of population with only 6.4% of income. Agricultural laborers had 4.4% of population with only 2.1% of income. The incomes of these two latter groups were only half the sample average.

By 1987 former landlord households had 1.5 times the average income. Former tenants had raised their share of total income by 14%, but they still had only 0.6 of the average income in 1987. Agricultural laborers had raised their share of the income 43% not counting various welfare programs outside the land reform.

Table 7.12
Land Reform, Class, and Income Inequality
Welfare, Lunches, and Ration Shop Not Included
Nadur Village Kerala 1971 to 1987

| Class | Percent of Sample | | Percent of Income | | 1971 Avg | 1971 Ratio to Avg | 1987 Avg | 1987 Ratio to Avg | 1971 to 1987 Gain in Rupees | Index |
|---|---|---|---|---|---|---|---|---|---|---|
| | 1971 | 1987 | 1971 | 1987 | | | | | | |
| Landlord | 1.3 | (0.0) | 8.1 | (1.8) | 11,135 | 6.5 | (9,850) | (1.5) | (-1,285) | (88) |
| Professional | 6.9 | 6.5 | 16.3 | 23.6 | 4,067 | 2.4 | 24,792 | 3.7 | 20,725 | 610 |
| Service | 4.4 | 5.3 | 8.1 | 9.2 | 3,187 | 1.9 | 11,946 | 1.8 | 8,759 | 375 |
| Craft | 6.3 | 8.2 | 9.7 | 8.6 | 2,664 | 1.6 | 7,153 | 1.1 | 4,489 | 268 |
| Farmer | 6.9 | 13.5 | 4.3 | 12.1 | 1,069 | 0.6 | 6,137 | 0.9 | 5,068 | 574 |
| Petty Trade | 15.0 | 10.6 | 13.9 | 10.5 | 1,596 | 0.9 | 6,744 | 1.0 | 5,148 | 423 |
| Recipient | 15.6 | 17.6 | 13.9 | 11.7 | 1,530 | 0.9 | 4,432 | 0.7 | 2,902 | 290 |
| Laborer | 26.9 | 33.5 | 17.1 | 21.4 | 1,092 | 0.6 | 4,280 | 0.6 | 3,188 | 392 |
| Tenant | 12.5 | (0.0) | 6.4 | (7.3) | 883 | 0.5 | (3,949) | (0.6) | (3,066) | (447) |
| Agricultural Laborer | 4.4 | 4.7 | 2.1 | 3.1 | 824 | 0.5 | 4,291 | 0.6 | 3,467 | 521 |
| Totals and Averages | 100.2 | 99.9 | 99.9 | 99.9 | 1,717 | 1.0 | 6,789 | 1.0 | 5,016 | 395 |

Note: Numbers in parentheses refer back to former categories; that is, how much of 1987 income is held by the 1971 landlord and tenant class households.

We see here, as with caste, that income once highly concentrated in a few hands has been distributed across many households so that the negative economic effects are very clear at the top. The benefits are harder to measure because they are spread across a larger group of households. Nevertheless, the Kerala land reform *has* reduced class inequality by moving income from the most privileged classes to some of those lower on the hierarchy.

This income redistribution can also be seen by looking at the far right hand columns of Table 7.12. The two landlord households maintained only 88% of their 1971 incomes while former tenants had 447% of their 1971 income, a gain of 5 times more than the former landlords.

A dramatic finding computed from the table is the ratio of income between landlords and tenants. In 1971 the landlord households had on average 12.6 times the incomes of their tenants; by 1987 the former landlords had only 2.5 times the income of their former tenants.[18] Similar patterns obtain between the landlords and the laborer and agricultural laborer classes. At the same time, new forms of income inequality have been created or strengthened: professionals had 4.6 times the income of tenants in 1971, but by 1987 this had gone up to 6.3 times. Professional incomes have clearly replaced landlordism as the main source of extreme income inequality, but with three differences: (1) the new inequality is not (yet?) as great as with landlordism of the past, (2) professionals do not require the direct exploitation of other members of the community as did landlords, and (3) professionals contribute to the development of the economy as teachers or government officers in ways far more useful and less parasitic than did landlords.

Income inequality has also declined in terms of size of rice land ownership. In 1971, owners or jenmies with one acre or more rice land had incomes more than 3 times that of tenants and 3.6 times that of non owners. Tenants with more than one acre had 1.22 times the income of the landless, while smaller tenancy holders had almost exactly the average incomes of the landless. In 1987 those owning one acre or more had 1.9 times the average income of landless while those owning less than one acre had 1.05 times the incomes of the landless.

With house compound land almost exactly the same situation obtains. Owners or jenmies of one or more acre house compounds had 3.6 times the income of non owners in 1971 while for owners of less than one acre the ratio was 1.8. In 1987 owners of more than one acre house compounds had only 1.7 times the income of those owning less than one acre. With house compounds there are no landless in Nadur.

These observations can be sustained statistically with correlation coefficients as was done with the caste analysis above. In 1971 the two landlord households had incomes correlating almost 1 to 1 with each type of land holding while in 1987 the correlation was almost minus 1 in both cases.[19] The correlation of income change and land change is also about 1. For 1971, the recipient class had the highest correlation with rice land tenancy and income at 0.59* while the 20 tenants had a figure of 0.44. In 1987 the former tenants' incomes correlated 0.57* with agricultural land owned and 0.74** with house compound land owned. The correlations with change in income for the former tenants are 0.57* with change in agricultural land owned and 0.65* for change in house compound land owned. By contrast, farmers in 1971 had low correlations between land and income; those in 1987 also had low correlations, indicating the importance of non-farm sources of income at both periods even to those making their most important income from the land. Petty traders had high correlations of land and income in both periods, suggesting either that they were investing profits in land for security, or that returns from the land were helping put them into business. In fact both processes were taking place, the former primarily with small Muslim shopkeepers and the latter with a couple of Nambudiri households that used past landlord incomes to start such enterprises as bottled soda distribution. Service workers also had high correlations of land ownership and income in both periods: they too have used the land reform as a means of security. One bus driver, for example, holds 1.69 acres of rice land and 2.45 acres of house compound, both received from the land reform. The rice land produced 2,916 rupees in 1987 before production costs, which left rice worth 1,637 rupees profit. The house compound land contains 30 coconut trees, 8 mango trees, and several other varieties. In addition to the income from the land, the job of the household head's son as bus driver brings in Rs 800 per month or Rs 9,600 per year along with another household member's job at a bank worth Rs 200 per month or Rs 2,400 per year. The 12,000 rupees derived from service sector employment far outweigh the income from the substantial land holdings of the household, but the land provides security and food for household consumption. This example and the correlations underscore the importance of the land reform not for creating a new class of small farmers dependent mostly on the land they received, but rather for spreading small amounts of rice land for security or supplementary investment for households bringing in income from many other sources as well as from the land. In Chapter 12 we shall see case studies of the interplay between land reform and other features of Nadur such as education, household structure, and luck.

## Conclusions

Our analysis of Nadur's land reform can now be summarized as follows:.

**1. The land reform redistributed substantial amounts of land from the biggest owners to small holders and the landless.** In Nadur, abolition of rice land tenancy resulted in the transfer of 52.25 acres of rice land from 2 large landlords and 5 smaller jenmies (4%) to 47 tenants (29%) who became fully entitled small holders. Not affected by the rice land reform were 103 landless households (64%).

The abolition of house compound tenancy benefited 92% of households. Rights to 47.87 acres were transferred to 156 households. The poorest laboring families gained title only to small and often inferior plots.

**2. The land reform reduced both land and income inequality.** In Nadur, the Gini Index for rice land ownership inequality dropped 13 points, and that for house compound land dropped by 39 points between the two surveys. During the same 16 year period, the Gini Index for income inequality declined by 5.3 points. Although forces outside the land reform pulled towards both greater and less inequality, land reform must have caused much of this decline in income inequality. Now that the reform is complete, small landowners have the difficult task of producing enough incomes from their plots to keep pace with rising professional and other incomes; otherwise, the effects of the reform will be swallowed up in the next generation.

**3. The high caste landlords found means to offset their land losses.** Nadur's Nambudiri caste landlord households adopted effective strategies to survive the land reform and maintain their high incomes. Some sold land to tenants before the reform to acquire capital for investment in other undertakings. As we shall see in Chapters 11 and 12, all got their children into higher education to make professional employment the chief landlord response to the reform. This response has benefited Nadur because formerly parasitic landlords have become teachers, administrators, and small business people who contribute to the economy in ways their ancestors did not.

**4. The land reform undermined the material basis of caste and class inequality.** In Nadur, a reduction in caste inequality is one of the clearest consequences of the land reform. The Nambudiri hold on land and high incomes has been broken. The land basis for caste inequality and caste exploitation has been entirely eliminated by the land reform. No material basis exists in Nadur for caste privilege or exploitation since the land reform. Nambudiri incomes rose far less rapidly than those of other castes. Nair and Mannan caste households gained the most while the lowest caste Pulayas raised their relative position only slightly. Mannans and Pulayas probably gained more from programs other than the land reform such as affirmative action. The political conditions for these programs, however, included the power of tenants and their allies in the land reform movement. Land reform struggles reinforced the leverage of these lowest caste groups and allowed them to move upwards economically.

Nadur's class structure was altered dramatically by the elimination of landlord and tenant classes. Former landlords dropped from garnering 6.5 times the sample average income to 1.5 times the average. Former tenants did not gain much on average, but several occupational groups slightly improved their economic position. Professionals raised their share of income from 2.4 to 3.7 times the sample average in the land reform period. Households depending primarily on farming raised their relative share of income from 60% of the average to 90%. Land reform played an important but not exclusive role in these class changes.

**5. The land reform reduced exploitation of the poor by the rich.** One of the most effective components of Kerala's land reform has been the elimination of landlords threats of eviction of tenants from either rice land or house compounds. The success of the land reform, however, has produced new tensions. In place of the struggle between tenants and landlords, former tenants are now at odds with their hired agricultural laborers (Herring 1989). Where once the poor were pitted against the rich, now the poor are pitted against the slightly less poor. This problem cannot be solved by further land reform aimed at spreading private ownership since too little land is available for redistribution.

Land reform alone, however, is not Kerala's only redistribution program. Landless laborers have organized unions, won wage increases, and garnered certain welfare benefits that further reduce inequality. We turn to these programs in the next two chapters.

### Notes

1. Sankaranarayanan and Karunakaran (1985:69-91) list 30 to 40 varieties of tenures and sub-tenures. Varghese (1970) traces the histories of several of the most important of these tenures in the various regions of the territory that became Kerala State in 1956.

2. In much of Travancore, tapioca (cassava) is grown on the drier lands found there instead of rice (Ninan 1986).

3. Jenmies and kanam lease holders carried out additional eviction battles in Malabar. The statement in the text refers only to verumpattam lease holders who usually lost their eviction cases.

4. Panikkar (1989:30-31) presents data from the 1920s in Malabar indicating that cultivators got from 13% to 20% of the after-cost harvest. The kanam lease-holders took 74% to 80% in rental payments, but passed only 2% to 12% to the jenmies. Such a high proportion kept by the intermediate landholder makes sense only if the jenmies held vast estates.

5. Varghese (1970:143-146). Paulini provides a detailed examination of the proposed act of 1957 (1979:241-252); of the watered-down 1963 version (1979:257-260 and 267-272); and of the eventual Kerala Land Reform Amendments Act of 1969 that became the effective land reform (1979:292-296).

6. Herring (1983:180-216) details the intricate political, legal, and on-the-ground battles surrounding the culmination of the land reform act and its implementation.

7. The land ceiling is discussed in United Nations 1975: Chapters IV and V.

8. As of 30 November 1990, the Kerala state government (GOK 1991:A119) lists 2,603,610 rice land ownership certificates issued (some households may have recieved more than one), and 278,712 kudikidappu (hutment) certificates of ownership (probably one per household).

9. The Government of Kerala *Agricultural Census, 1985-86* (cited in Padhi and Nair 1992:7) gives a Gini of 62.0 for 1986 for "size group of holding." The authors citing the data do not indicate whether landless households are included or whether they are referring to rice land only or to combined rice land and house compound land. Combining the two forms in Nadur among all owners would produce a statistic close to that of the Agricultural Census, but would blur the important differences between the two forms of land ownership spelled out in this chapter.

10. Research in Karimpur village in western Uttar Pradesh shows a decline in the land ownership Gini from 58.4 in 1925 to 49.8 in 1984 (Wadley and Derr 1989:105). Despite this decline, attributed in part to a 1950 land reform (1989:102), Brahmins owned 58% of the land in 1985, compared with 74% in 1925. This continuing Brahmin hold on the land contrasts sharply with Nadur and may help explain Karimpur's paradoxical "growing abundance of food coexisting with a growing abundance of hunger and poverty in the village" (1989:84). In another restudy in 1984, the researchers were able to conclude only that "the proportion of the population that is poor has not risen in the past decade" (1989:111).

11. In the Maharashtra village of Malegaon, Attwood (1992) traced changes in land ownership with squared correlation coefficients (similar to regression $r$s). Using his methods, we calculated that the rice land ownership distribution in Nadur in 1971 explained only 3% of the variance of the 1987 distribution. For

Malegaon, landholdings in 1930 still accounted for 18% of the variance for 1980 (Attwood 1992:157). In other words, the Kerala land reform caused more ownership change in Nadur between 1971 and 1987 than occurred in Malegaon over 50 years.

12. We have not attempted a quantitative analysis of the value of the land. It may be possible to indicate roughly the differences by using respondent statements of their land value, land tax data, or a stand-in such as number of coconut trees per acre.

13. Radhakrishnan (1989:163) states that 99% of the Kerala-wide land transfers were completed by 31 March 1982.

14. For the 1987 survey we have respondent data on costs and output which are factored into the 1987 income data. We hope in a future publication to present a detailed input-output analysis of post-land reform agriculture in Nadur.

15. Radhakrishnan (1989:227-228) found similar land and caste transfer results in the Malabar village of Kodakkad, which he surveyed in 1979. Nieuwenhuys (1991) had a less positive impression of the extent of land transfers to Ezhava laborers in the central Kerala coastal village of Poomkara.

16. These numbers differ from those on Table 6.7, which summarizes the effects of *all* redistribution programs combined.

17. Although these correlations are not returned as statistically significant by SPSS because of the small sample size, we can see that there was a great impact of the land reform on these 12 households' incomes.

18. Herring (1983:182) cites Kerala government statistics indicating that landlords averaged only 2.6 times the income of their tenants in the mid-1960s. Those statistics may greatly underestimate the advantage of the landlords who probably could hide much of their income to researchers doing large-scale surveys.

19. In 1971 the correlation of rice land owned or jenmied with house compound land owned or jenmied was 0.95**, while for rice land tenancies and house compound tenancies, it was only 0.18. In 1987 the correlation of house compound land with rice land was 0.38**.

# 8

---

# Unions, Wages, Work, and Survival

Kerala stands out among all the states of India for its early and militant labor struggles and organizations. These struggles have extended unions into the difficult to organize agricultural labor sector. Kerala's radical trade unions grew out of the caste improvement associations described in Chapter 4, joined with the land reform movement outlined in Chapter 7, and gave support to the Communist Party to agitate for and legislate higher wages, better working conditions, and selected welfare programs for the poorest workers and their families. Unions are neither strong nor highly visible in Nadur, but union-won gains have spilled over into the village from Alleppey, Palghat, and other union strongholds.

Agricultural laborers are the poorest, most exploited, lowest caste, most heavily female, and most generally oppressed of all Kerala's people. A redistribution strategy thus must attempt to improve the lives of these laborers.

## Prior Conditions of Agricultural Laborers

Nineteenth century Kerala agricultural laborers were agrestic (rural) slaves. They could be bought and sold. They owed service to their masters. They were held in categories identical to those used for ownership of land:

1. *jenmom*, fully owned.
2. *kanom*, held on a long term lease, and
3. *pattom*, held on a shorter lease, whereby the slave could be hired out annually.

Although slavery was abolished in Kerala in 1855, agricultural laborers effectively remained slaves into the 20th century (Tharamanga-lam 1981:52-53). As we saw in Chapter 7, an important hold over labor-ers was the house compound tenancy system under which they could be threatened with eviction until after the land reform of 1969.

Laborers were on call to their masters 24 hours a day. In addition to field labor, they could be forced to cut firewood, beat up the master's enemies, and do other odd jobs. A laborer who rebelled faced eviction by the master's thugs, who would appear suddenly one morning, throw the laborer's few belongings out of the hut, pull it down, or burn it quickly to ashes. One or two such incidents from time to time undoubt-edly sufficed to remind potentially recalcitrant laborers to stay in their place (Tharamangalam 1981:56-57).

Because laborers were low-caste, their subjugation was reinforced by caste behavior prescriptions and proscriptions such as we described in Chapter 4. Laborers addressed their employers as "master" (*thampuran*) or "lord" (*melan*) while referring to themselves as "slave" (*adiyan*) (Tharamangalam 1981:57). According to laborers in Kuttanad, where unions began earliest, high-caste landlords could take sexual advantage of female low-caste laborers or their children with impunity (Tharaman-galam 1981:58).

Along with these social and psychological humiliations, workers had to suffer numerous "petty exactions" from their hard-earned wages. They could not challenge the size or shape of the containers used by the masters to measure the rice paid them as wages for harvesting or other field labor. They had to give fruit and coconut from their house com-pounds more or less on demand to their masters in return for cloth or food given them when in need, but could not easily ask for a fair ac-counting of the transactions. Since their working hours were not fixed, landlords could manipulate their wages in the fields. House chores demanded of them added further to the work day (Kannan 1988:235). To the grim account of life for Pulaya caste members in Chapter 4 —virtually all of them agricultural laborers—we can add K. P. Kannan's sociological observations (1988:236) of the patron-client relationship that obtained between agricultural laborers and their bosses:

> Everything the landowner gave had the aura of charity and patronage and was invariably accompanied by various exactions and low wages which was all concealed under the implicit (when necessary explicit) authoritarian command of the landowner.

In short, agricultural laborers lived in poverty, servitude, obedience, and humiliation. Individually or as a small group confronting their own landlord, they could do little to better their lives. As part of a large social movement that included trade unions in other sectors of the economy, however, they were able to overcome many of their former indignities. To see what historical circumstances led to their partial emancipation, let us look briefly at the history of Kerala's trade union movement with emphasis on its role in organizing and protecting agricultural laborers.

### History of Trade Unions in Kerala

Kerala's first union was the Travancore Labour Association (TLA), formed among coir workers in Alleppey in 1922. Initially it was a company union (Isaac 1983:1,12). Wage cuts from the Great Depression began to hit coir workers in 1928, causing the union to turn to militancy (Kannan 1988:105). The influence of the caste improvement associations, especially the association of Ezhavas (see Chapter 4) who made up most of the coir workers in Alleppey, led the union from militancy to radicalization and its eventual alliance with the Communist Party (Isaac 1983:14-25). Throughout the 1920s to 1940s coir workers led in organizing their own unions and supporting other workers in their struggles to organize (Isaac 1984; Jayadevadas 1983).

Other unions began to form. In Malabar railway workers struck in 1928 (Kannan 1988:107). During the 1930s, unions sprang up in tile and textile factories, among toddy tappers and coconut tree climbers, harbor workers, cigarette (beedi) rollers, cashew nut processors, head-load carriers, and others (Tharamangalam 1981:68). In 1938 the Coir Factory Workers Union—an outgrowth of the TLA—carried out a general strike in which some wage demands were won and arrested strike leaders were released (Isaac 1983:46-56). By the early 1940s, workers had formed a labor federation, the All Travancore Trade Union Congress (ATTUC) (Tharamangalam 1981:68).

In 1939, out of the growing strength and militancy of the unions, led by the coir workers, the Travancore Agricultural Labor Union (TALU) was organized among farm workers in Alleppey (Alexander 1980:A72-A73). In 1952 the TALU was able to win a 20% wage increase for male workers; the following year the union won a similar increase for female agricultural laborers, along with some restrictions on working hours, and the right to 1/2 hour's rest at noon (Alexander 1980:A73). In 1961-62, 5% of Kerala's total work force was unionized compared with 2% for all-India (Nossiter 1982:59).

In the late 1960s, during one of the most intense moments in the struggle for land reform, the CPM began spreading the agricultural workers movement outside the Alleppey area. Other political parties followed suit with less success. In 1966, 54 agricultural labor unions were registered with the Kerala Labour Department; by 1976 this had risen to 205 (Jose 1984:57). The CPM-oriented Kerala State Karshaka Thozhilali Union (KSKTU) claimed 130,000 members by 1972 (Jose 1984:61). The strongest areas were Alleppey with 35,000 members and Palghat with 42,000 (Alexander 1980:A73). Palghat District borders Trichur in which Nadur is located. In 1975 KSKTU membership reached 159,000 (Tharamangalam 1981:80), and in 1981 it was up to 485,000 (Kannan 1988:254). Kerala's agricultural laborers are probably the best organized in all of India (Krishnan 1991:A89-A90).

How did Kerala's workers achieve such spectacular growth in union membership? One factor appears to be the relatively high percent of workers in rural jobs *other* than field labor. In 1971, Kerala ranked first among all Indian states with 45% of its rural work force in non field (nonagricultural) production. Assam, the nearest competitor, had only 27%. By contrast, only 34% of Kerala's rural laborers are listed as engaged in agricultural labor, ranking the state 6th in that category (Kannan 1988:10). These data are important for two reasons. First, a high proportion of Kerala's nonagricultural workers have been in strategic sectors such as plantations, toddy tapping (production of a mildly alcoholic coconut drink), coir production, and other pursuits such as tile factories where conditions favored the building of strong unions. These non field but rural unions in turn became bases for extension of radical labor activity into the more difficult agricultural sector. As a result, Kerala farm laborers have had organizational and political support from powerful and strategic unions in nearby sectors. A second factor has been the building of a strong Communist Party organization in large part via the nonagricultural unions *and* the tenants who were struggling for the land reform. Kerala's several Communist and Left Front governments, starting in 1957, have been sympathetic to agricultural workers.

Along with the occupational structure and the rise of the Communist Party, we must add that Kerala's workers and their leaders have also demonstrated tremendous courage, self-sacrifice, and resistance to corruption in generating their union organizations. Over the years, hundreds of workers, union organizers, Communist Party cadre, and bystanders were killed in police shootings and *lathi* (nightstick) charges against picketers and demonstrators. Thousands more were injured in these same clashes while many others were murdered or beaten in their homes, at union offices, or in the rice fields by thugs hired by local landlords (Isaac 1983:49-52; Tharamangalam 1981:72-78, 82-83; Kannan 1988:158, 200, 250-251). Today's benefits were paid for by Kerala's many working class martyrs. Some of these martyrs are memorialized with small shrines along village roads, often at or near the site where they gave their lives for the advancement of their fellow workers.

## What Have Agricultural Laborers Won?

Unions have improved the lives of Kerala's agricultural laborers in many ways. Most observers agree on the following points.

1.  Removal of indignities. Agricultural laborers no longer feel the need to address their employers as "master." Many respondents replied to K. P. Kannan, "We are no longer looked upon as slave-like people." These rural workers saw the union's power as the main cause of their rise in social status vis à vis the landowners (1988:255; cf. Herring 1989:104). As summarized by Tharamangalam (1981:95):

Not long ago, the agricultural labourers of Kuttanad were unorganized, powerless and oppressed, and divided among themselves by caste and patron-client bondage. Today, they have not only organized strength but a sense of their strength and power.

2.  Ban on evictions. The land reform overcame the threat of evicting landless agricultural workers from their house plots. This gave them additional strength to organize unions and demand other reforms.[1]
3.  Fixed working hours. In Kuttanad and Palghat where the unions are strongest, fixed daily working hours can be enforced. Eight hours is the longest day allowed.
4.  Rice land distribution. As of March, 1980, 76,120 landless and virtually landless laborer households had received an average of 0.63 acres of paddy land as part of the ceiling provision of the land reform. As we noted in Chapter 7, this represented only a tiny portion of landless households (Kannan 1988:266).

These 4 improvements have had differing impacts in different parts of Kerala. Nadur residents are keenly aware of the changes in the behavior and self-image of the lowest-caste, agricultural laborers. As one respondent put it "They no longer have their backs bent over."

Two other reforms are more controversial: the Kerala Agricultural Workers' Act (KAWA) of 1974, and union-won wage gains.

## The Kerala Agricultural Workers' Act

In 1974 the Kerala government attempted to codify certain rights for agricultural laborers. The Kerala Agricultural Workers' Act contains 6 major components:

1. Security of employment: preference is to be given to workers who worked the same lands during the previous season.
2. Provident Fund: to be made up of a matching contribution of the landowner to a contribution by the worker of 5% of wages. In 1975 the fund was suspended, but partly replaced in 1982 by agricultural laborer pensions (see Chapter 9).
3. Fixed working hours: statewide codification of the gains won in Alleppey for 8 hours maximum daily work for adults and 6 hours for adolescents.
4. Minimum wage: to be set from time to time by the government. All wages for harvest work are to be paid on the threshing floor; no rice can be removed prior to payment.
5. Dispute settlement machinery: tribunals and inspection officers to carry out regulations on settlement of grievances, including power to exact penalties for noncompliance.
6. Civil courts excluded: the civil courts which had interfered so frequently in land reform legislation on the side of landlords, are barred from taking up matters covered by the KAWA. (Paulini 1979:313-314; cf. Kannan 1988:281-285). In theory this strengthens the unions and workers who have better representation in the tribunals.

Implementation of the KAWA has met with extreme difficulty. It has come into full force only in such areas as Kuttanad where the agricultural workers' union is strong enough to carry it out through confrontation with employers (Kannan 1988:283). One important dilution occurred when landowners with less than one hectare (2.47 acres or 247 cents) were excluded from the Act (UN 1975:95). In 1975, the Minister for Agriculture estimated that the one hectare exclusion meant that only 350,000 of 2 million agricultural laborers would be technically included under the KAWA (Paulini 1979:314). More recent observers believe that even the 350,000 is a substantial overestimate since machinery to enforce the law was not put in place rapidly. In the Nadur sample, only one landowner in 61 holds more than the 2.47 acres of rice land necessary to come under the provisions of the KAWA. Because of the dispersed, small-scale nature of agricultural production, the desperate poverty, and the need for work among laborers, landowners flouting the law are unlikely to be brought before the reconciliation tribunals anyway. Farmers who resorted to casual labor or who imported workers from across the state line in Tamil Nadu could be challenged only where the union was strong. But where the union was strong, it had already achieved many of the provisions of the Act (Kannan 1988:281-285; Herring 1989:109; Pushpangadan 1992).

Although the KAWA may have done less than its supporters hoped, it may also signify more than its detractors claim. The KAWA helps set a climate in which the rights of agricultural laborers to certain benefits become accepted as just. The agricultural laborers pensions discussed in Chapter 9 may be an example. An Act on paper is also an organizing tool for the farm laborers and their unions. In future years, implementation could become a political issue. Limitation on working hours might spread from areas where unions are agitating to enforce a government act to nearby villages.

Nadur laborers are not conscious of benefiting from the KAWA. Not a single agricultural laborer in Nadur thought that the KAWA was relevant to his/her wages or working conditions, and none had apparently ever attempted to get any provision enforced. This lack of awareness may result from the weak union presence in the village.


## Wages in Kerala

The passage of the KAWA in combination with the long years of agitation by agricultural laborers seems associated with increases in wages for agricultural laborers. In Kerala, harvest wages reached about 17% of the share of the harvest in the early 1980s, possibly the highest share in all-India (Kannan 1988:263). Where the unions are strongest and have been active for the longest time, wage rates for women are also more nearly equal to men than in areas where unions are weaker and newer (Kannan 1988:261).

Wages for male rice field laborers rose faster in Kerala than most parts of India after 1957 when the first Communist Ministry came to power. Comparative nationwide data for female laborers do not appear to be available. In 1957 Kerala workers earned 1.45 rupees per day, the 3rd highest rate after Punjab and Assam. In 1972 Kerala laborers averaged 4.90 rupees per day, 2nd only to Punjab which offered 6.93. Kerala's rate of increase in the 15 year period was 238%, the largest in the country (UN 1975:87). "Real" wages for Kerala's farm laborers—corrected for the consumer price index for the agricultural labor population —rose an estimated 51% in Kerala, 2nd to Uttar Pradesh which experienced a 72% increase between 1957 and 1972. Agricultural laborers' daily real wage rates in Kerala for 1987 were the 3rd highest in India, behind Punjab and West Bengal (Krishnan 1991:A83).

## Wages in Nadur

For the period since 1971, wages in Kerala seem to have increased about the same as during the period 1957-1972. In Nadur they have gone up more rapidly since 1971. To compute wages for 1971 in Nadur we constructed a composite of stated wages in rupees and wages in unhusked rice multiplied by the all-Kerala market price of unhusked rice for that year. For 1987 data, wages are the average of those stated by respondents.[2] Data for Nadur and for the Thrissur District in which Nadur is located are presented in Table 8.1.

Table 8.1
Average Daily Rice Field Wages in Rupees
Thrissur District, Nadur Village, and all-Kerala 1961-1987

| Year | Thrissur | | All Kerala | |
|---|---|---|---|---|
| | Males | Females | Males | Females |
| 1961-62 [b] | 2.41 | n.a. | 2.22 | n.a. |
| 1970-71 | 3.00 [a] | 1.75 [a] | | |
| | 5.62 [b] | n.a. | 5.09 | n.a. |
| 1976-77 | 8.58 | 5.38 | 8.44 | 5.89 |
| 1980-81 | 12.46 | 8.38 | 11.13 | 7.91 |
| 1984-85 | n.a. | n.a. | 23.60 [c] | 11.89 [c] |
| 1985-86 | n.a. | n.a. | 26.08 [c] | 15.10 [c] |
| 1986-87 | 20.00 [a] | 12.00 [a] | 28.36 [c] | 16.39 [c] |

Sources: Government of Kerala 1985a.
*a. Figures are for Nadur Village from sample survey. b. Kannan 1988:253. c. Government of Kerala 1990:21.*

From Table 8.1 we can see that male wages in Kerala in 1987 were 557% of the 1971 rate (28.36/5.09x100). Since the Agricultural Laborers Consumer Price Index in 1987 was 368 (base year 1970=100; GOK 1988:119), we can say that real wages increased by 51% (557/368x100). This is the same as for the period 1957-72 (see above).

For Nadur wages were 667% in 1987 of the 1971 average (20/3x100). Since the Agricultural Laborers Consumer Price Index in Thrissur District was 367 (base year 1970=100; GOK 1988:119), we can say that real wages for field laborers increased by 82% (667/367x100). These rising wages are no doubt a component of the 5.3 points decline in the Gini Index observed in Tables 6.2 and 6.3. How much of that 5.3 point decline is directly from the land reform and how much from the increase in wages we cannot say.

We can also see from Table 8.1 that female wages remain well below those of male wages, 58% in 1971 and 60% in 1987. The all-Kerala female wage rate in 1987 was 58% (16.39/28.36x100) that of males. Nadur is thus right at the all-Kerala average.

## Unemployment in Kerala

Unemployment and underemployment cut deeply into the potential incomes of agricultural field laborers in Kerala. Unemployment in Kerala has been high since at least 1961. In that year the work participation rate—the percentage of main workers to total population—was 34% for Kerala (UN 1975:75) compared to 43% for all-India (Rajeev 1983:51). In 1977-78, Kerala's unemployment stood at 26% for rural males and 29% for rural females, compared to all-India rates of 8% for rural males and 10% for rural females (GOK 1984:128).[3] The 1981 Indian Census gives all-India unemployment rates of 12% for rural males and 14% for rural females (Prakash 1989:12). A survey by the Kerala Department of Economics and Statistics (DES), found Kerala's rates in 1987 to be 17% for rural males and 19% for rural females (cited in Prakash 1989:9).

Unemployment is defined differently in different surveys. The most recent DES survey took unemployment to mean having had no work at all in the previous year. Such a definition obviously does not capture the full extent of effective unemployment. The DES therefore added the category "underemployment" to refer to workers who had worked fewer than 183 days the previous year, but were available for more work than that (Prakash 1989:8). That definition yielded another 13% of rural males and 19% of rural females for totals of effectively unemployed rural males of 30% and for females of 60%. In actual numbers, the combined unemployed + underemployed totaled 3,631,000 out of a rural labor force of 9,256,000. Urban unemployment rates in Kerala were just as high (Prakash 1989:9).

## Work and Unemployment in Nadur

How severe is unemployment in Nadur? Because the 1971 survey had incomplete information on individual occupations, we cannot make a statistical comparison. For 1987 we collected data for all 1,035 individuals listed as members of the 170 sample households. Of these, 317 were under 15; we counted them as children. Another 88 were 65 or older; we counted them as elderly, although some agricultural laborers continue to seek work as long as they can walk to the fields. The remaining 630 individuals were classified according to their main occupation as given in Table 8.2.

Table 8.2 indicates that unemployment in Nadur is as severe as in Kerala generally. It is the largest single category with 23.3% of the individuals. The second highest category is "household affairs," which describes mostly females of working age who are tending the household. Agricultural labor and house compound and general labor combined make up 28%. These first four categories together account for 73% of all able-bodied workers in the sample.

The ratio of 287 males to 343 females in the row marked "subtotal" is obviously too low. Absent laborers sending remittances add another 45 males and one female to the occupational chart. The addition of these workers, reported by respondents in the sample survey, results in totals of 332 males to 344 females. This gives a ratio of 1,036 females to 1,000 males, very close to the 1981 Kerala average of 1,032 to 1,000 (GOI 1983:xxiii),[4] and suggests that our occupational count is pretty accurate. We will discuss these workers shortly.

### Workers and Dependents

When examining work and unemployment, we need to consider the number of dependents the employed household members must support.[5] Table 8.3 shows the distribution of dependents—children, aged, and unemployed—and workers—village workers resident in Nadur and absent workers sending remittances.

Table 8.3 reads like this: 45 households have no children, 98 have no aged, 91 have no unemployed, and so on. Twenty households have 4 children, 5 households have 4 unemployed. Combining the various

Table 8.2
Main Occupation of Household Members
Ages 15 Through 64

| Occupation | Males | Females | Total | Percent |
|---|---|---|---|---|
| Unemployed | 51 | 96 | 147 | 23.3 |
| Household Affairs | 11 | 126 | 137 | 21.7 |
| House Compound Labor | 89 | 23 | 112 | 17.8 |
| Agricultural Labor | 7 | 57 | 64 | 10.2 |
| Student | 25 | 23 | 48 | 7.6 |
| Petty Trade | 30 | 3 | 33 | 5.2 |
| Skilled Labor | 29 | 1 | 30 | 4.8 |
| White Collar | 10 | 4 | 14 | 2.2 |
| Service | 12 | 4 | 16 | 2.5 |
| Farmer | 11 | 0 | 11 | 1.7 |
| Professional | 5 | 2 | 7 | 1.1 |
| Pensioner | 3 | 1 | 4 | 0.6 |
| Servant | 1 | 2 | 3 | 0.5 |
| Unknown | 2 | 1 | 3 | 0.5 |
| Religious Services | 1 | 0 | 1 | 0.2 |
| Subtotal | 287 | 343 | 630 | 99.9 |
| Absent Laborer | 45 | 1 | 46 | -- |
| Total | 332 | 344 | 676 | -- |

dependents—children, aged, and unemployed adults—we get the distribution in the fourth row: total dependents. These work-related demographic features of the households are shown by caste, class, and income quintile on Table 8.4.

### Household Dependents to Worker Ratios

To compile our data into the most inclusive units, we computed a dependency ratio: the number of workers in the household divided by the number of dependents not including the workers themselves. The worker/dependency ratio thus tells us how many workers are in the

Table 8.3

Number of Households With Numbers of Workers and Nonworkers
Nadur Village Kerala 1987

| Member Type | Number in Household | | | | | | | | | | | |
|---|---|---|---|---|---|---|---|---|---|---|---|---|
| | 0 | 1 | 2 | 3 | 4 | 5 | 6 | 7 | 8 | 9 | 10 | 11 |
| Children | 45 | 37 | 35 | 21 | 20 | 9 | 1 | 1 | 0 | 1 | | |
| Aged | 98 | 57 | 14 | 1 | | | | | | | | |
| Unemployed | 91 | 36 | 23 | 15 | 5 | | | | | | | |
| Total Dependents | 12 | 27 | 28 | 41 | 25 | 11 | 11 | 3 | 6 | 5 | 0 | 1 |
| Village Workers | 4 | 8 | 30 | 43 | 36 | 22 | 12 | 13 | 2 | | | |
| Absent Workers | 134 | 28 | 6 | 2 | | | | | | | | |
| Total Workers | 0 | 10 | 25 | 40 | 35 | 27 | 12 | 18 | 2 | 1 | | |

Row Totals = 170

household to support each non-working member. The range goes from 0 to 3.5. No apparent relationship exists between the worker/dependency ratio and household income. The correlation coefficient is virtually zero. When we consider only the 43 households with agricultural laborers or the 72 households with rural laborers of all kinds, the coefficient remains virtually zero.

From Table 8.4 we can see that 6 sets of averages differ enough to be statistically significant. Using one-way analysis of variance (ANOVA), we computed the significance of each set of averages across each set of categories. The results appear as single or double asterisks above the columns to which they apply. The relation between absent workers and occupational classes results mostly from the definition of the classes themselves, since one category—recipients—is made up primarily of households receiving remittances. We can ignore this relationship.

The most significant patterns appear among the castes. The variation in numbers of children ranges from the Nambudiris with a low of 0.6 children average per household to the Muslims with a high of 3.1.

Table 8.4
Average Dependents Per Worker by Caste, Class and Income Quintile
Nadur Village, Kerala, 1987

| | Children | Aged | Unem-ployed | Total Depend-ents | Village Wor-kers | Absent Workers | Total Workers | Worker/ Depend Ratio |
|---|---|---|---|---|---|---|---|---|
| **Caste** | * | | ** | ** | | ** | | * |
| Nambudiri | .6 | .8 | 1.3 | 2.8 | 3.5 | .1 | 3.6 | .7 |
| Nair | 1.8 | .5 | .8 | 3.1 | 3.6 | .5 | 4.1 | .8 |
| Craft | 1.5 | .4 | 0.0 | 2.0 | 4.3 | .1 | 4.4 | .5 |
| Ezhuthasan/ Chetty | 1.4 | .4 | .7 | 2.5 | 3.5 | 0.0 | 3.5 | .6 |
| Muslim | 3.1 | .3 | 1.8 | 5.2 | 4.4 | .1 | 4.4 | 1.3 |
| Ezhava | 1.7 | .5 | .9 | 3.2 | 3.0 | .2 | 3.2 | 1.1 |
| Mannan | 2.0 | 1.2 | 1.0 | 4.2 | 3.5 | 0.0 | 3.5 | 1.3 |
| Pulaya | 2.1 | .8 | .3 | 3.2 | 3.6 | 0.0 | 3.6 | .9 |
| **Class** | | | | | | ** | | |
| Professional | 1.6 | 1.0 | .4 | 3.0 | 2.8 | .2 | 3.0 | 1.2 |
| Service | 2.2 | .3 | 1.4 | 4.0 | 4.8 | .1 | 4.9 | .7 |
| Craft | 1.6 | .6 | .4 | 2.6 | 4.4 | .1 | 4.4 | .6 |
| Farmer | 1.6 | .7 | 1.1 | 3.5 | 3.4 | .5 | 3.9 | 1.0 |
| Petty Trade | 2.1 | .4 | .8 | 3.3 | 3.8 | .1 | 3.9 | 1.0 |
| Recipient | 1.6 | .5 | .7 | 2.8 | 3.2 | .7 | 3.9 | .8 |
| Laborer | 2.0 | .4 | 1.0 | 3.5 | 3.9 | .1 | 4.0 | .9 |
| Agricultural Laborer | 2.1 | .4 | .1 | 2.6 | 3.9 | .1 | 4.0 | .7 |
| **Household Income Quintile** [a] | | | | | | | | |
| 1. 9,200-54,000 | 1.8 | .6 | 1.0 | 3.4 | 4.3 | .3 | 4.6 | .9 |
| 2. 6,000-9,199 | 2.1 | .5 | .9 | 3.5 | 4.2 | .2 | 4.4 | .8 |
| 3. 3,920-5,999 | 2.3 | .6 | .8 | 3.6 | 4.0 | .3 | 4.3 | .9 |
| 4. 2,900-3,919 | 2.0 | .4 | 1.1 | 3.4 | 3.5 | .3 | 3.7 | 1.0 |
| 5. 840-2,899 | 1.2 | .5 | .6 | 2.2 | 2.6 | .3 | 2.8 | .8 |
| Totals | 1.9 | .5 | .9 | 3.2 | 3.7 | .3 | 4.0 | .88[b] |

a. *For household income we used correlation coefficients since all the variables are numeric.*
b. *For 1981, the estimated Kerala state average of all persons of working age to child and aged dependents was .75. (Gulati 1990:342). Using the same method, we computed the 1987 Nadur sample dependency rate at .62 with absent workers and .67 without them.*

* *Significant at $p \leq -.01$ (ANOVA)*    ** *Significant at $p \leq -.001$ (ANOVA)*

The number of unemployed by caste also varies significantly. Here Muslims are also the highest with 1.8 unemployed workers per household while Namdudiris follow with 1.3. The craft castes report no unemployed members, reflecting the ability of the males in each generation to take up work with their fathers, while some females work as part time agricultural laborers to supplement the craft income. Also very low in reported unemployment are members of the Pulaya caste in which nearly all adult members report themselves as agricultural laborers. Even if they are getting very little work, they do not consider themselves actually unemployed as would an educated Nambudiri who was seeking work in the professional or service sector.

The total numbers of dependents also differ significantly by caste. Since this column is made up mostly of the children and unemployed, two sets already significant, it does not require separate consideration. Household members 65 and over are distributed across a fairly wide range from 1.2 among the Mannan and 0.8 among Nambudiris to 0.3 among Muslim households. Partly because of the reversal among Nambudiris and Muslims with regard to children and aged, the significance level for all dependents is lower.

Finally, we see that the worker/dependency ratio also differs significantly among the castes. Mannans and Muslims have a high of 1.3 dependents for each household worker to support. The craft castes have the lowest average at only 0.5. Since the Mannans have high average incomes and the Muslims low incomes (see Table 6.7), we can predict that the ratio will not likely be a significant factor in explaining income. The correlation coefficients are not significant with or without the Mannan caste households in the computation.

## Absent Workers and Remittances

On Table 6.3 we saw that remittances make up 9% of the income of the Nadur sample households. On Table 8.2 we saw that 46 members work away from 36 Nadur households and send money back. One female works as a maid in New Delhi. The 45 males include three working in the Middle East Gulf states, 16 working as laborers in Madras, and 26 dispersed throughout other parts of India. These workers send an average of Rs 159 per month per worker to households in Nadur. Because some households have more than one absent worker, the remittance per household averages Rs 201 (Table 8.5).

Among absent workers, Nairs account for 41 (89%) of the 45. Two are Ezhava, and one each comes from the craft, Nambudiri, and Muslim castes. Nairs account for 94% of remittance households. We saw on Tables 4.2 and 6.7 that Nairs are 49% of the sample population. Why have they been so much more active than other castes in sending out young males for absentee labor?

Migration from Kerala is a complex subject. We can offer a few speculations. Two different forms of migration occur from Kerala: overseas migration far more than any other Indian state, and internal migration within India that may be similar to that in several other states. Nadur's migrant workers stay mostly within India. At least three factors are at work: (1) education, (2) household structure, and (3) unemployment.

First, existing research suggests that Kerala migrant workers are generally better educated than Kerala village workers (Oberai *et al* 1989:29). As we will see in Table 11.3, Nadur's Nair males are better educated than males of all other castes except Nambudiris and Mannans.

Second, Nair households have flexible, open, female-centered structures, as we saw in Chapter 4. The absence of male household members may not cause the strains in such households that would occur in others; because Nair wives, sisters, mothers, and uncles are accustomed to the tradition of raising children with absent fathers. They can depend on their maternal relatives for help with child care and household maintenance or can move into those houses.

Education and household structural flexibility combine with the desperate needs of unemployed household members to find work to support their families. Education and the traditional caste household structure thus combine to produce an adaptation to economic hardship among Nair households. Among Nairs, remittances constitute 16% of income.

Correlations of class and of household income with number of village workers (0.13), absent workers (0.01), or total workers (0.13), are not statistically significant. Separating households with and without absent workers does not produce significant correlations. Even among Nairs, the number of absent workers correlates hardly at all with household income. But it does correlate strongly with the amounts of the remittances. Data on Table 8.5 show this.

We see that for remittance households, the rupees amounts of the remittances account for 34% of household income. For Nair caste households, remittances are a statistically significant component also. Clearly, households with earning capacity outside Nadur depend heavily on those earnings.

Table 8.5
Remittance and Non Remittance Households
Nadur Village Kerala 1987

|  | Remittance Households | Nair HHs | Non Remittance | All |
|---|---|---|---|---|
| Number of Households | 36 | 83 | 134 | 170 |
| Percent of Sample | 21 | 49 | 79 | 100 |
| Average Monthly Remittance in Rupees | 201 | 74 | 0 | 43 |
| Average Annual Remittance in Rupees | 2,412 | 891 | 0 | 511 |
| Average Household Income | | | | |
| With Remittances | 7,078 | 6,704 | 6,815 | 6,871 |
| Without Remittances | 4,664 | 5,813 | 6,815 | 6,360 |
| Remittance as Percent of Income | 34 | 16 | 0 | 9 |
| Correlation of Remittance with Household Income | .54** | .26* | 0 | .16 |

## Underemployment in Kerala

For both remittance and non remittance households, another factor powerfully influences income: days of work. Agricultural labor opportunities become available only when rice land owners have tasks to do: diking, ditching, hoeing, sowing, weeding, transplanting, applying pesticides and fertilizer, harvesting, threshing, and parboiling. This long list supplies far less than full time employment. And other rural labor such as rubber tapping and coconut tree maintenance makes up only part of the shortfall.

Kerala suffers from substantial underemployment. For high wage professional and service workers, this may not be a major problem. For those farmers who can feed their households from their rice land

Table 8.6
Average Working Days Per Year
Kerala Agricultural Laborers

| Year | Males | Females |
|------|-------|---------|
| 1956 | 201 [a] | 131 [a] |
| 1964-65 | 198 | 165 |
| 1974-75 | 169 | 128 |
| 1983-84 | 147 | 115 |

Sources:GOK 1985b:34, survey of 336 villages.
a. *Tharamangalam 1981:62, Travancore-Cochin only.*

and from sale of coconuts and other house compound crops, it may also be unimportant. For labor and agricultural labor households, however, the number of days of work is a crucial as the wage level in affecting their ability to support their households.

For Kerala generally the working days per year for agricultural laborers seem to be declining to crisis levels. Data from some recent studies are given in Table 8.6.

Table 8.6 indicates severely declining work opportunities for both males and females in agriculture. Because the figures are averages, they hide the worst cases. Joan Mencher (1980:1783) found in one village in Palghat and one village in Kuttanad in 1970-71 that average days of work per year were only 71 and 73 respectively. For 1980, Ronald Herring found in Nallepilli Village in Palghat District that average days of employment were "just under 99" (1989:106).

## Underemployment in Nadur

How severe is underemployment in Nadur? We asked workers to estimate their annual days of labor. We broke the questions down into farming seasons to make it easier to remember how much work there had been. We independently asked farmers how many days' labor they hired for each specific production task. The farmers' estimates were very close to what we would expect if the workers' estimates were accurate. In addition, we asked several general questions about work availability and work shortage.

Table 8.7
Days Worked by Agricultural Labor Households
Nadur Village Kerala 1987

| Number of Laborers | Number of Households | Percent of Households | Days Worked Per Laborer | HH Income (No Welfare) |
|---|---|---|---|---|
| 0 | 127 | 75 | 0 | 7,580 |
| 1 | 26 | 15 | 62 | 4,636 |
| 2 | 13 | 8 | 52 | 3,674 |
| 3 | 3 | 2 | 60 | 5,742 |
| 4 | 1 | 1 | 60 | 6,000 |
| Totals | 170 | 101 | 59 | 6,789 |

## Underemployment of Agricultural Laborers

First we consider the degree of underemployment among agricultural laborers. Table 8.7 provides the data on estimated numbers of days worked on the rice fields of others in the previous two farming seasons. The households are broken down by number of agricultural laborers in them.

From Table 8.7 we can see that the average household income of households without agricultural laborers is far higher than that of those containing agricultural laborers. The average income of the 43 households containing at least one agricultural laborer is Rs 4,454. The most dramatic data on Table 8.7 are the days worked per agricultural laborer. With only 59 days work, rice field labor clearly provides insufficient employment across the year in Nadur.

## Underemployment of Other Rural Laborers

Many agricultural laborers supplement their field labor with labor on house compounds (*parambas*), sometimes of the same households on whose rice fields they labor, sometimes on the house compounds of others. Some laborers work on nearby rubber or pineapple estates. Total days worked by the 64 agricultural laborers in the Nadur sample are therefore made up of rice field labor strictly speaking plus other rural labor.

Another 89 sample members work only in house compounds or

Table 8.8
Days Worked by Rural Labor Households
Nadur Village Kerala 1987

| Number of Laborers | Number of Households | Percent of Households | Days Worked Per Laborer | HH Income (No Welfare) |
|---|---|---|---|---|
| 0 | 98 | 58 | 0 | 8,589 |
| 1 | 30 | 18 | 93 | 4,267 |
| 2 | 24 | 14 | 87 | 3,992 |
| 3 | 11 | 6 | 93 | 4,384 |
| 4 | 7 | 4 | 80 | 5,782 |
| Totals | 170 | 100 | 90 | 6,789 |

estates. Table 8.8 gives the maximum overall rural employment in Nadur.

Comparing Table 8.8 with Table 8.7, we see that the average days worked increases from 59 to 90 for all rural labor jobs combined. This figure is still only 49% of the 183 days threshold of employment considered by the Department of Economics and Statistics and only 35% of the 260 days the laborers would probably work if they could. Average income for the 72 households with one or more rural laborer comes to only Rs 4,340, slightly less even than that for the 43 households with agricultural laborers shown on Table 8.7 The relationship between days worked per rural laborer and income of the household is complicated by the structure of dependents that we will reexamine shortly. First, however, let us look at the distribution of rural labor days by caste, class, and income quintile.

### Rural Labor Work Days by Caste and Class

The distribution of rural work days is given on Table 8.9. This Table reveals a number of important features of rural labor in Nadur. First, we see that the craft castes have by far the lowest average days of rural labor. This comes about because the rural labor of the craft households is all small-scale supplementary harvest work by wives. Ezhava, Muslim, and Ezhuthasan/Chetty castes get the most days of work. Nair and Pulaya get about 20% less: these 2 castes include most of the agricul-

Table 8.9
Work Days and Work Shortage
Nadur Village Kerala 1987

| | Number of | | Average Days Work | |
|---|---|---|---|---|
| | Agricultural Laborers | Rural Laborers | Agriculture | All Rural Labor |
| **Caste** | | | | |
| Nambudiri | 0 | 0 | 0 | 0 |
| Nair | 37 | 59 | 60 | 82 |
| Craft | 3 | 3 | 45 | 45 |
| Ezhuthasan/Chetty | 3 | 5 | 60 | 101 |
| Muslim | 1 | 30 | 90 | 99 |
| Ezhava | 1 | 11 | 60 | 113 |
| Mannan | 0 | 0 | 0 | 0 |
| Pulaya | 19 | 31 | 54 | 86 |
| **Class** | | | | |
| Professional | 0 | 0 | 0 | 0 |
| Service | 1 | 1 | 75 | 75 |
| Craft | 4 | 4 | 50 | 50 |
| Farmer | 3 | 5 | 16 | 71 |
| Petty Trade | 1 | 4 | 40 | 101 |
| Recipient | 9 | 11 | 66 | 90 |
| Laborer | 29 | 91 | 56 | 96 |
| Agricultural Laborer | 17 | 23 | 73 | 73 |
| **Household Income Quintile** | | | | |
| 1. 9,200-54,000 | 4 | 4 | 58 | 65 |
| 2. 6,000-9,199 | 17 | 34 | 63 | 99 |
| 3. 3,920-5,999 | 17 | 45 | 71 | 101 |
| 4. 2,900-3,919 | 9 | 26 | 47 | 99 |
| 5. 840-2,899 | 17 | 30 | 50 | 67 |
| Totals | 64 | 88 | 59 | 90 |

*Note: The class segment of the column labeled "Number of Agricultural Laborers is the same as the 1987 column labeled "Number" on Table 5.3.*

tural laborers. Agricultural laborers are not able to get as much supplementary house compound or estate work as those who do such work regularly throughout the year. This fact shows up in the class breakdown where laborers get 96 days versus only 73 for agricultural laborer household workers.

The relation of days of rural labor and household income begins to show up on this table. The highest income quintile has only 65 days average because the high incomes do not derive from rural labor: only 4 rural laborers are found in that quintile. Looking at quintiles 2 through 5, we see that the bottom quintile has strikingly fewer average days work than quintiles 2 through 4.

### Effective Unemployment in Nadur

The data on work days can be used to estimate the etic or effective unemployment rate for agricultural and rural labor households. We took the conservative (low) figure of 183 days work per year as used by the Kerala State Department of Economics and Statistics to be the threshold of full employment. For each rural worker, we divided the number of days worked by 183. We added this figure in place of the whole number one to the number of workers in the household and added the difference to the number of unemployed. For all days on which an agricultural or other rural laborer doesn't work, the laborer counts as a dependent. Such transformations for all 72 households containing rural workers produced the data in Table 8.10.

The emic ratio on Table 8.10 is a copy of the worker/dependency ratio column on Table 8.4. We see that computing the etic unemployment rate has no effect on the dependents to worker ratios for Nambudiris, Mannans, professionals, petty traders, or the highest income quintile households.

Among the castes, we see the biggest changes for Nairs, Muslims, and especially Pulayas, the latter registering a 211% increase in the worker/dependency ratio. For the classes, agricultural laborers are affected the most, while the lowest 2 income quintiles also show big changes. The overall sample dependency ratio increases by 47% from .88 to 1.29. The effective unemployment figure means that each worker on average must support 1.29 persons in addition to himself/herself.

For the 72 rural labor households only, the dependency ratio correlation with household income changes from +.06 with emic unemployment to -.22 ($p \leq .031$) with the etic rate. The negative direction is the one we would expect, but the regression $r^2$ is only .04. Each increase of 1 in the dependency ratio causes a drop in income of only 277 rupees

Table 8.10
Dependents, Etic Workers, and Dependency Ratios
Nadur Village Kerala 1987

| | Etic | | Worker/Dependency Ratios | |
| --- | --- | --- | --- | --- |
| | Unem-ployed | Total Workers | Emic | Etic |
| **Caste** | ** | | * | ** |
| Nambudiri | 1.3 | 3.6 | .7 | .7 |
| Nair | 1.0 | 3.8 | .8 | 1.1 |
| Crafts | .2 | 4.2 | .5 | .6 |
| Ezhuthasan/Chetty | .9 | 3.4 | .6 | .9 |
| Muslim | 1.8 | 4.4 | 1.3 | 1.7 |
| Ezhava | 1.0 | 3.1 | 1.1 | 1.3 |
| Mannan | 1.0 | 3.5 | 1.3 | 1.3 |
| Pulaya | 1.7 | 2.3 | .9 | 2.8 |
| | | | | |
| **Class** | * | | | |
| Professional | .5 | 3.0 | 1.2 | 1.2 |
| Service | 1.5 | 4.8 | .7 | .7 |
| Craft | .6 | 4.4 | .6 | .7 |
| Farmer | 1.2 | 3.8 | 1.0 | 1.1 |
| Petty Trade | .9 | 3.8 | 1.0 | 1.1 |
| Recipient | .9 | 3.8 | .8 | 1.2 |
| Laborer | 1.4 | 3.6 | .9 | 1.3 |
| Agricultural Laborer | 1.7 | 2.6 | .7 | 2.6 |
| | | | | |
| **Household Income Quintile** [a] | | * | | |
| 1.  9,200-54,000 | 1.1 | 4.5 | .9 | .9 |
| 2.  6,000-9,199 | 1.2 | 4.2 | .8 | 1.1 |
| 3.  3,920-5,999 | 1.1 | 3.9 | .9 | 1.3 |
| 4.  2,900-3,919 | 1.3 | 3.5 | 1.0 | 1.4 |
| 5.   840-2,899 | .9 | 2.5 | .8 | 1.8 |
| | | | | |
| Totals (N=170) | | | .88 | 1.29 |

a.  For household income we used correlation coefficients since all the variables are numeric.
*  Significant at $p \leq -.01$ (ANOVA)    **  Significant at $p \leq -.001$ (ANOVA)

below 5,006 rupees.[6] Considering only the bottom quintile, only laborers and agricultural laborers, or only Nairs and Pulayas, also does not produce significant correlations.[7] Unemployment and underemployment are important, but apparently not determining mathematical factors in household income levels.

## Coping with Underemployment

While unemployment and underemployment may produce inconclusive statistical results, they are real and severe, especially for poor households at certain times of year. To supplement the self-estimates of number of days worked in various rural labor jobs, we asked in a different section of the questionnaire whether members of the household experienced any times of year when they did not have enough work to continue supporting the household. The results of this question appear in Table 8.11.

As can be seen, no Nambudiri and Mannan caste members report a short time of year, while all Pulayas experience work shortage. Professional and service class households have enough, while 82% of laboring households and 100% of agricultural labor households say they do not. Of the 64 agricultural laborers in the sample population, 59 (92%) are in households reporting a short time of year. For the 88 other rural laborers, 72 (82%) are in households facing shortage.

When are the "short times?" For nearly all respondents they are the months of March through May or March through July. As we saw in Chapter 3, August is the month of the major harvest in Nadur. This is followed by several months of adequate rice supply for small landowners and the onset of the short rainy season in which field labor commences in September. January sees the small harvest and is followed in February by dry season house compound labor. As this labor tapers off, and March becomes hotter, the rice supplies from the little monsoon season get used up. By April the poorest households begin to feel the labor pinch; there is little work now until the monsoon rains come again in late May or early June. From March on, the lowest income agricultural and other rural laboring households must find ways to make ends meet with almost no employment. We asked the 78 households reporting a work shortage "How do you manage when there is not enough work?" Several choices were given as possible responses, along with the opportunity to fill in other mechanisms we had not considered.[8] Respondents were also free to select more than one choice. Most did. The results of this question are summarized on Table 8.12.

Table 8.11
Work Days and Work Shortage
Nadur Village Kerala 1987

|  | Enough Work? Number of Households Answering | |
| --- | --- | --- |
|  | Yes | No |
| **Caste** | | |
| Nambudiri | 13 | 0 |
| Nair | 51 | 32 |
| Craft | 6 | 5 |
| Ezhuthasan/Chetty | 7 | 5 |
| Muslim | 7 | 15 |
| Ezhava | 4 | 9 |
| Mannan | 4 | 0 |
| Pulaya | 0 | 11 |
| **Class** | | |
| Professional | 11 | 0 |
| Service | 8 | 1 |
| Craft | 8 | 6 |
| Farmer | 18 | 5 |
| Petty Trade | 14 | 4 |
| Recipient | 23 | 7 |
| Laborer | 10 | 47 |
| Agricultural Laborer | 0 | 8 |
| **Household Income Quintile** | | |
| 1.   9,200-54,000 | 30 | 4 |
| 2.   6,000-9,199 | 17 | 17 |
| 3.   3,920-5,999 | 11 | 23 |
| 4.   2,900-3,919 | 16 | 18 |
| 5.     840-2,899 | 18 | 16 |
| Totals | 92 | 78 |

As can been seen, work-short households adopt a variety of strategies. The 27 households (35%) with the highest incomes within this subgroup stretch money saved during peak work periods. An even

Table 8.12
Survival Strategies in Season With Work Shortage
Work Shortage Households Only
Nadur Village Kerala 1987

| Characteristic | Number of Households | Percent of Households | Average Household Income |
|---|---|---|---|
| **Has Money Saved?** | | | |
| Yes | 27 | 35 | 5,609 |
| No | 51 | 65 | 4,132 |
| | | | |
| **Borrows Money** | | | |
| Yes | 69 | 88 | 4,571 |
| No | 9 | 12 | 5,191 |
| | | | |
| **Borrows Food** | | | |
| Yes | 25 | 32 | 5,126 |
| No | 53 | 68 | 4,415 |
| | | | |
| **Eats Less Food** | | | |
| Yes | 18 | 23 | 3,578 |
| No | 60 | 77 | 4,962 |
| | | | |
| Totals | 78 | 100 | 4,643 |

greater number—88%—borrow money during this period. Average
loans in this category are about Rs 300 to 500. They range from formal
loans at the local cooperative society at 18% interest to "friendly adjust-
ments" with kinspeople and neighbors, without interest according to
respondents. A smaller group of 25 households borrows food, either as
credit from local merchants who allow short delays in payment for
purchases, or from family and neighbors. Finally, 18 households stated
that they cut their food intake sharply because they simply cannot afford
to eat normally during the short periods. These 18 households have the
lowest average household income of all the subgroups on Table 8.11:
only 53% of the total sample average and 77% of the work-short households average. They represent 11% of all households, but contain 34% of
all agricultural laborers in the Nadur sample. Short of work, not having
money saved because the peak work periods are themselves insufficient,

not able to borrow enough money or food, these 18 households can be considered Nadur's "poorest of the poor." Ten of the 18 households are Nair, 6 are Pulaya (55% of the caste), and one each is Ezhava and Muslim. Three agricultural labor class households, 9 labor households, 4 recipients and one each farmer and petty trade household are among them. Workers in the 18 food-short households are responsible for 1.1 dependents (2.4 etic) compared with 0.9 (1.5 etic) for the 60 households that manage to get by on savings, loans, and borrowed food. Fifteen of the 18 food-short households have no money saved for short periods, 17 borrow money and 6 borrow food while still ending up short. There is little difference in average days worked between the food-short and the food-sufficient households, but this is not surprising when we recall how few are the rural work days anyway. Fourteen of the 18 households have no rice land and of the 4 owners, 2 have plots of 0.10 and 0.15 acres. None of the 18 households has more than 0.39 acres of house compound. The average is 0.19 acres compared with 0.33 for the 60 work-short but food-sufficient households and 0.76 for those with enough work.

### Conclusions

Our survey shows that unions have won for Nadur agricultural and other rural workers large increases in wages since 1961, but in 1987 they had far too few days of work. Survival strategies include sending male workers outside the village for jobs along with saving, borrowing, and cutting down on food.

In the next 2 chapters, we shall see additional Kerala reforms that lessen the burdens on worker households. These include the unemployment, pension, and targeted development programs examined in Chapter 9, and public food distribution to be analyzed in Chapter 10.

### Notes

1.  Forced evictions were brought under some control in Travancore in 1945 and in Malabar in 1957 by the strength of radical movements (Kannan 1988:256).

2.  For both years, we excluded plowing from the computation of averages, since only a few people get this privileged work and it would skew up the average. In 1971, plowing netted 5 rupees per day and all plowing in Nadur was done with bullocks. In 1987, 60% of plowing costs went to a tractor service hired from a nearby town. Rates were 50 rupees per day for bullock plowing which remained necessary on some land parcels not accessible to the tractor and for

some farmers who could better use their bullocks than pay a tractor service. The ratio of plowing to field labor was 1.67 to 1 (5 to 3) in 1971 and 2.5 to 1 (50 to 20) in 1987.

3.  Unemployment and the work participation rate are approximately the reverse of each other. We use the unemployment rate for all years we can locate it. Otherwise, we substitute the work participation rate which is available for a larger number of years.

4.  As we stated in Chapter 1, Note 2, Kerala's 1991 ratio rose to 1,040 females per 1,000 males, while the all-India ratio dropped from 934 in 1981 to 929 in 1991 (Bose 1991:67).

5.  The overall composition and structure of the household may also play a role. We plan to examine this complex issue in a future publication.

6.  The 5,006 rupees is the intercept for the regression of etic dependency ratio on income. It is the average amount the regression equation predicts if no dependency effects were present.

7.  Among Pulayas only, the correlation changes from +0.20 to -0.53, the latter with $p \leq 0.45$. Among agricultural labor households only, the change is from -0.30 to -0.51 ($p \leq 0.10$).

8.  Nieuwenhuys (1990) provides evidence on child labor as a household survival strategy for the central Kerala coastal village of Poomkara.

# 9

# Workers, Welfare,
# and Targeted Advancement

Two of Kerala's most remarkable reforms are unemployment insurance and pensions for agricultural laborers enacted by a Left Front
government in 1980. Both of these programs were severely curtailed
when a conservative coalition came to power in 1982, but were expanded again during another Left Front government from 1987 to 1991.

## Insurance and Pensions in Kerala

Unemployment insurance in Kerala was paid to 205,556 persons in
1987. To qualify, a person had to register on a government employment
exchange, and had to be out of work for more than 3 years. (GOK
1990:110). These are difficult conditions for rural workers to meet: they
must also be prepared to accept any employment that comes to them via
the exchange, which may be far away or otherwise difficult to accept. In
Nadur, 3 individuals in 2 sample households were receiving unemployment compensation.

More accessible are the agricultural laborer pensions. To qualify, a
worker must be 60 years or older and the household income must be less
than Rs 1,500. Plantation workers, cashew nut processors, toddy tappers, and some other rural workers are covered by separate pensions.

Workers submit their applications for agricultural labor pensions to
the local village executive officer who refers it to a village verification
committee. This committee consists of the elected village head along
with other members including at least 1 representative of the local agricultural trade union (Gulati 1990:340).

In 1982, 99,000 of the intended 240,000 agricultural labor beneficiaries were receiving their pension of 45 rupees per month (computed from

Kannan 1988:286). By 1986 200,000 pensions were being dispersed
(Nossiter 1988:105; GOK 1988:88). In 1987 the number of beneficiaries
rose to 286,733 and the payment was increased to 60 rupees per month
(GOK 1990:110).[1] In addition, small numbers of rural households receive widows pensions and pensions for handicapped family members.
Two others received payments for physical handicap and 1 household
was getting a widow's pension.

How inclusive are these pensions in coverage? Kerala had 1.9 million agricultural workers in 1981 (Gulati 1990:340). Using the 1987
pension disbursement numbers, we arrive at a figure of 15% of the work
force. This is close to the percent of agricultural laborers above age 60
which was estimated for 1981 at 13% (Gulati 1990:340). By 1987 most
agricultural laborers may have been covered; 56% of recipients were
women (GOK 1990:111).

How valuable are the pensions to the beneficiaries? Forty-five
rupees per month ($41.86 per year using 1987 payments and conversion
rates) amounted to 27% of the official Kerala per capita income in 1986.
In Nadur in 1987 Rs 45 would feed 1 adult for at least 10 days per month,
or about 1/3 of the time. Other observers have found the pensions
economically more significant than our estimate would suggest. Herring
(1989:103) claims they "far exceeded the most generous treatment in the
traditional system and approached the average income of those still
labouring in the fields." Gulati (1990:341) argues that they cover essentially all of the food costs of the retiree when the subsidized prices of the
ration shop are considered, which we shall examine in the following
chapter. She also notes that the pensions increased the acceptability of
aged household members according to 97% of those interviewed in a
survey (1990:341). In the Nadur sample, agricultural labor pensions
equaled 23% of the total wage earnings of field laborers in strictly rice
field labor and 5% of the total of all rural labor wages during the survey
period.

In addition to pensions and welfare programs, Kerala state also
provides a nominal subsidy of 35 rupees per child per school year to
members of designated former untouchable castes. In the case of Nadur
Village, this subsidy applies to Pulaya school children.


## Pensions and Welfare in Nadur

How important are government pensions and welfare programs in
Nadur? Our survey indicates that 25 households (15%) were receiving
18 total agricultural laborers pensions, 6 other welfare payments, and 13

Table 9.1
Pension/Welfare Recipients Versus Nonrecipients
Nadur Village Kerala 1987

| Characteristic | Recipient Households | Non Recipient Households |
|---|---|---|
| Number of Households | 25 | 145 |
| Percent of Sample | 15 | 85 |
| | | |
| Average Household Income | | |
| Without the Payments | 4,009 | 7,273 |
| With the Payments | 4,563 | 7,273 |
| | | |
| Average payment in Rupees | 555 | 0 |
| | | |
| Average Percent of Household | | |
| Income from Pensions | 16.5 | 0 |
| Gini coefficient | | |
| Without the Payments | 45.4 | |
| With the Payments | 44.8 | |

school subsidies worth a total of Rs 13,865. This sum represents 1.2% of the total income of the sample. Among the 16 agricultural labor pension households, 4 are Pulaya (36% of the caste), 1 is Ezhava (8%), and 11 (13%) are Nair. One craft class household has a pensioner along with 2 from petty trade, 5 each among recipients and laborers, and 3 among the 8 agricultural labor class households. Thirteen (72%) of the individual pensioners are women. Six of the pension households are among the 18 reporting a food shortage that we described in Chapter 8. That means 38% of pension households experience some food shortage, compared to 8% of the nonpensioners. These data show: (1) that the pensions are going to those most in need, and (2) that they are not enough.

## Pensions, Welfare, and Income Inequality

Up to now, we have been using income figures that do not include these welfare programs. This allowed us to give a more accurate estimate of the effects of the land reform and the gains won by unions. By

Table 9.2
Features of Pension Households
Nadur Village Kerala 1987

| | Recipient Households | | Total Amount Received | Percent of Income |
|---|---|---|---|---|
| | Number | Percent | | |
| **Caste** | | | | |
| Nambudiri | 0 | 0 | 0 | 0 |
| Nair | 12 | 14 | 8,120 | 1.5 |
| Craft | 0 | 0 | 0 | 0 |
| Ezhuthasan/Chetty | 2 | 8 | 1,620 | 2.0 |
| Muslim | 0 | 0 | 0 | 0 |
| Ezhava | 1 | 8 | 540 | 0.9 |
| Mannan* | 0 | 0 | 0 | 0 |
| Pulaya* | 10 | 91 | 3,585 | 7.1 |
| | | | | |
| **Class** | | | | |
| Professional | 0 | 0 | 0 | 0 |
| Service | 0 | 0 | 0 | 0 |
| Craft | 1 | 7 | 540 | 0.5 |
| Farmer | 0 | 0 | 0 | 0 |
| Petty Trade | 2 | 11 | 1,620 | 1.3 |
| Recipient | 6 | 20 | 3,600 | 2.6 |
| Laborer | 12 | 21 | 6,205 | 2.5 |
| Agricultural Labor | 4 | 50 | 1,900 | 5.2 |
| | | | | |
| **Household Income Quintile** | | | | |
| 1.  9,200-54,000 | 1 | 3 | 1,080 | 0.2 |
| 2.    6,000-9,199 | 3 | 9 | 680 | 0.3 |
| 3.    3,920-5,999 | 11 | 32 | 6,580 | 4.0 |
| 4.    2,900-3,919 | 1 | 3 | 540 | 0.5 |
| 5.      840-2,899 | 9 | 26 | 4,985 | 6.7 |
| | | | | |
| Totals | 25 | 15 | 13,865 | 1.2 |

*\* Former Untouchables*

adding the agricultural labor pensions and other welfare payments back into the income data, we arrive at the income actually reported by respondents in 1987. We can then recompute the Gini coefficient on the incomes with these payments included. The data appear in Table 9.1.

From Table 9.1 we see that the Gini drops 0.6 points from 45.4 to 44.8 when pensions and welfare payments are added. When we look at the beneficiaries of the payments more closely, we see that the payments are 16.5% of their incomes. Without them, household income would decline from Rs 4,563 to Rs 4,009. From Table 9.1 we can see that the average recipient household earns far less than the nonrecipients.

### Caste, Class, and Pensions

How are the pensions distributed among the various income and social groups in Nadur? Table 9.2 summarizes the data.

Looking first at the castes, we see that the formerly most oppressed castes are receiving by far the greatest percent of pensions. The formerly untouchable Mannan caste got no payments, but received other benefits to be described in the case studies in Chapter 12. We see that 91% of sample Pulaya households received some government welfare and 26% of all welfare payments were received by this caste. Of all the castes, Pulayas received the greatest share of their income from government payments, 7.1%.

Among the classes, agricultural labor households have the greatest percentage of participation in pensions at 50%. They constitute 5% of the sample, but acquired 14% of all welfare monies, while laborer households are 34% of the sample but received 45% of the rupees disbursed. Professional, service, and farmer class members received no payments. The bottom 60% of the sample (quintiles 3 through 5) received 87% of all welfare payments. The bottom quintile got 36% of the payments while the 4th quintile received 4%. Only 1 household in the 4th quintile was receiving a pension.

In sum, agricultural laborers' pensions and other similar welfare payments lowered the inequality level by onely a small amount. But the payments constitute a large portion of the incomes of many of the poorest households.

### Resource Transfer Programs: IRDP

Kerala State's programs of redistribution are supplemented by several programs of the Indian national government. The Integrated Rural Development Programme (IRDP) was started in 1980 as an extension of the earlier Community Development Program. Unlike earlier programs, IRDP was intended to be client-specific, aimed at households below the poverty line, including small farmers and rural laborers. According to one of its original statements of purpose, the program was to

> provide gainful employment and increased purchasing power for the rural poor, particularly landless labour, marginal farmers, artisans, women and children.... (quoted in Maheshwari 1985:117; cf. Parthasarathy 1981).

In the early 1980s households with incomes below Rs 3,500, were to be identified in each development block of about 20,000 households each. Of the 10,000 to 12,000 likely eligible households, approximately 2,000 would be assisted in the first 5 year period, with up to 3,000 after 1986. Following identification of the eligible households, the implementing bureaucracy was to encourage submission of loan plans, assist with details of the financing, and monitor the projects. Local public and private banks could be lending agencies, with substantial government subsidies and loan guarantees backing up the program. Government funding is divided 50:50 between central and state governments.

In Kerala in 1986, 87,006 households participated in the IRDP. Average loans were Rs 6,254 for new participants and Rs 3,927 for continuing projects. Scheduled caste and tribal households accounted for 37% of the recipients (GOK 1988:105). Purchase of cattle, other animals, wells, pumps, and small business investment have been the main uses of IRDP loans in Kerala. The official poverty line for eligibility was Rs 6,400 in 1987 (GOK 1990:85). Kerala claims the greatest targeting effectiveness of its IRDP program, with only 2% of ineligible households getting into the program compared with the Indian national average of 11% (GOK 1989:93).

According to the village development block officer (*gram savak*), the IRDP in Nadur in 1987 included 60 households. Of these, 23 are in the sample population. Scheduled caste households account for 6 (23%) of the projects in the sample population. The projects and their loan amounts are given in Table 9.3

From Table 9.3 we can see that cattle purchase makes up the largest category. If goats and she-buffaloes are included, purchase of animals accounts for 39% of loans. The machinery projects include 1 sewing machine and 3 blacksmiths' grinder motors.

The largest average loans go to the households that own petty shops. These loans are greatly favored by Nadur's gram savak who considers them the most economically effective.

Table 9.3
IRDP Loans: Amounts and Purposes
Nadur Village Kerala 1987

| Number of Households | Loans Total | Loans Average | Loan Purpose | Average HH Income |
|---|---|---|---|---|
| 147 | 0 | 0 | -- | 7,143 |
| 5 | 17,000 | 3,400 | Cattle | 3,857 |
| 4 | 12,500 | 3,125 | Well/Pumpset | 5,365 |
| 4 | 8,350 | 2,088 | Machinery | 5,820 |
| 3 | 7,375 | 2,458 | Agriculture | 2,306 |
| 3 | 17,000 | 5,667 | Business | 9,654 |
| 2 | 2,400 | 1,200 | Goats | 3,390 |
| 2 | 8,000 | 4,000 | Buffaloes | 5,654 |
| Total | 72,625 | 3,158 | | 6,871 |

Agricultural purposes cover 3 of the loans. These include purchase of banana seedlings for a house compound and other similar undertakings. If the well/pumpset loans and those for buffaloes are considered as agricultural, then 9 of the 23 loans (39%) would be for agriculture.

IRDP loans in Nadur carry interest rates of 4.5% or in a few instances 10% according to household respondents. Loans on the open credit market go for 18% at the local cooperative society bank and 19% at the local State Bank of India branch, which also finances many of the lower rate IRDP loans. Many of the IRDP loans do not have to be repaid in full. A loan for cattle, for example, may be Rs 4,000, but only Rs 3,000 have to be repaid.

Despite the favorable terms and the targeting of the loans to the poorest households, adequate use of the IRDP actually seems to require some start-up resources. Even with the assistance of the best-intentioned gram savak, 2 cows cannot be well tended for unless the household can provide adequate food supply and sanitary conditions for the animals. Likewise, a low-income blacksmith whose grinding motor breaks, may have trouble getting it back into operation. Perhaps for this reason the very poorest participants in the Nadur sample chose goats, which are the least destructible and most easily fed and tended of the animals.

Are IRDP loans reaching the poorest households? Shopkeepers had the highest average household incomes among the IRDP loan recipients.

Next came those borrowing for well/pumpsets, then machinery. Very low incomes were held by those asking to purchase buffaloes, cattle, and finally, goats. Agricultural loans went to the very poorest IRDP beneficiaries.

### Housing Programs and RLEGP

Kerala has conducted the most extensive program for house construction for low-income households of all the Indian states. The 1 *lakh* (lakh = 100,000) housing scheme was begun in 1972. It constitutes a follow-up to the land reform. The idea was to build housing for landless workers who had not received homesteads under the land reform. In each of Kerala's 960 village units or *panchayats* approximately 100 houses were to be constructed. As we described them in Chapter 3, each had 250 square feet of floor space, with 3 rooms, a hard foundation, cement floor, sun-dried brick walls, and a tile roof on teak beams taken from the state's forests (UN 1975:196). The plan cost far more than originally envisioned, but 57,000 houses were built by 1978 and 33,000 additional house sites had been distributed (Panikar and Soman 1984:59). In 1979 another 12,000 houses were built, in 1980 36,000, and in 1981 39,000 (Panikar and Soman 1984:58). In 1971 Kerala had the best rooms-to-people ratio and was 7th out of 15 Indian states with 46% of its housing described as "reasonably good" (ICSSR 1983:89-94).

In 1986-87 over 8,000 houses were built in Kerala under a continuation of the 1 lakh scheme. In Nadur 6 such houses were just finished or under construction at the time of the survey. Two were funded by the Indian national government under the Rural Landless Employment Guarantee Programme (RLEGP) which also employs rural workers to build roads, latrines, and irrigation canals. The other 4 houses were being built on funds from the "housing board," but had the same conditions as the RLEGP loans. In addition, several better-off households were doing major repair or upgrading of their houses with loans from the private credit market.

The 2 RLEGP houses are part of an upgrading of 1 of Nadur's 4 Pulaya (former outcaste) neighborhoods. The loans can include up to Rs 8,000 for a house, Rs 1,200 for latrine and Rs 12,500 for a well to be shared by 5 households. The 2 households constructing their new houses in 1987 had borrowed Rs 6,000 each, of which Rs 4,500 had to be repaid. Both households subsisted entirely from agricultural and house compound labor. One of these households was also receiving an IRDP loan to purchase 4 goats.

The 4 other houses were being built by 1 Ezhava rubber estate worker household, 1 Nair agricultural labor household which also contained a member doing servant work for a wealthy Nambudiri household, and 2 Nair laboring households whose income sources include house compound labor supplemented by agricultural labor.

### Rural Employment: Nadur's Spinning Co-op

We saw in Chapter 8 how Kerala's and Nadur's severe unemployment undermine development efforts. Rural light industry makes a small contribution towards overcoming it. The All-India *Khadi* (Handloom) Board started up in 1923, influenced by Mahatma Gandhi, who wanted to create low-tech, indigenous, employment-generating industries to counter British colonial control of the economy. Hand-woven cloth and garments provide Gandhi's main economic heritage. The Kerala Assembly created a statewide Khadi and Village Industries Board in 1957. By 1980, 95,000 looms were available in Kerala, employing 250,000 persons across the industry (Sankaranarayanan and Karunakaran 1985:253).[2] Prices and wages were set by the Khadi Board to produce a split of 55% for wages, 21% for materials, and 20% for management (Prem 1985:21).[3]

Nadur houses a unit of the *Kerala Khadi and Village Industries Association*, which employed 29 young women from 3 villages in in 1987 in a spinning cooperative.[4] Nadur's cooperative was first set up in 1971, but moved to a nearby village until 1981, when local political pressure brought about the creation of a new subunit in Nadur. The women, ages 15 to 33, hand crank spinning machines called *charkas*. These charkas turn masses of ground and twisted cotton called *sliva* into refined thread that can be woven on handlooms into cloth for saris or other clothing items. Technically, their work is called "rewinding," but they and Khadi officers usually refer to it as a stage of spinning.

The work is monotonous and unhealthy. The charkas are not hooked up electrically. The women sit before the machines for hours, resulting in frequent complaints of backache, stomach pain, chest pain, and bronchial disorders. Cotton dust fills the poorly lighted and poorly ventilated room. Appropriate technology is not automatically beneficial; small is not always beautiful.

Because the spinning work is difficult and because the young women also have substantial household chores, most find it impossible to work every week of the month. The 29 women in the coop during the survey period worked an average of 2.3 weeks per month, producing

224.6 bundles of thread for an average monthly wage of Rs 103. Wages are paid according to the amount produced in a formula that also brings a small management fee to the coop. In addition to their wages, the women earn credits in a welfare fund that provides clothing at *Onam* and severance pay with interest when they stop working.

Despite the physically difficult conditions, rewinding sliva at the charkas attracts young women from poor households because of the regular work and the relatively high pay. Rs 103 per month for 12 months—Rs 1,236 for a year—is more than a male agricultural laborer can earn in the rice fields. Twenty of the coop workers came from Nadur, of which 11 were members of 9 of the sample households. Six came from 4 labor households, 2 from craft, 2 from petty trade, and 1 from a farmer household. Nine were from 7 Nair households, with 1 from a blacksmith household and the other from the Mannan caste.

The average income of the 9 households with spinners was Rs 4,540, compared to Rs 7,001 for nonspinners. Spinners held 0.13 acres rice land compared with 0.32 for nonspinners. For house compound land, the figures also show spinner households with less, 0.36 acres versus 0.56 acres for the nonspinners.

Although spinning wages accounted for for only 1% of total sample income, they made up an average of 29% of spinner household income, ranging from 6% to 100%. Coop workers stated that they used 78% of their wages for household expenses on average, with the remainder going for items such as magazines to read during work and, rarely, for other personal needs. Like the many other programs detailed in this study, Khadi Coop employment helps poor households offset low income and seasonal shortages. Because the young women mostly work only until marriage, it does not provide a means of mobility or advancement, however.

### Wages, Work, Welfare, and Survival: Case Studies

We now have enough information on conditions in Nadur to look at some particular households. We conclude Chapter 9 with some cases representative of the variety of experiences of Nadur sample households containing 1 or more agricultural laborers. In Chapter 12 we shall present 18 additional cases.

*Case 1: Spinners Support the Household.* Govindan is 49, his wife Lakshmyamma is 39. They are members of the Nair caste. Both have 3 years of education. Lakshmyamma has worked all her adult life as an agricultural laborer. They have 4 daughters. In 1971 Govindan worked as a temple servant, but has more recently depended on agricultural labor himself. Both he and his wife have health problems which reduce their working ability.

The household's 8 members live in a 6 room house along a secluded path just behind the main village road. They have only bare furnishings in the house, and the latrine is a covered pit. The house had a palm leaf roof in 1971, but now has a tile roof. Their water supply is a well shared with several other households. This well is conveniently just outside their .10 acres house compound to which they received title in the land reform. But during the dry season the well often goes dry, and the household women walk 250 meters to the well of a Nambudiri former landlord for all their water needs. They have 5 coconut trees on the small compound.

Govindan and his wife manage to find 75 days each of agricultural field labor, transplanting, weeding, harvesting, and threshing. This brings in Rs 1,800, which is far below the needs of a family of 8. Their income is more than doubled by the work of daughters Amaru, 19, and Karthyayani, 18, at the Nadur spinning cooperative. Amaru's and Karthyayani's combined earnings are Rs 400 per month, or Rs 4,800 in the year—73% of the household total. This brings the total household income to Rs 6,600, or Rs 825 per person, about 1/3 of the Kerala State average per capita of Rs 2,361 in 1987.

Govindan's household benefited from the land reform, because the .10 acres house compound they now own had previously cost them 3/10 para of paddy in rent per year. Now there is no rent. Govindan stated that he feels much freer than his father who had been dependent on the jenmy who controlled the house compound. But he wishes he could get some agricultural land.

Amaru and Karthyayani work hard at the thread turning machines. Both girls feel that because their parents are not well, they cannot quit the spinning jobs although they often suffer bronchial irritations, headaches, and back pains. One day during our research, Govindan came to the spinning cooperative to take Amaru home to meet the family of a prospective husband. Both girls are exceptionally attractive and have received several marriage offers, but this was the first which did not include the demand for a dowry. When Amaru marries, she will quit her coop job and the household may have to send the 3rd daughter, Chinnamaru, now 16 and studying in the 10th standard, to crank the charkas.

In 1987, Govindan was given a Rs 6,000 low-interest loan to rebuild the house. Rs 4,500 of this amount must be repaid. The loan will come in several stages. First, money is granted for the foundation. Upon verification by the block development officer that the foundation has been constructed, money will be released for the walls and latrine, and finally the roof.

Govindan and Lakshmyamma are often forced to borrow money in July and August to meet a work shortage. Still, the household moved between surveys from the 3rd to the 2nd income quintile because of the income from the 2 working daughters. The 2 youngest daughters ages 7 and 5 get lunch free at school and at the nursery which is less than 1/2 kilometer from their house. Govindan says that the agricultural workers unions should struggle to get higher wages and permanent jobs for agricultural laborers. He also wishes the government would offer loans for purchase of agricultural land.

*Case 2: Extended Household Combines Several Incomes.* Rajan, aged 75 and his wife Mukhami, aged 68 are both Nair caste members. They live with their extended family in a 7-room house with a tiled roof and little furniture along the main Nadur road near a junction with a few shops. The roof was already tiled in 1971. They have a well and 16 coconut trees on their house compound, but only a covered pit for a latrine. The family of 11 members includes their 48-year-old daughter Janaky who is an agricultural laborer and her husband Madhavan who works in a tea shop. Also living in the household are 21-year-old granddaughter Lakshmy who is unemployed and her husband Krishnan who works for the railroad as a laborer. Four other grandchildren and 1 two-year-old great-granddaughter complete the household.

Janaky finds 40 days work per year in Nadur's rice fields, mostly for 1 wealthy Nambudiri landowner and about 20 days work tending the coconut trees of the same Nambudiri household, bringing her wages to Rs 600 per year. She also receives a *theerpu*, or gift of 2 *mundus*, or lower body wrap-arounds from her main employer each year. Her husband Madhavan earns Rs 450 per month in the tea shop as does Krishnan with his railroad work, bringing total household income to Rs 11,400. The household's .32 acres house compound land has 16 coconut trees yielding enough fruit for Rs 1,000 in sales along with what the household consumes.

On top of these income sources, both Rajan and Mukhami receive agricultural laborer pensions of Rs 540 per year each. This brings the household's total income to Rs 13,480 of which 8% comes from the pensions.

Despite the highest overall income among the 43 Nadur sample households with agricultural laborers, the household is forced to borrow money from merchants during some lean months. They do not have to eat less, however. Rajan says his father had more income relative to expenses than the present household has. They have recently planted 6 arecanut trees on their house compound land from which they hope to derive additional cash income in future years. The household owns a cow.

*Case 3: All Agricultural Laborers.* Chakkan is a 52-year-old Pulaya caste agricultural laborer. His wife Radha is 40. She also works in the fields as do their 22- and 19-year-old sons Chammy and Kunju. Their nuclear household has 7 members including 2 children and Chakkan's 85-year old mother Pariyani. Their 4-room house stands on .10 acres of land which formerly belonged to a wealthy Nambudiri who lives on the other side of the hill and to whom the household was formerly attached. The Nambudiri side faces the rice fields. It is cool, expansive, and shaded by many coconut trees. The side with Chakkan's house is steep and rocky. He has planted 3 coconut trees, but they are not yielding. The house has a leaf roof and mud walls. In 1971 the roof was made of hay, the house had just 1 room and the house compound had no trees at all. In 1987 the roof remains of leaf and there is no furniture, only some cooking utensils. The house is larger, however, with 4 rooms. The latrine is open air.

Chakkan, Radha, Chammy, and Kunju all work as agricultural laborers. They average 65 days per worker per year, earning Rs 2,200 in 1986-87. Pariyani gets an agricultural laborer's pension of Rs 540, equal to 25% of what the younger members can earn combined. They have no other source of income.

During months when they get no field labor, Chakkan and Radha borrow from merchants and friends but eventually have to eat less. In 1971 the household had 1 goat. In 1987 they received an IRDP loan for Rs 300 to purchase 3 goats.

*Case 4: Building on Government Programs.* Manikandan is a 60-year-old Pulaya former rubber estate worker who now is a house compound laborer. His wife Kaly is 50 years old and works as an agricultural laborer.

The nuclear household of 7 members lives in a 5-room house with a tiled roof, and no furniture. In 1971 the roof was tiled but there were only 2 rooms. The house and compound are located on a steep, rocky hillside with a spectacular view of the rice lands of other households and the foothills of the Western Ghat Mountains.

Manikandan gets 90 days of house compound labor in a year. Kaly gets the same along with 30 days of rice field labor. This nets the household Rs 3,900 per year. The household recently received an IRDP loan of Rs 800 to purchase 4 goats. They also got a subsidized loan of Rs 6,000 from the RLEGP to build a new house. There is currently a protected well at their house site which goes dry in the late dry season months of April and May. The road junction 350 meters from their house site has a water pipe connected to a nearby town supply. The pipe is shared with many households.

Manikandan and Kaly are illiterate. An 18-year-old daughter got through the 6th standard. Her 22-year-old brother made it only to standard 3. But the oldest son Ayyappan passed the Secondary School Leaving Certificate (SSLC) exam in the 10th standard and is now a B. A. student. With government reservation (affirmative action) programs, Ayyappan has a good chance at a government job with a reasonable salary and benefits. Another son and daughter each are at third and fifth standards in the Nadur government school.

### Notes

1. In August, 1991, the payment went to Rs 70 per month. Beneficiaries for 1990-91 numbered 316,509 (GOK 1992:121).

2. About 23,000 loans were in cooperatives and 22,000 in households. Small factories like that in Nadur numbered about 2,000, but not all of those were coops under the Khadi Board (Sankaranarayanan and Karunakaran 1985:253).

3. The remaining 4% presumably goes for losses and unexpected costs.

4. The Kerala Khadi and Village Industries Association is a division of the Khadi Board which includes marketing and purchasing agencies as well as the local production facilities.

# 10

## Public Food Distribution

Kerala's redistribution programs bring food to large numbers of people throughout the state at primary health care centers, special feeding centers for tribal and slum-area children, school and nursery lunch programs, and the fair price or ration shops.

### School and Nursery Lunches

School feeding programs originated in the princely states of Travancore and Cochin in the 1940s (UN 1975:41). The expansion of the program to all school children was proposed during the first Communist Ministry of 1957-59 as part of the Kerala Education Bill (Sathyamurthy 1985:394). The bill also envisaged free textbooks and writing materials. Right-wing Catholic and Congress Party forces opposed the bill with the same hysteria as they opposed the land reform act proposed by the same ministry. Initially they prevented its implementation. But, like the land reform, subsidized food eventually came into being in piecemeal fashion. The lunch program was partly realized in 1961 with the assistance of Cooperative for American Relief Everywhere (CARE), which provided most of the foodstuffs until just a few years ago. The program is now primarily funded by the Kerala State Government.

Until June 1987 the program offered all students in Standards (grades) 1 to 4 a hot lunch each day. In the early 1970s about 70% of eligible students were being covered. Thirty percent of parents preferred to feed their children at home. By 1987 over 2 million children were receiving the meals which were designed to provide about 410 calories and 15 grams of protein (UN 1975:42; GOK 1988:88). In June of 1987 the newly-elected Left Democratic Front government expanded the program to cover standards 5 through 7, raising the number of beneficiaries statewide to 3.2 million.[1] The LDF government also reinstituted the textbook and writing slate program in 1987, 30 years after the initial proposal. In the early 1970s village nurseries were feeding more than 150,000 women and infants (UN 1975:41). By 1988, 9,227 feeding centers were serving 265,000 women and infants (GOK 1989:97).

## A Nadur Nursery

In Nadur Village 6 nurseries provide food to preschool children and to pregnant and lactating mothers. They serve a total of 240 infants and women in the entire *panchayat* or government unit, which is slightly larger than the Nadur census block.

Most infants and women in the sample population were fed in a nursery that was founded in 1974. It was housed in the library building near the school until 1977, when a new site was found and a new building was constructed. The new building was sited on .05 acres of land donated by a wealthy Nambudiri. The land given was rocky house compound, but the site is convenient for most of the households that use the nursery. The Kerala state government put up Rs 1,000 along with Rs 3,000 from CARE and a public collection in Nadur raised the remaining Rs 4,000. Local people donated all construction labor.

The nursery capacity is 40. In 1987, 35 students were enrolled. Children from all castes except Nambudiris are present at the nursery. It is run by the *Mahila Samojam* (Women's Organization) of Nadur on user fees supplemented by funds from the state government. The fees are Rs 1 for initial membership and then Rs 0.25 per month for all services including food. Infants not attending the nursery can still be brought for meals.

The nursery employs a Nambudiri woman as teacher at a salary of Rs 175 per month. She takes care of the children from 9:00 am to 5:00 pm, teaching them songs, dances, and preschool exercises such as learning to make up stories based on pictures she shows them. The nursery has few toys; the building is small and the latrine, while cemented and sealed, is connected to the main building. This forces the teacher to keep the back door closed making the nursery building very hot.

## Nursery Meals

Nursery meals are designed to provide 65 grams per person. US bulgur wheat from the World Food Program is cooked with soybean oil to make a porridge. Children present range from ages 2 1/2 to 5. Seventeen of the children receive a double feeding, once at 11:00 and again with all the children at 3:30 pm. The double feeding is offered after verification by a doctor that the infant or mother needs extra feeding. A doctor is supposed to visit annually, with travel costs paid by the nursery, but Nadur had not had a physician at the nursery for 2 years. The nursery remains open the entire year.

At meal time, the children line up outside the kitchen, a small cubicle on one side of the 5 meters by 7 meters building. Each child and mother present receives an aluminum bowl about 12 centimeters (5 inches) wide into which is dipped the *upama*, or porridge. After receiving their food, the children and mothers sit with crossed legs, reaching into the bowls with their right hand and rolling the glutinous porridge into balls which they put into their mouths. After eating, everyone washes his or her hands and mouth. The nursery is close to a water tap that is not yet functioning, but the cook brings buckets of water from a well nearby.

## School Meals

Nadur's school children get to eat more than their nursery counterparts. At noon, classes stop; the morning shift is over. Children in standards 1 through 4 go to the verandahs that form the front of the U-shaped school building facade. At the far end of the U-opening is a well with an electric pump. Near the well stands a small shack with a palm leaf roof. Smoke wafts upwards from the shack. Inside the cook prepares rice and green gram for 300 students. Each will also receive one pappadam (fried gram chip).

After the children have been sitting quietly for a few minutes, a teacher brings out stacks of the 12 centimeter aluminum bowls. She walks down the verandah corridor, handing one bowl to each child. Near the end, she runs out of bowls; another teacher quickly arrives with banana leaves, the traditional plates of Kerala.

The cook appears. He and several teachers ply down the rows of sitting children with buckets filled with rice or green gram. Cook and teachers ladle out hefty portions of rice and smaller amounts of gram; while the students are eating, one more teacher comes along with a pappadam for each child. After lunch, students line up girls together and boys together at the water pump for hand and mouth cleaning. As they wash, they look up the hill towards the library 200 meters above where once one of the nurseries was located. Out front on the grass some men sit playing cards. Students from the morning shift can go home.

## Lunches and Income Inequality

Have school and nursery lunch programs reduced income inequality in Nadur? Only households with young children or pregnant or lactating women receive these benefits. Characteristics of lunch and non lunch households are shown on Table 10.1.

As can be seen from Table 10.1, 39 sample households received at least one lunch. This included 20 infants fed at local nurseries, along with 6 pregnant/lactating women. At school, 39 children in standards 1 through 4 were fed, for a total of 65 meals. Households receiving the food were less well off than the non recipients who included mostly wealthy children but a few poor households as well. In some households respondents stated their children did not like the food and came home for lunch.

On Table 10.1 we have created a sub sample of households with eligible children for school or nursery lunches. By age 11 virtually all children have completed the 4th standard; many complete it by age 8 or 9. Households with one or more child of age 10 or below constitute the group with eligible children. Within this sub sample, the participation rate is 36% of households. Nonusers average Rs 1,984 more than users. Clearly the feeding programs are more popular among the less well off. But how much difference do they make?

If we assume an income value of Rs 0.50 per meal and 200 days feeding per year at the school or nurseries, the rupees value per beneficiary comes to 100. We arrive at the Rs 0.50 figure by taking the average market price of rice during the survey period which was Rs 3.75 per kg. This makes 100 grams equal to Rs 0.375. One hundred grams of rice provide 346 calories according to Indian food tables (Gopalan *et al* 1985:61). Since the lunch officially provides 410 calories, this requires 118 grams of rice equal to a price of Rs 0.44. We round the figure up to Rs 0.50 to include calories for the 15 grams of protein that would require purchase of some legumes, eggs, milk, or fish.[2] The overall rupees effect of the lunches is small; the Gini coefficient declines from 44.8 to 44.6. Nonetheless, participating households gained the equivalent of 2.7% of their incomes from the lunches.

How do the lunches affect caste, class, and income groups? The data appear on Table 10.2. From Table 10.2 it can be seen that the top quintile received the least return, but the other lunches were distributed fairly evenly among quintiles 2 to 4. The bottom quintile received only 4 lunches among 3 households.

The caste distribution indicates greater redistribution. Muslim households with children have a 69% participation rate for the lunches,

Table 10.1
Lunch Recipients and Non recipients
Nadur Village Kerala 1987

| Characteristic | Recipients | Non Recipients |
|---|---|---|
| Number of Households | 39 | 131 |
| Percent of Sample Households | 23 | 77 |
| Number of Beneficiaries | 65 | 0 |
| | | |
| Average Household Income | | |
| Without the lunches | 6,122 | 7,094 |
| With the lunches | 6,288 | 7,094 |
| | | |
| Households with Children | | |
| Under 11 Only (N=102) | 37 | 65 |
| Percent of Sub Sample | 36 | 64 |
| | | |
| Average Household Income | | |
| Without the Lunches | 6,167 | 8,151 |
| With the Lunches | 6,337 | 8,151 |
| | | |
| Average Value in Rupees | 170 | 0 |
| Average Percent of Household | | |
| Income from Lunches | 2.7 | 0 |
| | | |
| Gini Index | | |
| Without Lunches | 44.8 | |
| With Lunches | 44.6 | |

an important fact when one considers the data from Table 9.2 where we saw that they receive nothing from the pension and welfare programs. Thirty-six percent of Pulaya households with children were receiving lunches.

Looking at the occupational/ownership classes, we see that laborers received 33 lunches in 19 households. Only 28% of households with children were participating in the program. Agricultural laborers also fared poorly, partly explained by the fact that a few of their children were not attending school.

The clearest set of associations are between lunches and amount of rice from own land.  We see from Table 10.2 that possession of even small amounts of rice land leads to nonparticipation.  Presumably children in households with almost any amount of rice from their own fields will be given that rice in place of food from the school or nursery.

In sum, it appears that school lunches in Nadur provide slight income redistribution, including some effects by caste.  The lunch program also provides employment for several cooks and for the nursery teachers and assistants.

## Food Distribution Through Ration Shops

Food distribution via ration shops or "Fair Price Shops" is Kerala's most extensive and important program next to the land reform.  In one way public distribution of food is even more significant than the land reform, since it reaches landless as well as landed.

Public food distribution in Kerala began during the first world war, but became important in the state after 1964 when food shortages in India caused the state government to purchase rice and wheat to make sure enough was available (Gwatkin 1979:248).

### Historical Struggles for Subsidized Food

Food rationing was not simply the gift of enlightened administrations.  Workers and tenant farmers struggled for decades to control landlords and other high class and caste forces that were exploiting them.  During the Indian independence movement, at a high point of local struggles in 1946, the Kerala peasants front in Malabar organized a campaign against hoarding and black-marketing of food that included forcible prevention of the movement of grain from the area so it could be kept in local ration shops.  During a famine in 1942-43, the *All-Malabar Karshaka Sangham*—one of the land reform organizations—set up a food committee which organized unofficial ration shops.  This action helped lead to the creation of official rationing through consumer co-operatives in 1944 (Oomen 1985:50).  In 1948, Malabar peasant activists, inspired in part by the famous Telangana uprising in the Andhra Pradesh region of India, forced landlords to sell their surplus grain at a "fair price".  The intensity of these struggles can be measured by the fact that many activists were killed, including 22 in a single slaughter inside a prison in 1950 (Sathyamurthy 1985:176).  Although these struggles involved other issues such as land reform, the idea of a non exploitative price for

Table 10.2: Features of School Lunch Households
Nadur Village Kerala 1987

| | Households With 1 or More Lunches | Number of Lunches | Rupees Amount |
|---|---|---|---|
| **Caste** | | | |
| Nambudiri | 0 | 0 | 0 |
| Nair | 12 | 23 | 2,300 |
| Craft | 1 | 1 | 100 |
| Ezhuthasan/Chetty | 4 | 8 | 800 |
| Muslim | 12 | 18 | 1,800 |
| Ezhava | 5 | 8 | 800 |
| Mannan | 0 | 0 | 0 |
| Pulaya | 5 | 7 | 700 |
| **Class** | | | |
| Professional | 1 | 1 | 100 |
| Service | 1 | 1 | 100 |
| Craft | 1 | 1 | 100 |
| Farmer | 5 | 8 | 800 |
| Petty Trade | 5 | 6 | 600 |
| Recipient | 5 | 12 | 1,200 |
| Laborer | 19 | 33 | 3,300 |
| Agricultural Laborer | 2 | 3 | 300 |
| **Household Income Quintile** | | | |
| 1.   9,200-54,000 | 4 | 5 | 500 |
| 2.   6,000-9,199 | 13 | 23 | 2,300 |
| 3.   3,920-5,999 | 8 | 17 | 1,700 |
| 4.   2,900-3,919 | 11 | 16 | 1,500 |
| 5.    840-2,899 | 3 | 4 | 400 |
| **Amount of Rice From Own Land** | | | |
| 100% | 1 | 1 | 100 |
| 75% | 0 | 0 | 0 |
| 50% | 3 | 4 | 400 |
| 25% | 2 | 8 | 800 |
| None | 33 | 52 | 5,200 |
| Totals | 39 | 65 | 6,500 |

food became a mass popular demand to which successive Kerala governments have had to respond.

Since the large-scale expansion of the program in 1964, Kerala's fair price or ration shops have become the most extensive and effective in India. By the 1970s, they accounted for 15-16% of total calorie intake and 19-20% of total protein in the state (Gwatkin 1979:249). We can see from Table 1.3 that 99% of Kerala's villages are served by a shop within 2 kilometers, as compared with only 35% of villages in all-India. Other Indian states have ration shops, but Kerala is 20 years ahead of even the most advanced other states such as Tamil Nadu, Gujarat, Andhra Pradesh, and Karnataka, which began extending shops into rural areas in the 1980s. In the remaining Indian states, the shops are generally accessible only to urban people (Gwatkin 1979:248; Subbarao 1989:25-26).[3]

In 1987, 4.7 million ration cards were issued to Kerala households for purchasing price-controlled rice, wheat, sugar, palm oil, and kerosene in 12,783 shops (GOK 1988:17). In addition 171 "Maveli" Stores sell an even broader range of products at controlled prices (GOK 1988:19). Both ration and Maveli shops offer special additional goods on festival occasions such as *Onam*, the Kerala harvest and New Year celebration in late August or early September, which was described in Chapter 3.

On the average, ration shops are within 2 km of the 360 households which they serve. Some stores are cooperatives while most are owned by private businesses that receive a fixed profit on their operations (GOK 1988:17-19).

In 1961-62 ration shops accounted for only 13% of the cereals consumed. By 1971-72 they accounted for 37%, but the bottom 30% of the population got 2/3 of its rice and wheat from the shops (UN 1975:43,48).[4] The greater use by lower income groups comes from the structure of the ration system in which the amount of rice available is inversely related to the amount of rice land owned. We will examine this below after we describe Nadur's ration shop.

### Nadur's Ration Shop

Nadur's first ration shop was opened in 1962 in a nearby village. It closed in 1968 but reopened in 1975. In 1987 the shop served households with a total of 600 ration cards, about 1.5 times the official state average. The shop is located at Nadur City—which we described in Chapter 3. It is open Monday through Saturday from 8 to 12 in the morning and again from 3:30 to 7:30 in the afternoon and evening. Crowded with sacks of rice, tins of cooking oil, and drums of kerosene, it is electrified but

poorly lit. From the open front of the shop one can look across the dirt
road of Nadur City to the barber shop and a goldsmith's workplace.

Nadur's ration shop is owned privately by a Chetty caste household.
The owner's son works for a salary weighing the goods; a daughter is
employed as bookkeeper. On rice and wheat sales the owner is allowed
a commission of Rs 7.21 per quintal (100 kg), Rs 9 per 100 liters of kerosene and Rs 4.5 per quintal (100 kilograms) of sugar. From the commission he must pay transportation costs from the nearest distribution
center 10 kilometers distant, along with his rent, electricity and license
fee. A Kerala state sales tax is paid by customers in the prices.

Nadur's ration shop owner seems to be doing well by local standards. The household property is less than 1/4 kilometer from the store.
Located on the top of the ridge, the compound has a deep well and
several coconut trees. The house itself is furnished with chairs and a
sofa with plastic upholstery. One son of the household works in the
Gulf state of Dubai where he earns a good salary. This may be the
source of capital for the shop.

The shop is rarely without a customer. Households buy quantities
as large as allowed. Parents and children carry their goods home across
paddy fields and coconut groves in large sacks on the tops of their
heads. They transport kerosene in 5- or 10-gallon square metal drums;
distant households cart heavy loads of kerosene or rice on the bus to a
stop close to their house. During the survey period the ration shop
always had rice available. Some goods such as cooking oil are less reliable. In the 1970s many Kerala ration shops sometimes ran short of rice,
but this problem did not recur in Nadur up to 1987.

### Rice Land and the Ration Shop

How much rice can a household buy at subsidized prices? Households are given cards that allot ration units at 1 per person under 12
years of age and 2 per adult. Each unit allows the holder to purchase 770
grams of rice weekly. Units are further divided in full portion for 12
months for households with less than 1/2 acre of land; full ration for 4
months of the year (=1/3 ration) for owners of 2-crop rice land of more
than 1/2 acre, and no rice ration (but other goods are available) for those
with 2 acres or more. In Nadur, households owning more than 1.5 acres
of 2-crop land do not use a rice ration. The relation between ration shop
purchases and rice land owned is set out in Table 10.3.

From Table 10.3 we see that Nambudiris purchase only 24% of their
rice at the ration shop. The remainder is produced on land owned by

Table 10.3: Ration Shop Use and Rice Land Farmed

| | N | Percent of Rice at Shop | Rice Land Owned | Percent of Rice From Own Land | | | | |
|---|---|---|---|---|---|---|---|---|
| | | | | None | 1/4 | 1/2 | 3/4 | All |
| **Caste** | | | | | | | | |
| Nambudiri | 13 | 24 | 71 | 5 | 0 | 0 | 0 | 8 |
| Nair | 83 | 59 | 34 | 47 | 11 | 12 | 7 | 6 |
| Craft | 11 | 69 | 2 | 10 | 1 | 0 | 0 | 0 |
| Ezhuthasan/Chetty | 13 | 45 | 49 | 8 | 1 | 0 | 2 | 2 |
| Muslim | 22 | 49 | 28 | 15 | 2 | 4 | 1 | 0 |
| Ezhava | 13 | 63 | 5 | 12 | 0 | 1 | 0 | 0 |
| Mannan | 4 | 24 | 19 | 3 | 0 | 1 | 0 | 0 |
| Pulaya | 11 | 59 | 9 | 10 | 0 | 1 | 0 | 0 |
| **Class** | | | | | | | | |
| Professional | 11 | 28 | 50 | 7 | 0 | 1 | 0 | 3 |
| Service | 9 | 41 | 56 | 4 | 0 | 2 | 2 | 1 |
| Craft | 14 | 67 | 6 | 12 | 1 | 1 | 0 | 0 |
| Farmer | 23 | 25 | 76 | 6 | 2 | 5 | 2 | 8 |
| Petty Trade | 18 | 51 | 46 | 9 | 5 | 2 | 1 | 1 |
| Recipient | 30 | 76 | 30 | 17 | 3 | 4 | 3 | 3 |
| Laborer | 57 | 58 | 8 | 49 | 3 | 3 | 2 | 0 |
| Agricultural Laborer | 8 | 54 | 15 | 6 | 1 | 1 | 0 | 0 |
| **Household Income Quintile** | | | | | | | | |
| 1. 9,200-54,000 | 34 | 32 | 60 | 17 | 2 | 3 | 3 | 9 |
| 2. 6,000-9,199 | 34 | 57 | 30 | 24 | 2 | 4 | 2 | 2 |
| 3. 3,920-5,999 | 34 | 58 | 25 | 21 | 7 | 2 | 2 | 2 |
| 4. 2,900-3,919 | 34 | 67 | 23 | 24 | 2 | 6 | 2 | 0 |
| 5. 840-2,899 | 34 | 55 | 15 | 24 | 2 | 4 | 1 | 3 |
| **Ration Shop** | | | | | | | | |
| Users | 139 | 66 | 11 | 107 | 14 | 15 | 3 | 0 |
| Nonusers | 31 | 0 | 120 | 3 | 1 | 4 | 7 | 16 |
| **Rice Land** | | | | | | | | |
| Owners | 61 | 31 | 85 | 1 | 15 | 19 | 10 | 16 |
| Non owners | 109 | 67 | 0 | 109 | 0 | 0 | 0 | 0 |
| Totals | 170 | 54 | 31 | 110 | 15 | 19 | 10 | 16 |

the household or purchased on the open market. More details about these relationships appear later in this chapter. On our nutrition survey, we asked households to estimate how much of their rice needs they met from their own rice lands. Landless households obviously chose none as the answer, while large rice land owners gave 100% as the response. As can be seen from Table 10.3, many households gave answers of 1/4, 1/2, or 3/4. These answers are summarized on Table 10.3 along with the average rice land holding for each group. The average rice land holding for Nambudiris is 0.71 acres. Five Nambudiri households produce no rice on their own lands, while 8 households produce all their rice needs on their own holdings. One rice land owner on Table 10.3 is listed as producing no rice from its own land. This Nambudiri household with 0.31 acres of rice land claimed all its production was used for religious offerings. The household's holding is small enough to qualify them for full ration shop usage.

Nairs get 59% of their annual rice intake from the ration shop. The average rice land holding for the caste in 1987 is 0.34 acres. Forty-seven Nair households own no rice land, 11 get 1/4 of their rice from their plots, 12 manage half their needs, 7 get 3/4, and 6 produce all they need from their own lands. Ezhavas and Pulayas, the traditional rice land landless, have the least production from their own lands along with the craft castes. Of the 170 households in the Nadur sample, only 16 (9%) are able to produce all their rice needs from their own land, 10 (6%) can produce 3/4, and 19 (11%) produce 1/2 of their needs.

We see on Table 10.3 that 7 of 23 farmer class households meet 100% of their rice needs while 8 households meet none of their needs. The 8 rice land landless farmers produce coconuts and other house compound crops for sale. Laborers and agricultural laborers have the least production along with craft households, but recipient class households claim the largest use of the ration shop. The highest quintile gets 32% of its rice from the shop and averages 0.60 acres of rice land while the lowest quintile gets 55% from the shop and averages 0.15 acres of rice land.

Looking at the bottom lines on Table 10.3, we see that ration shop users as a group have only 0.11 acres rice land per household and 107 of the 139 user households have no land. By contrast, households not using the shop average 1.2 acres of rice land and only 4 of the 31 have no rice land. These latter 4 households include high-income professionals who prefer to eat the highest grade open-market rice which is not available at the shop. High-income households do use the shop for some purchases such as cooking oil at holiday seasons, however.

The 61 households owning rice land average 0.85 acres and get only 31% of their rice at the shop while the 109 without rice land average 67%

of rice needs met at the shop. Overall, the shop supplies 54% of the rice eaten by Nadur sample households.

## The Ration Shop and Income Inequality

Does the ration shop reduce income inequality? Our research into the effects of the ration system in Nadur involved several questions about the ration shop and an examination of each sample household's ration card. By examining the ration card directly, we are able to have high confidence of the reliability of the data on ration use.

To evaluate the effects of the shop for rice, we computed the opportunity cost of the ration rice purchases. Because the shop also provides wheat, sugar, and fuel oil, our use of rice alone as an indicator *under*estimates the real effect of ration shop purchases.

We took weekly price records at a village store on all food and other major consumer items. During the period of the household survey, the average open market price of medium-grade rice was Rs 3.75 per kg. while the ration shop price was Rs 2.71. The difference was thus Rs 1.04. Next we took data from the survey questionnaire on how many units of ration the household was entitled to. This was multiplied by 0.77, the kilograms allowed per week, and then by 52 weeks to give the estimated yearly household purchase at the shop. When multiplied by the Rs. 1.04 opportunity cost figure, the rupees value of the shop to the household is estimated. This amount can be added to household income for recomputation of inequality.

How much redistribution does the ration shop effect through sale of rice? The data are shown in Table 10.4.

From Table 10.4 we can see that more than 8 out of 10 households purchase rice at the shop. This figure is actually rather low. The all-Kerala estimate is that 97% of households use the shop for rice purchases (George 1979:23). The average household income of the users is substantially below those of the nonusers. Thus, the overall income effect must be redistributive. For households using the shop, nearly 8% of income is from the opportunity cost savings of the shop. If we add the income value of the ration shop rice subsidy to those households purchasing there, the Gini index declines 2.4 points or 5.4% from 44.6 to 42.2. This is the most egalitarian form of the income distribution of the Nadur sample population in 1987, and represents a decline of the Gini by 8.5 points or 16.8% compared with the index for 1971. This is the final inequality adjustment we can measure, and is the same as the column marked "with ration shop" on Table 6.5.

Table 10.4
Ration Shop Users Versus Nonusers
Nadur Village Kerala 1987

| Characteristic | Users | Nonusers |
|---|---|---|
| Number of Households | 139 | 31 |
| Percent of Sample | 82 | 18 |
| Average Benefit in Rupees | 466 | 0 |
| Average Household Income | | |
|   Without the Shop | 5,439 | 13,446 |
|   With the Shop | 5,906 | 13,446 |
| Average Percent of Household | | |
|   Income from Ration | 8 | 0 |
| Average Percent of Rice Needs | | |
|   From Ration Shop | 66 | 0 |
| Gini Index of Inequality | | |
|   Without the shop | 44.6 | |
|   With the shop | 42.2 | |

*Note: Lunches and pensions are also included in these computations.*

To obtain the average percent of rice needs met by the ration shop, we multiplied the number of adult equivalents in each household by 0.4 kilograms of rice (400 grams), the daily amount recommended for a minimum diet by the Indian Council on Medical Research (Gopalan *et al* 1985:29). We then multiplied by 365 days. The amount of rice purchased at the shop was then divided by this total in order to obtain a figure of percent of needs met by the shop. The range of variation was small although some discrepancies occurred because some households have ration units for members who are currently out of the village and thus their ration percent may be exaggerated. The figure of 66% corresponds exactly to what researchers have estimated for the poorest groups in Kerala generally (UN 1975:48). The characteristics of users and nonusers by caste, class, and income quintile appear on Table 10.5.

Table 10.5 shows percent of household income derived from the

Table 10.5
Features of Ration Shop User Households
Nadur Village Kerala 1987

| | Households | | |
|---|---|---|---|
| | Number | Percent | Percent of Income |
| **Caste** | | | |
| Nambudiri | 5 | 38 | 2 |
| Nair | 69 | 83 | 9 |
| Craft | 11 | 100 | 6 |
| Ezhuthasan/Chetty | 9 | 69 | 6 |
| Muslim | 19 | 86 | 8 |
| Ezhava | 13 | 100 | 9 |
| Mannan* | 2 | 50 | 4 |
| Pulaya* | 11 | 100 | 10 |
| **Class** | | | |
| Professional | 5 | 45 | 1 |
| Service | 5 | 56 | 3 |
| Craft | 14 | 100 | 7 |
| Farmer | 10 | 43 | 3 |
| Petty Trade | 15 | 83 | 7 |
| Recipient | 27 | 90 | 11 |
| Laborer | 55 | 96 | 10 |
| Agricultural Laborer | 8 | 100 | 10 |
| **Household Income Quintile** | | | |
| 1. 9,200-54,000 | 18 | 53 | 3 |
| 2.   6,000-9,199 | 31 | 91 | 6 |
| 3.   3,920-5,999 | 30 | 88 | 9 |
| 4.   2,900-3,919 | 30 | 88 | 10 |
| 5.     840-2,899 | 30 | 88 | 11 |

* *Former untouchables*

ration shop subsidy. We see that the top quintile has an even division between users and nonusers, deriving much the least income from the shop. As we go down the quintiles, the ratio of users to nonusers becomes stable but the percent of income increases as income declines.

Among the castes Nambudiris make the least use of the shop and therefore their incomes are least affected. Most other castes have heavy use and large income effects. The Pulayas gain most, averaging 10% of income from the shop. Muslims and Ezhavas, two other poor castes, on average also gained among the highest percents of income from the shop.

Recipients, laborers, and agricultural laborers are heavy users and relatively larger beneficiaries in income terms than higher income occupational groups such as farmers, service workers, and professionals. In sum, we see that rice rationing in Nadur has a significant redistributive impact. The Nadur data confirm the findings of other studies (George 1979; Kumar 1979) for Kerala. By contrast, a 2-village study of the Noon Meals Scheme and ration shops in neighboring Tamil Nadu State found no redistributive effects (Harriss 1991:80-81).[5]

## Food Distribution and Food Intake

Have the lunches and the ration shop brought adequate calorie intake to Nadur's people? This question has 2 parts. First we must ask whether the nutritional level of the sample population is adequate. Second, can we show that the lunches or ration shop have a significant impact on the observed nutritional level? These questions arise in the context of the Kerala nutrition debate.

### The Kerala Nutrition Debate

Studies of nutrition in Kerala have produced contradictory findings. During the 1950s and 1960s surveys seemed to indicate about 1,600 calories per person per day, far below the 2,400 calorie Indian minimum standard. Economists at Kerala's Centre for Development Studies (CDS) were suspicious of both these figures. Kerala's long life expectancy and low infant mortality rates seemed implausible at such low calorie levels. CDS staff set out to reconsider the calorie requirements for Kerala on the one hand and the available calories on the other.

First they considered the state's female to male ratio which is the highest of all Indian states (see Chapter 1). They then factored in the high unemployment in Kerala and the fact that the higher educational level meant more people working in office and technical jobs requiring fewer calories per worker. This led them to revise the calorie standard down to 2,200 for a population like Kerala's (UN 1975:32). They then examined the food balance sheets used by researchers to estimate calorie intake in India. This led to the discovery that cassava and coconuts—2 of Kerala's most important foods—were not being counted. After conducting an exploratory nutrition survey near the research institute in which cassava and coconuts were counted in the diet, they tentatively concluded that Kerala's people were obtaining about 2,339 calories per person per day, 6% above their revised minimum (UN 1975: Chapters II, III and Annex II).

The CDS average figures, however, can be read as a continuing sign of food inadequacy. Since the average intake is very close to the minimum, we can guess that substantial numbers of individuals would fall below it. The calorie distribution in the CDS sample survey suggested wide variations among households by income (UN 1975:186). Local calorie studies in the 1970s, again indicated serious calorie deficits. Anthropologist Loes Schenk-Sandbergen reported for 1979 that among 61 Kudumbi servant households in Alleppey town, "58 families could not even afford elementary food items such as milk and sugar." In the lean months of March and April, 50 households were reduced to one meal per day (1988:25). Joan Mencher (1980:1789) and CDS economist P. G. K. Panikar found for 1976 and 1977 in 27 and 29 households from villages in Kuttanad and Palghat—the latter region near to Nadur—that average per capita calorie intakes were just 1,894 and 1,488 respectively. The lowest sample households received just 1,472 and 744.

Like findings prior to the CDS revisions, these surveys are difficult to reconcile with Kerala's long life expectancy and low infant mortality. When calorie intakes dropped to 910 per person per day in the 1940s, death rates increased by as much as 250% (Panikar and Soman 1984:22-23). The health and survival of Kerala's children may be influenced by the superior sanitary conditions and health services enjoyed by the state's people. The dispersed settlement pattern in Kerala inhibits the spread of infectious diseases. More accessible health care facilities lessen the dietary effects of diseases. The importance of these factors is highlighted by a recent observation that "One heavy attack of dysentry can drain away six or more months of very careful nutritional build-up, and worms and intestinal parasites can consume more of the food than the body can appropriate" (Mitra 1985:153).

Additional data support the view, however, that Kerala's food intake situation is among the best in India. Height and weight surveys for the period 1975-1979 had indicated that 16% of Kerala's children were normal in weight for age. In 1982 32% were normal. This placed Kerala first among 10 Indian states surveyed. West Bengal came in a distant second with 21% normal. Only 2% of Kerala's children were listed as severely malnourished, placing it second behind West Bengal.

Other states ranged from 5% in Tamil Nadu to 15% in Gujarat.[6] Kerala's high rankings in the study should be qualified with the fact that the high-income states of Punjab and Haryana were not included in the survey (Subarrao 1989:13). The average of 8 Indian states for 1982 was 17% of children normal in weight for age while 6% were severely malnourished (Kumar and Stewart 1987:3). Other research indicated negligible protein deficiency in Kerala compared with 2 to 7% in Andhra Pradesh and up to 9% in Uttar Pradesh. Iron deficiency in Kerala ranged from 5% to 17% while in Andhra Pradesh it was 3% to 28% and from 26% to 57% in Uttar Pradesh (Mahadevan and Sumangala 1987:40). In 1974, Shubh Kumar found in a sample of 43 households with incomes in the lowest 50-60% of the population of 3 villages in the Trivandrum region, that 60% of children 6 months to 3 years were below the Indian average on weight for age. But, on the measure of height for age, nearly 70% were above average. Considering the fact that the children came from households in the bottom half of the income distribution, Kumar concluded that "while current [1974] nutritional status for these children falls a little below the Indian average, their prenatal and neonatal nutrition appear to have been superior, giving them a better start on height" (1979:26). Finally, our measurements on 135 Nadur children ages 1 month to 13 years in 1987, indicate that 34% were normal on weight for age, using the same standards of the Indian Academy of Pediatrics used for the other Indian data (Franke 1988:27).[7] The nutrition debate in Kerala thus remains unresolved. How well nourished are people in Nadur?

## Composition of the Diet in Nadur

Nadur villagers usually take breakfast of rice porridge, steam cakes (*iddilies*), or pancakes (*dosai*), sometimes supplemented with pappadams (fried gram chips) and pickle. Coconut and chili-spiced sauces are added to the cakes. During the months of February through May the pickle is made of mango which is abundant in many house compounds. A single tree may produce hundreds of fruits that can be eaten in curries, pickled, or sold. The midday meal is the biggest. It includes steamed rice with a small curry for the poorest households. To this the wealthier add pappadams, buttermilk, curd, additional pickle and a second curry. The evening meal is made up of leftovers from lunch. Wealthier households may add a late afternoon snack of fruit with coffee or tea. Better-off non vegetarian households eat small amounts of fish or even a little beef or eggs once to several times per month. The wealthier vegetarian households make extensive use of curd and pulses for protein.

Table 10.6
Percent of Calories in the Diet
Nadur Village Kerala 1987 and Kerala State

| | Nadur 1987 | | Kerala State |
|---|---|---|---|
| Food | February | July | 1961-1971 |
| Rice | 65 | 73 | 39 |
| Tapioca (Cassava) | 1 | 1 | 27 |
| Coconuts | 7 | 5 | 11 |
| Cooking Oil | 8 | 6 | 7 |
| Other (chilies, fruit) | 4 | 2 | 7 |
| Sugar | 9 | 7 | 4 |
| Eggs/Meat/Fish | 1 | 3 | 2 |
| Vegetables/pulses | 3 | 2 | 1 |
| Milk/Curd | 2 | 2 | 1 |
| Totals | 100 | 101 | 99 |

Source: The Kerala state averages are from George 1979:62.
*Note: Included in the Other foods for that table are 3.5% from wheat and 3.0% from fruit.*

Even the poorest households drink tea in the morning, and on working days some farm and general laborers eat *iddilies* with small amounts of a chili-spiced sauce called *sambar* from local tea shops where they may also read the newspapers and argue politics or gossip. Table 10.6 shows the basic components of the diet for the two survey periods, compared with the all-Kerala breakdown for the years 1961-1971.

As can be seen from Table 10.6, Nadur residents eat mostly rice and almost no tapioca—the major alternative staple to rice in the southern Kerala region of Travancore. There soil and water conditions do not lend themselves as well to rice production as in the rolling hills and well-irrigated valleys of the central Kerala region of Cochin where Nadur is located. Coconuts supply a smaller portion in Nadur than the all-Kerala average.

Prices affect the seasonal changes in diet. On Table 10.7 we compare prices for 27 February, the mid-point of the first nutrition survey, with those of 10 July, the week of the second survey.

We computed the calories per rupee figure by taking first the number of calories per 100 grams as given in the Indian food tables

Table 10.7
Calories per Rupee: Selected Foods
Nadur Village Kerala 1987

| Food | Calories Per 100 gms | Rupees Per 100 grams | | Calories Per Rupee | |
|---|---|---|---|---|---|
| | | 27 Feb | 10 July | 27 Feb | 10 July |
| Ration Shop Rice | 346 | 0.27 | 0.27 | 1,277 | 1,277 |
| Tapioca | 157 | 0.13 | 0.12 | 1,256 | 1,308 |
| Open Market Rice | 346 | 0.35 | 0.44 | 989 | 795 |
| Sugar | 398 | 0.65 | 0.68 | 612 | 585 |
| Green Gram | 334 | 0.60 | 0.70 | 567 | 477 |
| Coconut Oil | 900 | 2.75 | 3.25 | 327 | 277 |
| Mango | 74 | 0.25 | 0.15 | 296 | 493 |
| Milk | 67 | 0.25 | 0.25 | 268 | 268 |

(Gopalan *et al* 1985). We divided that number by the rupees price per 100 grams. The open market prices for all items were available directly in units of 100 grams or one kilogram, except milk. Here the sales unit is one *naazhi*, a traditional rice measuring container about 1/2 liter in volume. The price was stable throughout the survey period at Rs 1.25 per naazhi which comes to Rs 2.5 per liter, or Rs 0.25 per 100 grams.

On Table 10.7 we see that some major food items varied greatly over the 5-month period between the 2 surveys. The average of high-grade and low-grade open market rice gives 989 calories per rupee on 27 February but only 795 in July. Coconut oil drops from 327 in February to 277 calories per rupee in July. Sugar and green gram also decline while mango increases in caloric value per rupee as does tapioca. Contrary to expectation based on prices alone, tapioca does not become a July alternative to open market rice. Tapioca goes from 1,256 to 1,308, an increase of 52 calories per rupee. Open market rice drops 194 calories per rupee, or 3.7 times as much. At the same time, ration shop rice remains at 1,277 calories per rupee, slightly higher in February and slightly lower in July than tapioca. The difference at both periods is probably not enough to affect taste preferences: Nadur residents prefer rice over tapioca. Ration shop rice becomes more cost-beneficial to the Nadur diet as the July monsoon season develops. The week of July 10 had the highest open market rice price of any week during the fieldwork in Nadur. Ration shop rice thus becomes an important alternative to both tapioca and open market rice in July.

## The Nutrition Surveys

To describe in detail the level of nutrition and to evaluate the nutritional role of the ration shop in Nadur, we conducted two 24-hour recall surveys of food intake among sample households.[8] The first survey was conducted during late February and early March of 1987. The second survey was taken in early July. A severe drought hit much of India in 1987, making March a difficult month. The first survey was taken while rice supplies from the minor monsoon harvest of January were still around, but laborers were starting to feel the pinch from work shortage. The first survey thus captures the end of the short period of plenty and the beginning of the long period of shortage. The major monsoon was adequate in June and July, 1987. Laborers and agricultural laborers were receiving regular work during the period just prior to the second survey. The two surveys reflect contrasting situations.

Of the 170 households surveyed, 2 declined to answer the nutrition questions. In July, 1 household head had died and another had left the village. The base sample for the nutrition surveys is thus 168 in February-March and 166 in July. Food amounts reported by respondents were multiplied by their calorie contents according to Indian food tables (Gopalan et al 1985). Total calories per household were divided by the number of adult equivalents in the household. We removed 11 cases of adult equivalent intake over 4,000 calories in the February survey and 6 such cases for July on the assumption that they represent unreliable reports. This results in an effective sample size of 157 for the February survey and 160 for July. We chose not to delete cases of extremely low calorie intake because of the low findings of other Kerala surveys as described above, and because we wanted to bias the data downward if at all so that any positive findings would be more supportable.[9]

To gain the most accurate calorie counts possible, we added school and nursery lunches separately. They were not included in the household recall estimates, but we asked each respondent how many children and/or women received meals. The number of school lunches and women eating at the nursery was multiplied by 410, the official calorie amount of the school meals. The nursery meals each were estimated at 231 calories, a number we arrived at by multiplying the official amount of 65 grams of bulgur wheat times 3.56, the number of calories per gram (Gopalan et al 1985:62).

Estimating tea shop meals was more complicated. We asked house-

Table 10.8
Calorie Intake Per Adult Equivalent
February and July 1987 Surveys
Nadur Village Kerala

| | February | | July | |
| | Without Lunches | With Lunches | Without Lunches | With Lunches |
|---|---|---|---|---|
| Sample Size | 157 | 157 | 160 | 160 |
| Average | 2,204 | 2,231 | 2,159 | 2,184 |
| Minimum | 849 | 849 | 1,104 | 1,104 |
| Maximum | 3,904 | 3,904 | 3,482 | 3,482 |
| **Calories** | **Number of Households** | | | |
| 3,200+ | 8 | 8 | 6 | 7 |
| 3,001-3,200 | 13 | 14 | 2 | 2 |
| 2,801-3,000 | 10 | 11 | 6 | 6 |
| 2,601-2,800 | 10 | 10 | 11 | 16 |
| 2,401-2,600 | 16 | 17 | 19 | 16 |
| 2,201-2,400 | 19 | 19 | 23 | 23 |
| 2,001-2,200 | 17 | 15 | 31 | 28 |
| 1,801-2,000 | 18 | 19 | 29 | 30 |
| 1,601-1,800 | 17 | 17 | 15 | 14 |
| 1,401-1,600 | 16 | 17 | 14 | 14 |
| 1,201-1,400 | 8 | 5 | 2 | 2 |
| ≤1,200 | 5 | 5 | 2 | 2 |

holds how many members had eaten how many meals in tea shops in the 24 hours prior to the survey. The number of adult equivalents for the person(s) eating at the shop divided by 3 (the number of meals per day) for each meal taken was subtracted from the denominator of the fraction, average calories over adult equivalent for the household. For each meal taken outside the home, the remaining calories were thus presumed to be available for all other members in greater amounts.

### Calorie Intake in Nadur

Results of the calorie intake survey are given in Table 10.8. We see that the average calorie intake at both surveys is very close to the CDS minimum of 2,200. However, 52% of included households in February and 56% in July remained below the minimum even after the addition of school and nursery lunches. In February, the lunches reduce the number of households below 1,400 calories from 13 (8+5) to 10; no other obvious effect appears on Table 10.8.[10]

### Caste, Class, Income, and Calories

How do caste, class, income, and land ownership affect calorie intake? The data appear in Table 10.9. Table 10.9 contains 5 statistically significant associations. For the categorical variables of caste, class, and percent of rice from own land, we used one-way ANOVA. For adult equivalent income we used the Pearson correlation coefficient. We see that in February, when land owning households are eating from their recent harvest supplies, caste is significant, while in July it is not. This is probably an effect of the continuing post-land reform association between caste and rice land ownership which can be seen on Table 7.5. In July, land-owning households are awaiting the major harvest and personal stocks are at their lowest. Pearson correlation coefficients for rice land owned per adult equivalent and calories per adult equivalent are 0.35** in February, but only 0.18 (not significant) in July.

Class also associates significantly with calories in February, but not in July. The correlation coefficient with adult equivalent income for February is 0.46** and for July 0.24*. Income has a greater statistical effect on calorie intake than does rice land ownership. The relationships are complex, however. As we noted in Chapter 7, rice land ownership helps to produce income, but income generated outside the rice economy can also lead in the post-land reform period to purchase of rice land as an investment.

Nambudiri, Nair, and Mannan caste members are calorie sufficient while Ezhavas remain below minimum at both periods. Pulayas average 7% above the minimum in February, but drop to the minimum in July. Muslims have the lowest calorie intake as a group with only 87% of minimum in February. In July, however, they increase to 102% as field and house compound labor opportunities become available. At both survey periods, Muslims show the largest increase from school and nursery lunches, as we would expect from the data in Chapter 9 which showed them making extensive use of the lunches.

Table 10.9: Calorie Intake by Caste, Class, Income, and Land Ownership
Nadur Village Kerala 1987

| | February/March | | | July | | |
|---|---|---|---|---|---|---|
| | Households | Calories | % of Min | House-holds | Calories | % of Min |
| **Caste** | | * | | | | |
| Nambudiri | 12 | 2,553 | 116 | 12 | 2,159 | 98 |
| Nair | 76 | 2,174 | 99 | 78 | 2,162 | 98 |
| Craft | 9 | 2,605 | 118 | 9 | 2,074 | 94 |
| Ezhuthasan/Chetty | 11 | 2,460 | 112 | 13 | 2,312 | 105 |
| Muslim | 22 | 1,920 | 87 | 22 | 2,234 | 102 |
| Ezhava | 12 | 2,060 | 94 | 11 | 2,132 | 97 |
| Mannan | 4 | 2,754 | 125 | 4 | 2,500 | 114 |
| Pulaya | 11 | 2,360 | 107 | 11 | 2,152 | 98 |
| **Class** | | * | | | | |
| Professional | 11 | 2,992 | 136 | 11 | 2,340 | 106 |
| Service | 8 | 2,296 | 104 | 9 | 2,467 | 112 |
| Craft | 11 | 2,426 | 110 | 12 | 1,981 | 90 |
| Farmer | 20 | 2,274 | 103 | 21 | 2,163 | 98 |
| Petty Trade | 17 | 2,197 | 100 | 17 | 2,082 | 95 |
| Recipient | 27 | 2,418 | 110 | 28 | 2,274 | 103 |
| Laborer | 55 | 1,974 | 90 | 54 | 2,174 | 99 |
| Agricultural Laborer | 8 | 1,954 | 89 | 8 | 1,982 | 90 |
| **Adult Equivalent** | | | | | | |
| **Income Quintile** | | ** | | | * | |
| 1. 1,951-8,308 | 27 | 2,641 | 120 | 31 | 2,407 | 109 |
| 2. 1,232-1,950 | 31 | 2,423 | 110 | 30 | 2,261 | 103 |
| 3. 857-1,219 | 33 | 2,261 | 103 | 33 | 2,110 | 96 |
| 4. 632-850 | 33 | 2,080 | 95 | 32 | 2,209 | 100 |
| 5. 267-621 | 33 | 1,803 | 82 | 34 | 1,982 | 90 |
| **% of Rice From Own Land** | | ** | | | | |
| 100% | 13 | 2,795 | 127 | 14 | 2,407 | 109 |
| 75% | 9 | 2,473 | 112 | 9 | 2,293 | 104 |
| 50% | 19 | 2,448 | 111 | 18 | 2,251 | 102 |
| 25% | 15 | 2,096 | 95 | 15 | 2,055 | 93 |
| None | 101 | 2,135 | 97 | 104 | 2,163 | 98 |
| Totals | 157 | 2,231 | 101 | 160 | 2,184 | 99 |

Professionals and service workers have more than enough while farmers are at the minimum in both periods. Laborers and agricultural laborers are 10-11% below minimum in February/March. Laborers improve in July to 1% below, while agricultural laborers are still 10% below minimum. The lowest adult equivalent income quintile is 82% of minimum in February and 90% in July. Households with 100% of need from their own fields average 27% above minimum in February and 9% above in July. Rice land landless are 3% below in February and 2% below in July.

## Work Shortage and Calorie Shortfall

We saw in Chapter 8 that 46% (78 households) of the Nadur sample population consider their work days inadequate and that 18 households (11%) stated that they reduce their food intake during work-short periods. How do these perceptions coincide with the nutrition survey data?

For the February survey, the work-short households averaged 1,960 calories while those with enough work got 2,433, a statistically significant difference (ANOVA $p \leq .0000$**). In July, the difference was 2,198 versus 2,116, not significant. During the week of the July survey, laborers and agricultural laborers were finding work on the rice fields and thus could purchase food or were being paid in (unhusked) rice. By contrast, in February-March, the calorie surveys reflect the declining days of work for the households that end up short of days.

The 18 households claiming food shortage displayed similar patterns, though neither ANOVA is statistically significant. Five of the 18 households did not experience calorie shortage on either food survey date, but 8 were more than 100 calories below the CDS minimum on one survey and 5 had 100 calorie plus shortfalls on both dates. In other words, 72% of these households experienced a shortage of 100 calories or more on at least one survey date. The lowest reported intake among this group was one Nair laborer household with only 1,352 calories per adult equivalent on the date of the February-March survey. The 18 food-short households include 4 of those we have chosen for case studies: Case 3 in Chapter 9; and Cases 15, 20, and 21 to appear in Chapter 12.

## Explaining Calorie Intake

To test the interactions of the variables presented in this Chapter, we ran several multiple regressions. The results appear in Table 10.10.[11]

The February survey is better accounted for mathematically. In both surveys, income and rice land owned play important roles. School and

Table 10.10  Variables Explaining Calorie Intake
Results of Multiple Regressions
Nadur Village Kerala, February and July 1987

| | Regression Coefficients | | |
| | Raw | Standardized | Signifi-cance |
| Variable | | | |
| --- | --- | --- | --- |
| **February 1987**  ($r^2 = .39$) | | | |
| Adult Equivalent Income | .16 | .40 | **.00 |
| Rice Land Per Adult Equivalent | 12.52 | .25 | **.00 |
| Recipient Class Membership | 287.66 | .18 | *.01 |
| Craft Caste Membership | 452.35 | .17 | *.01 |
| | | | |
| **July 1987**  ($r^2 = .26$) | | | |
| Lunch Calories Per Adult Equivalent | 2.62 | .32 | **.00 |
| Adult Equivalent Income | .08 | .27 | **.00 |
| Service Class Membership | 351.17 | .17 | .02 |
| Rice Land Per Adult Equivalent | 5.80 | .16 | .04 |
| Laborer Class Membership | 159.07 | .16 | .06 |
| Recipient Class Membership | 197.68 | .16 | .05 |

nursery feeding programs become statistically significant in July. This occurs despite their being present in only 39 (24%) of the households. Lunches increased the calorie intake by 5% among user households at both surveys. Those benefiting most were in the bottom 4 quintiles, Nair, Ezhava, and Muslim caste members, and households with 25% of rice needs met by their own land. These findings suggest that the lunches play an important seasonal role in calorie intake in Nadur even though the data earlier in this chapter showed that they have limited impact on income inequality.

The regression equations do not show the ration shop having a statistically significant impact on calorie intake overall in the sample population. But can we locate its effects with other methods?

### Seasons, Rice, and the Ration Shop

Table 10.9 shows that the seasons affect different socioeconomic groups in different ways. Nambudiri calorie intake declines because they are primarily rice land owners. In February they have the rice from the small monsoon harvest while in July they are awaiting the big harvest for which the wait has been longer.

Castes with heavy percentages of rural laborers—Muslim and Ezhava—improved their position in July over February. Pulayas were the exception. Labor class households increased their calorie intake by 10% over February, but agricultural workers did only 1% better. Although both laborers and agricultural laborers get more work during the planting and tending season, shortages begin to appear in the agricultural laborers' diets sooner, as their meager wages are depleted.

Households with the highest adult equivalent incomes drop 9% in calorie intake from February to July, but are still 207 calories above minimum on average. Those with the lowest incomes—mostly agricultural and other laborers—experience a 10% increase, but still remain 10% below minimum.

How much does the ration shop contribute to rice calories in Nadur by farming season? We asked on both nutrition surveys what were the sources of rice: the ration shop, own rice land or open market.[12] The results of the question for rice are shown on Table 10.11.

Table 10.11 shows the interplay between farming seasons, land ownership, income, and the ration shop among Nadur's castes and classes. Nambudiris exhibit about the same pattern in sources of rice calories at both survey periods. Most of their rice comes from their own land. This is consistent with their position as major land owners, even in the post-land reform era. At the other end of the hierarchy, Pulayas derive almost all of their rice from the ration shop, with very small supplements from the open market and some from rice land ownership. Muslims and Ezhavas display the same usage pattern as the Pulayas. The high-income but low land owning Mannan group in Nadur goes mostly to the open market for its July rice.

Among the classes, professionals exhibit the most nearly even distribution of sources, using the ration shop, their own land, and the open market about equally in February, but going more to the open market in July. Farmers depend greatly on home grown supplies in February and even in July. Craft households, laborers and agricultural laborers utilize the ration shop heavily in both periods. They have virtually no home grown rice in July: the rice land they own is mostly good only for one crop per year. Those supplies were used up months ago. In July, they are spending their entire incomes on rice or, in some cases, receiving it directly for field labor payments.

Households in the highest income quintile make the most use of the open market, but are also those most likely to have supplies from their

Table 10.11
Sources of Rice Calories by Season
Nadur Village Kerala February and July 1987

| | February Percent of Rice Calories From | | | July Percent of Rice Calories From | | |
|---|---|---|---|---|---|---|
| | Ration Shop | Own Land | Open Market | Ration Shop | Own Land | Open Market |
| **Caste** | | | | | | |
| Nambudiri | 8 | 67 | 25 | 8 | 67 | 25 |
| Nair | 50 | 39 | 11 | 68 | 11 | 21 |
| Craft | 67 | 11 | 22 | 56 | 0 | 44 |
| Ezhuthasan/Chetty | 55 | 36 | 9 | 62 | 23 | 15 |
| Muslim | 77 | 23 | 0 | 75 | 5 | 20 |
| Ezhava | 83 | 8 | 8 | 82 | 0 | 18 |
| Mannan | 50 | 25 | 25 | 50 | 0 | 50 |
| Pulaya | 73 | 9 | 18 | 77 | 0 | 23 |
| **Class** | | | | | | |
| Professional | 27 | 36 | 36 | 18 | 27 | 55 |
| Service | 38 | 50 | 13 | 50 | 33 | 17 |
| Craft | 64 | 18 | 18 | 67 | 0 | 33 |
| Farmer | 30 | 65 | 5 | 43 | 33 | 24 |
| Petty Trade | 41 | 47 | 12 | 65 | 12 | 24 |
| Recipient | 48 | 44 | 7 | 62 | 18 | 20 |
| Laborer | 82 | 11 | 7 | 83 | 1 | 16 |
| Agricultural Laborer | 50 | 25 | 25 | 75 | 0 | 25 |
| **Adult Equivalent Income Quintile** | | | | | | |
| 1. 1,951-8,308 | 26 | 52 | 22 | 39 | 32 | 29 |
| 2. 1,232-1,950 | 61 | 39 | 0 | 55 | 20 | 25 |
| 3. 857-1,219 | 61 | 36 | 3 | 64 | 7 | 29 |
| 4. 632-850 | 55 | 36 | 9 | 72 | 6 | 22 |
| 5. 267-621 | 73 | 12 | 15 | 90 | 0 | 10 |
| **Percent of Rice from Own Land** | | | | | | |
| 100% | 0 | 100 | 0 | 7 | 93 | 0 |
| 75% | 0 | 100 | 0 | 11 | 70 | 19 |
| 50% | 11 | 89 | 0 | 72 | 0 | 28 |
| 25% | 13 | 80 | 7 | 43 | 7 | 50 |
| None | 83 | 0 | 17 | 78 | 0 | 22 |
| Totals | 56 | 32 | 11 | 64 | 13 | 23 |

own land, while the very poorest become almost entirely dependent on the ration shop in July with a small supplement from the open market.

### Rice Land, Seasons, and the Ration Shop

Table 10.11 shows a striking association between the ration shop, amount of rice from one's own land, and the season. In February, households with 100% and 75% of needs from own land were making no use of the ration shop or of the open market. These households averaged 1.28 and 1.25 acres rice land respectively. In July, both groups made small use of the ration shop and the households with 75% of needs met by their own land also went to the open market. Those with no rice land got 83% of supplies from the shop in February and 78% in July.

Among the small and medium sized rice land owning groups we see the greatest seasonal variations in use of the ration shop. Households that met 50% of rice needs from their holdings (0.71 acres average rice land) purchased 11% of needs from the shop in February, but 72% in July. Those meeting 25% of needs on their holdings (averaging 0.36 acres of rice land) got 13% from the shop in February and 43% in July.

These differences indicate that the ration shop fills a seasonal need for small landholders whose rice land acquisitions from the land reform were not enough to produce rice self-sufficiency. *In the season of greatest need, the ration shop thus becomes an extension of the land reform for these households*. The less land the greater the dependence on the ration shop and the less the use of the open market. This can be seen by comparing the ration shop and open market columns in February and July with the percent of rice needs met by own holdings. Most of the small rice land owners are Nairs. The ration shop met 51% of their needs in February, rising to 68% in July, while rice from their own lands dropped from 39% in February to 11% in July. Labor class households show stable shop intakes.

These numbers indicate the great importance of the shop to the poor, the landless, and the low caste groups in the Nadur sample. They also indicate that in lean times such as July, one survival adaptation is to reduce the fruit, milk, and vegetable components of the diet. These foods, while nutritious, provide fewer calories per rupee and they are not available at the ration shop.

## Calories and Public Food Distribution

How important are lunches and the ration shop to actual calorie intake? Using certain supply and demand assumptions from classical economic theory, P. S. George (1979:37) estimated for 1974-75 that the lowest income groups would eat 14-18% less rice without the shop while higher groups would decrease their consumption by 2-10%. For the Nadur sample, we can say the following:

1. Lunches reduce income inequality by less than 1%.
2. Lunches provide the equivalent of 3% greater income for those households with children under 11 years of age who are receiving them.
3. Lunches raise the calorie intake of user households by 5%.
4. Because mostly low income households used the lunches, further redistribution probably resulted from the 1987 LDF ministry expansion of the lunches to standards 5 through 7.
5. Lunches become strategically more important to low income households in July, near the end of the long lean season before the August harvest.
6. The ration shop effectively reduces income inequality by 5.4%.
7. The ration shop provides the equivalent of 10% greater income for the bottom 2 quintiles which include mostly labor and agricultural labor households.
8. The ration shop provides an important food subsidy for the poorest households, but does not bring them up even to the CDS level of calorie sufficiency.
9. For small holder households, the ration shop constitutes an effective extension of the land reform by providing an important seasonal access to rice when their rice land ceases to be sufficient.
10. Lunches and the ration shop probably reduce debt among the poorest households.

## Conclusions

Without school lunches and the ration shop, many Nadur households would suffer great deprivation during the lean times. But our survey of the data also shows that the public distribution of food has limits as well as benefits. Greater income-earning ability for the lowest groups must join with the public distribution schemes outlined in this chapter. One of the most important of these income-earning devices is education, which we examine in the next chapter.

## Notes

1.  In 1989, however, the program was cut back to 2 million students and fed only 1.4 million in 1991. The State Planning Board's report (GOK 1992:124) gives no explanation for the reductions.

2.  The 1984 cost per meal in Tamil Nadu's Noon Meal Scheme was estimated at Rs 0.44 to Rs 0.90 (Harriss 1991:3).

3.  Venugopal (1992:168-213) details the recent Andhra Pradesh rural extension of public food distribution and provides additional comparisons with Kerala (1992:111). Étienne (1988) presents the more traditional technocratic view of food availability, although he does recognize the importance of organization among the poor to make land reform work (1988:229).

4.  In 1975 ration shops provided 56% of total rice consumed in Kerala compared with 9% in 2 Tamil Nadu villages studied in 1983 by Barbara Harriss (1991:78).

5.  Harriss also found the Noon Meals Scheme to be reinforcing rather than undermining caste barriers in Tamil Nadu (Harriss 1991:62-63 and 70-71).

6.  Alan Berg (1987:ix) reports that the World Bank's *Tamil Nadu Integrated Nutrition Project* reduced severe malnutrition among children in 9,000 targeted villages from 17-24% in 1982 to 7-10% in 1987. For $66 million (Berg 1987:10), the World Bank was thus able to bring Tamil Nadu close nutritionally to what Kerala had achieved on its own.

7.  Because considerable disagreement remains on which standards are appropriate and what they mean in terms of food intake and health, we present in the text only the most directly comparable figure with other recent Indian data. From our entire sample of 707 children, ages 1 month to 13 years, we found that 17% were normal on weight for height (Franke 1988:10-11).

8.  We designed a 24-hour recall version of the 7-day recall form developed by Scott and Mathew (1985:131) to reflect the foods typically eaten in Kerala.

9.  This is in keeping with our attempts to counteract any possible research bias as we explained in Chapter 2.

10. The distribution of Nadur households by calorie intake is very close to the all-Kerala rural distribution derived from the 1983 Indian National Sample Survey (Minhas 1991:14).

11. We used the combined methods of forced entry and step regression. This resulted in entering 20 variables, followed by the removal of the least significant to produce the equations in Table 10.10.

12. We asked similar questions for milk and sugar. We hope to analyze the responses in a future paper to see how much people depend on their cows for milk and how much the ration shop contributes to sugar availability.

# 11

## Education

### Mobility, Development, and Education

In Chapters 6 through 10 we examined the changing patterns of inequality in Nadur according to relative wealth and access to basic needs. In Chapters 11 and 12 we shall look at the mobility of households. As we noted in Chapter 4, households do not move out of or into different castes, but they can change their class position and their income. We can describe movement from one class category to another, and we can measure movement from one income quintile to another. How much mobility has there been in Nadur between 1971 and 1987? Can we relate the mobility to Kerala's redistribution policies? Before trying to answer these questions, we need to consider one more component of Kerala's recent development history: education.

A major goal of development is to increase economic and social mobility. This goal can be justified on both pragmatic and ethical grounds. Replacing ascribed with achieved status encourages greater participation in economic activity from all members of society, tapping the talents of those previously held back by artificial social barriers. Equal opportunity means a more just society according to widely accepted modern standards.

One of the most powerful tools for prying loose the traditional social structure is thought to be education which provides training and skills to persons otherwise held back. In addition, education in a progressive context can elevate self-conceptions of the poorest and most oppressed individuals so that they will participate more fully in the development process. In this chapter we shall survey the educational changes in Nadur within the context of Kerala's overall literacy and educational achievements.

## Educational Achievements in Kerala

Kerala stands out among all the states and regions of India for its remarkable achievements in raising the literacy level of its people. As we saw on Table 1.1, Kerala's literacy in 1986 was 1.8 times the all-India rate. On Table 1.2 we saw that Kerala's female and low-caste literacy rates in1981 were 2.6 times the all-India rates, while for rural areas Kerala was 2.3 times as literate.[1] Kerala's remarkable educational achievements stem from a combination of factors, including the nature of the British colonial presence, enlightened Travancore and Cochin rulers, and—most importantly—the workers and peasants movements.

## Struggles for Education in Kerala

Even before British colonial annexation of the Malabar coast in 1792, the region that became Kerala State in 1956 had a functioning system of traditional village schools. These schools, however, catered only to the upper castes and were focused on Brahmanic scriptures known as *vedas* which the male priests learned by rote. In addition, Hindu philosophy, logic, mathematics, *ayurvedic* (traditional Hindu) medicine, and architecture were taught to some of the Brahmin and upper (Kiriyattil subcaste) Nair males (Nair 1983:4).

The first impact of colonial rule on education came through missionaries who set upon the princely state of Travancore to convert the entire population to Christianity. Establishing schools in that area, they were initially successful in instructing and converting especially members of the lowest castes who had the most to gain by breaking free of traditional Hindu caste controls.

Travancore's rulers were favorably impressed with mission education, but wanted to prevent it from becoming a threat to established high caste interests. They thus attempted to bring the mission schools under government control. In 1817 the princess of Travancore issued an edict calling for state support for education so that

> there should be no backwardness in the spread of enlightenment in Travancore, that by diffusion of education the people would become better subjects and public servants and that the reputation of the state might be advanced thereby (quoted in Nair 1983:10).

For much of the 19th century a struggle ensued in which the local rulers attempted to spread Malayalam language government schools against the interests first of the missionaries, and then, after the 1830s, the British colonial government, both of whom preferred the more elite English language education. By 1894, there were 255 government schools and 1,388 government-aided private schools with a total enroll-ment of 57,314 (Nair 1983:17). In the 1860s attention began to be focused on education for girls, but progress was slow. By the early 20th century females and low caste persons were still largely illiterate.

In both Travancore and Cochin, the turn of the 20th century was a time of precedent-setting developments. In 1894-95, Travancore began a small program of grants for low caste children, and in 1902, lower educa-tion in Malayalam was mandated for all children, although it could not be enforced. In 1911-12 caste restrictions in government schools were formally abolished (Nair 1983:28-33). Cochin mandated free education in Malayalam in 1908.

The reforms of Cochin's and Travancore's rulers helped create an official environment of support for education. But literacy in Kerala is mostly the product of the land reform, trade union, and communist movements. In Chapter 8 we described some of Kerala's militant work-ing class history. The right to education became one of the first and most sustained peasant and worker demands of 20th century Kerala (Kannan 1988:35-88).

As the workers' movement spread in the 1930s, literacy became a major component in the strategy of awakening consciousness. Reading and writing circles were set up in villages, prominent authors wrote stories and poems with strong Marxist and pro-worker themes, and workers and tenant farmers themselves were encouraged to write and publish poetry and narratives in union-sponsored publications. Village libraries were opened.

The right to literacy in Kerala was transformed from a government-sponsored policy to a mass movement. By the early 1980s, Kerala had 4,977 officially recognized village libraries, supported by community contributions and small state government grants along with hundreds of smaller libraries not officially listed and operating solely on private funds (Mahadevan and Sumangala 1987:36).

Despite these developments, education of the lowest groups pro-gressed slowly. By 1945, Pulayas in Cochin had only 10% literacy compared with 1% in 1922 (Nair 1983:72). Under popular pressure, local governments continued with programs to expand literacy, introducing Arabic for Muslims in 1920 and Hindi language classes in standard 9 in 1937. At independence in 1947, plans were laid for an adult literacy campaign in Travancore (Nair 1983:43).

As education spread in Kerala a tension developed between the earlier government schools, government-aided private education, and the popular movement. This tension reached its height with the election of the first Communist Ministry in 1957.. That Ministry proposed a sweeping reform of the education system that would have brought private schools more closely into line with the government schools, an issue that had caused conflict for more than a century. The Kerala Education Bill aroused strong opposition from the Catholic Church which felt threatened by the secularization of education and the imposition of government standards and hiring and firing regulations in government-aided private schools. Along with the land reform proposed by the government, the education bill became the focus of right-wing protest that finally resulted in the dismissal of the Ministry by the Central Government in 1959 (Sathyamurthy 1985:382-420).

In addition to the public-private dispute, Kerala's education system is marked by three other features unique in India. First, unlike all other states, Kerala has focused educational expenditures on the primary levels, spreading basic literacy farther but resulting in higher education's being relatively less advanced (Nair 1979:85-90).

Second, the grassroots component of education in Kerala has also continued to develop. In 1963 the Kerala Peoples' Science Movement (KSSP) was formed with the aim of "mobilization of the people through science". During the 1970s the KSSP set up study classes in villages, and medical camps and literacy programs, along with statewide and national conventions and *jathas*, or parades which take science puppet shows, guerrilla theater, and other forms of informal education into neighborhoods and villages. The KSSP tries to raise environmental and other issues of concern in the state today (Sathyamurthy 1985:409-411; Isaac and Ekbal 1988). The KSSP also publishes a Malayalam language magazine and has established a wide following in the state. In Chapter 14 we will look briefly at Kerala's most recent educational achievement in which KSSP volunteer instructors made good a part of the 1947 adult literacy campaign, bringing Ernakulam District to 100% literacy in 1991.

Finally, Kerala has vastly expanded the program for low-caste scholarships and other school costs. In 1987 designated Scheduled Caste (SC) and Scheduled Tribe (ST) families (former untouchables) received over 500,000 scholarships. These scholarships benefited 79% of all SC and ST students in Kerala. Another 32,000 SC and ST students got scholarships for higher education while over 3,500 received subsidies for dormitory accommodations and clothing allowances to help them stay in school (GOK 1988:89).

Despite these impressive statistics, we can ask how much of Kerala's literacy gains have reached Nadur. Which groups have benefited from the village school? We shall first describe Nadur's school and library, then examine the changing educational levels of the castes and classes in the sample population.

## Nadur's School and Village Library

Nadur Village's school was built in 1930 by high-caste households for high-caste children. It was managed first by a Nambudiri committee, then by the temple board. In 1975, the government took over the management. The school was opened to all castes in 1945, but for several years only a few low caste students attended. In 1987 almost all village children were in school.

The Nadur government school offers classes from the first standard to the Secondary School Leaving Certificate (SSLC), for which students take examinations at the end of the 10th standard. Following the successful completion of the SSLC, a student can enter a pre-degree program for 2 years and then a 3-year bachelor's degree program. For Nadur students, as in most of Kerala, both pre-degree and bachelors degree institutions are close by. A 30 minute bus ride brings the student to a higher educational facility. Entry into the higher level institutions, however, is a more difficult matter for low caste children unless they receive government assistance. Even the daily bus fare of Rs 2 from Nadur works out to a sizable portion of a poor household's budget.

In 1987 Nadur's school had 1,094 students, 35 teachers, a headmaster, 2 cooks for the daily lunches, and a small additional support staff. The school yard featured a well with a motor-driven pump which insured safe water even in the dry season. Classes include English, history, geography, science, and Malayalam language and literature. Classes average 31 students per teacher. Although books are sufficient, other equipment such as laboratory items are virtually nonexistent. The facilities shortage forces a double shift with standards 1 to 4 in the morning and the remaining students coming from 12:30 to 4:30 pm.

Many students miss classes during peak agricultural work periods. The school year is not set according to the seasons in the village. July, for example, is a busy school month, but agricultural labor children are needed by their parents for field labor or tending the household on the precious days when work is available.

Nadur's library was formed in the early 1940s by upper caste villagers. The present building was put up in 1956 with local contributions of money, materials, and labor. In 1987 it contained 9,410 books, 1,700 in English and most of the rest in Malayalam. Many American and British

Table 11.1
Percent at Each Level of Education by Age Cohort
Nadur Village Kerala 1987

| Age Cohort | N | Percents Who Were | | | | Average Years of Education |
| | | Illiterate | Literate | Medium | SSLC+ | |
| --- | --- | --- | --- | --- | --- | --- |
| 15-29 | 304 | 7 | 16 | 63 | 14 | 7.9 |
| 30-45 | 166 | 25 | 33 | 39 | 4 | 5.4 |
| 46-60 | 132 | 46 | 31 | 17 | 6 | 3.5 |
| 61-75 | 96 | 55 | 31 | 13 | 1 | 2.1 |
| 76+ | 20 | 45 | 40 | 15 | 0 | 2.5 |
| Total N's | 718 | 185 | 184 | 293 | 56 | 5.5 |
| | | 26% | 26% | 41% | 8% | |

authors are represented along with several books in English and Malayalam from Soviet publishing houses. Average daily attendance is about 30 persons, and 1,520 books circulate per month according to records kept by the library committee. The library subscribes to several Kerala newspapers. Only a few people read them in the library, however. Most prefer the tea shops where snacks can be had and discussions are easier. The library is situated at a far end of the school grounds, and has a spectacular view of nearby Ghat mountain scenery. The grounds in front of the library are a favorite location for men to play cards. The library fee was one rupee ($.08 in 1987) per year. In 1987 there were 250 paid members with total contributions adding to Rs 900. Most funds for books came from a state government grant of Rs 2,200.

## Literacy in Nadur

What have the school and library achieved for residents of Nadur Village? In 1961, 35% of Nadur's population was listed as literate (GOI 1966 Part C:18). By 1971, 60% of the sample population over 14 was literate. In 1987 this had risen to 74%, a little above the all-Kerala average of 70% for 1981. In 1971, the average years of education were 3.6. By 1987 this had risen to 5.5.

One way to see the educational progress in Nadur is by breaking down the 1987 sample population into 15-year age cohorts. We start with age 15, since ages 0-14 are not usually counted in literacy statistics. We created cohorts of 15 years: ages 15-29, 30-44, 45-59, 60-74, and 75+.

We cross-tabulated the cohorts by 4 educational levels. Those with fewer than 3 years of schooling are classified as illiterate, those with 3-5 years are literate, and those with 6-10 years have medium education. Those who passed the SSLC and went beyond to pre-degree or other intellectual advancements (not skilled worker courses) we designate as SSLC+. The results are shown in Table 11.1.

From Table 11.1 we see that illiteracy has rapidly declined. For the cohort 15 to 29 years of age, 93% are literate, 77% have 6 years of education or more, and 14% have studied beyond the 10th standard.

If education expands this broadly, we can guess that all or nearly all groups in Nadur are gaining some access to it. But how are the levels of education distributed across caste, class, and gender?

### Caste, Gender, and Literacy

Results for castes by gender are shown in Table 11.2. From Table 11.2 we can see that both males and females from all castes have benefited from the expansion of education between 1971 and 1987 in Nadur. Nambudiris already had virtual 100% literacy in 1971. By 1987 they had raised their level of SSLC+ from 10% to 46%, with females increasing their SSLC+ percentage by 10 times. Nairs raised their literacy rate from 70% to 82%, with females gaining 13 points versus 7 points for males. Nairs also increased their SSLC+ percentage from 1% to 6% during period between the surveys.

Two striking cases are Muslims and Pulayas. In 1971 Muslims were only 9% literate, with females 100% illiterate. By 1987, 50% of all Muslims were literate, 47% of females. Among Pulayas, males went from total illiteracy in 1971 to 54% literacy in 1987, while females increased from 14% to 37%. Only 2% of Pulayas had gone beyond the SSLC, which is essential for access to high-paying professional employment. No Nadur sample Muslims had attained the SSLC in 1987.

Overall, females raised their literacy level 14 points compared to 12 points for males. Males increased their SSLC+ rate by 7 points compared to 4 for females.

Are the educational gains of 1971-1987 continuing? If we examine more closely the 15-29 age cohort, we can get insights into the educational developments of those who went to school during the period between 1971 and 1987. These data are given in Table 11.3.

Table 11.2
Educational Levels by Caste and Gender
Nadur Village Kerala 1971 and 1987

| Caste | N 1971 | N 1987 | Percent Literate 1971 | Percent Literate 1987 | Percent SSLC+ 1971 | Percent SSLC+ 1987 |
|---|---|---|---|---|---|---|
| Nambudiri | 58 | 57 | 95 | 96 | 10 | 46 |
| Males | 28 | 31 | 96 | 100 | 18 | 58 |
| Females | 30 | 26 | 93 | 92 | 3 | 31 |
| Nair/Variar | 287 | 340 | 70 | 82 | 1 | 6 |
| Males | 109 | 141 | 84 | 91 | 1 | 9 |
| Females | 178 | 199 | 62 | 75 | 1 | 5 |
| Ezhuthasan/ | | | | | | |
| Chetty | 40 | 51 | 50 | 76 | 0 | 6 |
| Males | 24 | 26 | 54 | 81 | 0 | 8 |
| Females | 16 | 25 | 44 | 72 | 0 | 4 |
| Craft | 37 | 52 | 65 | 86 | 0 | 4 |
| Males | 17 | 26 | 72 | 88 | 0 | 4 |
| Females | 20 | 26 | 60 | 85 | 0 | 4 |
| Ezhava | 37 | 46 | 54 | 60 | 5 | 0 |
| Males | 19 | 22 | 68 | 64 | 10 | 0 |
| Females | 18 | 24 | 39 | 58 | 0 | 0 |
| Muslim | 56 | 104 | 9 | 50 | 0 | 0 |
| Males | 31 | 55 | 16 | 53 | 0 | 0 |
| Females | 25 | 49 | 0 | 47 | 0 | 0 |
| Mannan | 22 | 19 | 82 | 79 | 9 | 10 |
| Males | 8 | 7 | 100 | 100 | 25 | 14 |
| Females | 14 | 12 | 71 | 67 | 0 | 8 |
| Pulaya | 37 | 49 | 8 | 45 | 0 | 2 |
| Males | 16 | 22 | 0 | 54 | 0 | 4 |
| Females | 21 | 27 | 14 | 37 | 0 | 0 |
| Totals | 574 | 718 | 60 | 74 | 2 | 8 |
| Males | 252 | 330 | 68 | 80 | 4 | 11 |
| Females | 322 | 388 | 55 | 69 | 1 | 5 |

Table 11.3
Literacy and Years of Education by Caste
Cohort Ages 15-29, Nadur Village Kerala 1987

| Caste | N | Percents | | Average Years of Education | |
|---|---|---|---|---|---|
| | | Literate | SSLC+ | Males | Females |
| Nambudiri | 20 | 100 | 75 | 12.8 | 11.6 |
| Nair | 136 | 98 | 14 | 9.0 | 8.3 |
| Craft | 23 | 100 | 9 | 8.9 | 8.4 |
| Ezhava | 20 | 100 | 0 | 7.0 | 7.6 |
| Ezhuthasan/Chetty | 24 | 92 | 8 | 8.7 | 7.8 |
| Muslim | 56 | 79 | 0 | 5.4 | 4.4 |
| Mannan | 4 | 100 | 50 | 11.0 | 11.0 |
| Pulaya | 21 | 81 | 5 | 5.2 | 5.4 |
| Totals | 304 | 93 | 14 | 8.1 | 7.6 |

(N = 150 males + 154 females = 304)

From Table 11.3 we see that among the students of 1971-1987, several castes already have achieved 100% literacy or are virtually there. Even the Pulayas and Muslims are at 81% and 79% respectively. Females are only 1/2 year behind males (8.1 minus 7.6) in average years of education among this age cohort.

We also see from Table 11.3 that substantial caste inequality remains. Muslims and Pulayas, two of the most oppressed groups of the past, have made great progress in literacy, but are producing few individuals with the SSLC.

By looking at the movement of average years of education by caste we can get an idea which castes are gaining education the most rapidly. The data are shown in Table 11.4.

Table 11.4 shows that all castes have raised their average level above that of 1971. Mannans increased their level by only 7%, while Nambudiris went up 39%. Nairs and Variars averaged a 54% increase. Pulayas raised their educational level by 460% while Muslims increased 650% between 1971 and 1987. The other castes were close to the Nambudiri level of increase.

Because Pulayas and Muslims raised their levels the most, we can

Table 11.4

Average Years of Education by Caste for Ages 15 and Over
Nadur Village Kerala 1971 and 1987

| | N | | Average Years of Education | | Years Increase | Percent Increase |
|---|---|---|---|---|---|---|
| Caste | 1971 | 1987 | 1971 | 1987 | | |
| Nambudiri | 58 | 57 | 7.1 | 9.9 | 2.8 | 39 |
| Nair/Variar | 287 | 340 | 3.9 | 6.0 | 2.1 | 54 |
| Ezhuthasan/Chetty | 40 | 51 | 2.6 | 5.9 | 3.3 | 127 |
| Craft | 37 | 52 | 3.4 | 5.7 | 2.3 | 68 |
| Ezhava | 37 | 46 | 3.0 | 4.2 | 1.2 | 40 |
| Muslim | 56 | 104 | 0.4 | 3.0 | 2.6 | 650 |
| Mannan | 22 | 19 | 6.7 | 7.2 | 0.5 | 7 |
| Pulaya | 37 | 49 | 0.5 | 2.8 | 2.3 | 460 |
| Totals | 574 | 718 | 3.6 | 5.5 | 1.9 | 153 |

say that educational equality by caste increased in Nadur between 1971 and 1987. But what are the practical consequences of this development? High-income employment requires attainment of certain absolute educational levels, not relative improvement. Muslims and Pulayas are moving towards educational levels where they can hope to get their SSLCs to compete with Nambudiris, Nairs, and Mannans, for white collar and professional jobs. But neither caste is very close to achieving this goal. In March 1989, 31 students out of 111 (28%) passed the SSLC exam. Of these 31 students, 16 were boys and 15 were girls. Only one was a Pulaya caste boy. This boy was one of 14 members of his caste who attempted the test. Two boys and 8 girls from the craft and Ezhava castes also passed out of a pool of 42 children from those castes who took the exam.

These data show that inequalities in education continue. If one Pulaya child per year passes the SSLC, however, this would mean 15 Pulaya graduates per age cohort. Such a figure, combined with Kerala's higher education scholarships and job reservation (affirmative action) programs, could open high-paying positions in the near future to Nadur Pulayas.

Table 11.5
Educational Levels for Ages 15 and Over by Class
Nadur Village Kerala 1971 and 1987

| Class | N | | Percent Literate | | Percent SSLC+ | |
|---|---|---|---|---|---|---|
| | 1971 | 1987 | 1971 | 1987 | 1971 | 1987 |
| Professional | 56 | 42 | 89 | 90 | 16 | 31 |
| Service | 28 | 46 | 93 | 96 | 0 | 9 |
| Farmer | 26 | 94 | 61 | 86 | 4 | 14 |
| Craft | 37 | 69 | 65 | 83 | 0 | 4 |
| Petty Trade | 71 | 75 | 46 | 68 | 1 | 3 |
| Recipient | 80 | 110 | 72 | 78 | 1 | 16 |
| Laborer | 137 | 248 | 36 | 62 | 0 | 2 |
| Agricultural | | | | | | |
| Laborer | 34 | 34 | 47 | 65 | 0 | 0 |
| Landlord | 10 | (14) | 90 | (100) | 0 | (43) |
| Tenant | 95 | (85) | 70 | (86) | 0 | (1) |
| Totals | 574 | 718 | 60 | 74 | 2 | 8 |

*Note: Numbers in parentheses refer back to former categories; that is, the educational levels in 1987 of the former landlords and tenants of 1971.*

### Class and Education in Nadur

Table 11.5 shows the distribution of educational levels of the sample individuals over age 14 by class. As we noted in Chapter 5, class membership changes, so the individuals at each survey time do not overlap to the degree they do with caste.

Table 11.5 shows that farmers, craft household members, petty traders, laborers, and agricultural laborers became literate rapidly during the period between the 2 surveys. Professionals, farmers, service household members and recipient household members experienced substantial increases in members at the SSLC+ level. Former landlords have the greatest percentage of SSLC+ members. Here we see statistical proof of our claim in Chapter 7 that the landlord class invested in higher education to reduce its losses from the reform. Former tenants raised their literacy level from 70% in 1971 to 88% in 1987. Only one former tenant household member had passed the SSLC by that year, but 11

Table 11.6
Average Years of Education by Class for Ages 15 and Over
Nadur Village Kerala 1971 and 1987

| Class | N 1971 | N 1987 | Average Years of Education 1971 | Average Years of Education 1987 | Years Increase |
|-------|--------|--------|--------|--------|--------|
| Professional | 56 | 42 | 7.3 | 9.1 | 1.8 |
| Service | 28 | 46 | 6.2 | 7.5 | 0.7 |
| Petty Trade | 71 | 75 | 2.9 | 5.1 | 2.2 |
| Craft | 37 | 69 | 3.4 | 5.7 | 2.3 |
| Farmer | 26 | 94 | 4.1 | 6.7 | 2.6 |
| Recipient | 80 | 110 | 4.0 | 6.1 | 2.1 |
| Laborer | 137 | 248 | 1.7 | 4.1 | 2.4 |
| Agricultural Laborer | 34 | 34 | 2.4 | 3.8 | 1.4 |
| Landlord | 10 | (14) | 5.0 | (9.1) | (4.1) |
| Tenant | 95 | (85) | 3.8 | (5.7) | (1.9) |
| Totals | 574 | 718 | 3.6 | 5.5 | 1.9 |

*Note:  Numbers in parentheses refer back to former categories; that is, the educational levels in 1987 of those who had been landlords and tenants in 1971.*

members (13%) had reached the 10th standard.

Table 11.6 shows the pattern of the increase in average years of education by class.  We can see that farmers were the most rapidly improving class in average years of education, followed by laborers, craft household members, and petty traders.  Those remaining or falling into the agricultural labor households between 1971 and 1987 experienced an increase from 2.4 to only 3.8 years.

## Effects of Education in Kerala

Kerala's educational achievements have produced a variety of consequences.  These include the highest newspaper reading rate in India (Jeffrey 1987), and a substantial Malayalam magazine and book publishing industry.

In addition, education has helped alleviate Kerala's severe unemployment, which we described in Chapter 8. Kerala exports educated employees to Bombay, New Delhi, and the Gulf States of the Middle East. Even Europe and the United States are making use of Kerala nurses. Literacy in Kerala's progressive and mobilized political environment further enhances political awareness. Villagers in Kerala can read about their demands and struggles in Malayalam magazines and newspapers (Nag 1989).

### Female Education, Age of Marriage, and Birth Rates in Nadur

One of Kerala's most dramatic achievements has been its dramatic decline in birth rates. As shown on Table 1.1, the 1986 rate was only 22 per 1,000, compared to the all-India rate of 32 in that year. Some observers have linked this low rate to Kerala's low per capita income and high unemployment rate or to changing attitudes towards the birth of sons (Mencher 1980; Basu 1986; Mahadevan and Sumangala 1987). Statistical studies show only weak connections between income and birth rates both for Indian states (Rouyer 1987:463) and for the various districts of Kerala, however (Krishnan 1976; cf. Mari Bhat and Irudaya Rajan 1990).

A more compelling explanation derives from the fact that the birth rate declined first in the districts of Travancore and Cochin, where public health measures and access to health care facilities were also developed earlier (Nair 1974; Panikar 1975; Ratcliffe 1977:136). Rouyer (1987:463) found that 70% of the variance in birth rates among Indian states could be accounted for statistically by the combination of literacy, infant mortality, and life expectancy. The logic for this finding is as follows: (1) lower infant mortality means greater expectation of child survival, (2) fewer births are needed to achieve desired family size, (3) higher educational levels increase the relative cost of raising children, and (4) better old age security through land reform and pension programs reduces the pressures to have large numbers of children for old-age support. As K. C. Zachariah (1983a:15) has summarized:

> In Kerala, the determinants came in the right order—a reduction in infant and child mortality, followed by or along with an increase in female education, followed by redistributive policies, and finally the official family-planning programme.

Zachariah's research (1983) led him to conclude that later age of marriage produced in part by rising years of female education played a

Table 11.7
Male and Female Education, Age of Marriage, and Births
Nadur Village Kerala 1987

|  | Females | | | Males | |
|---|---|---|---|---|---|
|  | Births | Age of Marriage | Years of Education | Age of Marriage | Years of Education |
| **Cohort** | | | | | |
| 15-29 | 1.9 | 19.2 | 7.6 | 23.6 | 8.1 |
| 30-44 | 3.5 | 19.6 | 5.1 | 27.4 | 5.8 |
| 45-59 | 5.0 | 19.1 | 3.0 | 27.0 | 4.3 |
| 60-74 | 5.2 | 19.3 | 1.2 | 27.8 | 3.2 |
| 75+ | 5.7 | 18.3 | 0.7 | 28.6 | 4.1 |
| **Educational Level** | | | | | |
| Illiterate | 5.1 | 18.2 | 0.2 | 25.8 | 0.5 |
| Literate | 3.9 | 19.2 | 4.0 | 26.6 | 3.8 |
| Medium | 2.6 | 20.4 | 8.4 | 28.0 | 8.5 |
| SSLC+ | 2.0 | 21.7 | 12.6 | 29.2 | 12.8 |
| Totals | 4.0 | 19.3 | 5.0 | 26.9 | 6.2 |
| N | 273 | 294 | 388 | 194 | 330 |

*Note: The total number of births equals 1,091 for the N of 273 women.*

significant role in lowering birth rates between 1965 and 1980 in the
districts of Alleppey, Ernakulam, and Palghat. What do the Nadur data
show on this issue?

### Education and Birth Rates in Nadur

Data on education, age of marriage, and birth patterns are shown on
Table 11.7.[2] Table 11.7 shows that births have been declining. The data
for cohorts 15-29 and 30-44 cannot be finalized since women in those age
groups can still have children. For the cohorts 45-59, 60-74, and 75+, we
have completed fertility data. The numbers move consistently downward. Looking at educational levels, we see that females have fewer
births as education increases. The Pearson correlation coefficient for age
of marriage with births is -0.31**. Males marry about 7.5 years later than

females. Nadur females with SSLC+ education marry 3.5 years later than illiterate females; for males the delay for education is 3.4 years.

Table 11.7 shows a consistent pattern among females in the years of education and births. The Pearson correlation coefficient is -0.45**. These data suggest that greater education among females is strongly related to later age of marriage and that later age of marriage is strongly related to smaller numbers of births. The reasons for these phenomena have been suggested by several observers. Women stay in school longer because it helps them to obtain better jobs. It also makes them more marriageable to better educated males who also go to school longer in hopes of obtaining better jobs. For men, later marriage may result from the need to stay in school longer to try to find better employment; males may also have to wait until their parents approve their starting a family. Kerala's and Nadur's substantial unemployment probably act as extensions on education, especially for men who cannot expect to marry until they have established some regular income. The delay in male marriage probably has no direct effect on number of children, however, since even females in the youngest cohort still marry early enough to have far more children than they do.

## Caste, Class, and Birth Rates

Zachariah (1983:56-57, 63) found that caste membership acted independently of other factors in influencing birth rates, though the effects were very small. Do caste and class correlate with the birth patterns in Nadur? The data appear in Table 11.8.

Table 11.9 indicates that caste and female age of marriage are statistically significant, but caste and number of births are not. As can be seen, some castes, such as Mannans, have low average age of marriage but the fewest average births. Craft castes and Nairs also have fewer births than might be expected from the age of marriage.

Class is not statistically related to either female age of marriage or number of births. But we do see that professionals have a higher average female age of marriage than do laborers or agricultural laborers while professionals have fewer births than do laborers or agricultural laborers. The petty trade group is producing the largest birth numbers, followed closely by agricultural laborers.

Household income associates negatively and significantly with female age of marriage. To test for the combined effects of the variables discussed here, we ran multiple regressions. Our sample included 273 mothers with 1,091 births, an average of 4.0. The results are summarized in Table 11.9.

Table 11.8
Average Births by Caste and Class
Nadur Village Kerala 1987

|  | N | Female Age of Marriage | N | Number of Births |
|---|---|---|---|---|
| **Caste** |  | ** |  |  |
| Nambudiri | 17 | 21.2 | 17 | 3.9 |
| Nair/Variar | 153 | 19.9 | 142 | 3.6 |
| Craft | 18 | 19.4 | 18 | 3.5 |
| Ezhuthasan/Chetty | 17 | 18.9 | 15 | 4.8 |
| Muslim | 42 | 16.8 | 40 | 4.4 |
| Ezhava | 20 | 20.6 | 16 | 4.8 |
| Mannan | 6 | 18.0 | 6 | 3.2 |
| Pulaya | 21 | 17.5 | 21 | 5.0 |
| **Class** |  |  |  |  |
| Professional | 16 | 20.8 | 16 | 3.1 |
| Service | 20 | 20.6 | 19 | 3.2 |
| Craft | 24 | 18.8 | 23 | 3.6 |
| Farmer | 39 | 19.2 | 38 | 4.3 |
| Petty Trade | 27 | 18.7 | 25 | 4.6 |
| Recipient | 49 | 18.6 | 44 | 4.2 |
| Laborer | 105 | 19.3 | 97 | 3.9 |
| Agricultural Laborer | 14 | 19.3 | 13 | 4.5 |
| **Household Income Quintiles** |  |  |  |  |
| 1. 9,200-54,000 | 60 | 20.1 | 58 | 3.8 |
| 2.   6,000-9,199 | 63 | 18.0 | 56 | 4.4 |
| 3.   3,920-5,999 | 62 | 19.3 | 61 | 3.9 |
| 4.   2,900-3,919 | 57 | 19.3 | 53 | 4.1 |
| 5.      840-2,899 | 52 | 19.6 | 47 | 3.7 |
| Totals | 294 | 19.3 | 275 | 4.0 |

Table 11.9 shows that age of the mother is the single biggest predic-
tor of number of births. Second comes the age of marriage followed by
the years of education, both of which associate strongly and negatively.
Caste membership shows up statistically only for Ezhavas while house-

## Table 11.9
### Factors Influencing Number of Births
### Nadur Village Kerala 1987

| | Regression Coefficients | | Signifi- |
| Variable | Raw | Standardized | cance |
|---|---|---|---|
| **Statistically Significant Variables** | | | |
| 1. Age | .07 | .43 | .00** |
| 2. Age of Marriage | -.20 | -.31 | .00** |
| 3. Years of Education | -.13 | -.20 | .001* |
| 4. Ezhava Caste | 1.31 | .12 | .001* |
| 5. Household Income | .00004 | .10 | .05 |
| Adjusted $r^2$ | .41 | | |
| **Variables not significant** | | | |
| 6. Rice Land | | | |
| 7. House Compound Land | | | |
| 8. Other Castes | | | |

hold income (entered as the numerical variable of the rupees amount rather than as quintile membership) has a small positive effect. These results are quite similar statistically to Zachariah's.

### Conclusions

Education in Nadur increased rapidly during the period between the 2 surveys. The best-educated, wealthy, high-caste households sent sons and daughters to post-secondary education. The poorest and lowest-caste households attained near complete literacy. The Nadur data support previous studies indicating that more years of education correlate with later age of marriage for both males and females. Later age of marriage in turn correlates in part with lower birth rates, one of Kerala's most notable accomplishments.

Despite these many changes, the education data show a possible barrier for Muslim, Ezhava, and Pulaya children in passing on from literacy or medium levels of education to the SSLC+ category that would open access to higher level salaried government or private sector employment. The existence of this barrier may constitute an important challenge to reformers in Kerala: can ways be found to provide openings to education for village-level low-caste children to go beyond the literacy and medium education offered by the village school?

Having examined Nadur's educational progress, we can now measure how much mobility households have experienced and how education and the redistribution programs described in Chapters 7 through 10 may have influenced that mobility. We take up these issues in Chapter 12.

## Notes

1.  1991 Indian census data cited in Note 2 of Chapter 1 show that Kerala maintained almost the same ratios over all-India averages.

2.  We asked respondents for numbers, ages, and causes of death to try to compute an infant mortality rate. Our questions, however, seem to have led respondents to mix deaths during the first year after birth with still births and spontaneous abortions. We decided not to probe this painful subject further in the interviews.

# 12

## Mobility

In Chapters 7 through 10 we saw how land reform, workers' struggles, welfare programs, and food rationing reduced inequality in Nadur. In Chapter 11 we saw that education reached the very poorest groups between 1971 and 1987, but that the traditional Nambudiri elite and other wealthy households also made substantial educational advances. We can now ask how much household mobility occurred in Nadur during the period between the two surveys. Household mobility by caste does not occur. Caste, however, can be a factor in other forms of mobility. We shall describe 2 forms of mobility: class mobility and income mobility. We shall also try to account for the mobility patterns with the data from Chapters 7 through 11.

### Class Mobility

How much class mobility occurred? The data are shown on Table 12.1. Table 12.1 shows that 93 households (58%) experienced occupational class change while 67 households (42%) remained in the same class in 1987 as they had been in at the time of the 1971 survey. (The 10 partitioned households were left off the table.) The 2 landlord and 20 tenant households were compelled to change class by the land reform. These 22 households represent 24% of class change households and 14% of the sample of 160 households for which data are available at both survey periods. In addition to direct land reform impact, we can thus say that 71 households (51%) changed occupational class out of a remaining sample of 138.

Among the castes, Nambudiris were most likely to change class, with 83% changing. Craft castes remained 100% within their craft class. Looking forward from the 1971 classes on Table 12.1, we see that the la-

Table 12.1
Class Membership Changes
Nadur Village Kerala 1971 to 1987

| | Number of Households | |
|---|---|---|
| | Class Changed | No Change |
| **Caste** | | |
| Nambudiri | 10 | 2 |
| Nair | 58 | 23 |
| Craft | 0 | 10 |
| Ezhuthasan/Chetty | 4 | 8 |
| Muslim | 10 | 8 |
| Ezhava | 5 | 7 |
| Mannan | 3 | 1 |
| Pulaya | 3 | 8 |
| **1971 Class** | | |
| Professional | 6 | 5 |
| Service | 5 | 2 |
| Craft | 0 | 10 |
| Farmer | 8 | 3 |
| Petty Trade | 16 | 8 |
| Recipient | 17 | 8 |
| Laborer | 14 | 29 |
| Agricultural Laborer | 5 | 2 |
| Landlord | 2 | 0 |
| Tenant | 20 | 0 |
| **1987 Class** | | |
| Professional | 5 | 5 |
| Service | 7 | 2 |
| Craft | 3 | 10 |
| Farmer | 18 | 3 |
| Petty Trade | 7 | 8 |
| Recipient | 21 | 8 |
| Laborer | 26 | 29 |
| Agricultural Laborer | 6 | 2 |
| Total Households | 93 | 67 |

bor class was 67% non mobile. Farmers and service workers had 73% and 71% change rates, respectively. Recipients were also highly mobile with 17 out of 25 (68%) moving to other classes. Recipients include pensioners and households living mostly off remittances from absent workers. As we noted in Chapter 5, both conditions are unstable: pensioners die and the household income shifts to the occupation of the highest-paid wage earner or to land returns, or some other source; absent workers return home or stop sending remittances, shifting the household to another income base.

Looking backwards from the 1987 classes on Table 12.1, we see a more stable picture. Farmers derive 86% from other classes—28% from former tenants—with service households coming in second with 78% from class change. Recipients derive 72% from changes while 50% of the professional class resulted from new members.

Both labor and agricultural labor households show high rates of change both from the perspective of 1971 and of 1987. Movement between the classes of laborer and agricultural laborer, however, means little since households in each group engage in the work of the other.

Table 12.2 shows the precise class-to-class changes. Classes are listed top to bottom for 1971 and left to right for 1987 from highest income and status to lowest.

Reading Table 12.2 across we see the movement from 1971 to 1987. Five professionals stayed professionals, 3 became farmers, and 3 became recipients. Reading the table down, we see the derivations of the 1987 classes from their 1971 origins. Five professionals originated as 1971 professionals, 3 derived from petty trade households, 2 from recipient households, and 1 from a partition.

From Table 12.2 we see that many households remained in the same class, and that most class changes occurred between occupational classes next to each other on the hierarchy. Among the 1987 professionals, 5 derived from 1971 professionals, 1 was a partition from a professional household, 3 were from petty trade and 2 came from recipients. No former tenants, 1971 laborers or agricultural laborers shot up to professional level. Service households include a former farmer, 4 recipients from 1971, one laborer, and one former tenant. The craft households include one former tenant and two former service households along with 10 traditional craft caste/class households.

Farmers for 1987 derive from the most diverse sources of all the 1987 classes. Three professionals, 1 service, 3 petty traders, 2 recipients, 2 laborers, 2 1971 landlords, 5 1971 tenants, and 2 partitions combined with 3 1971 farming households to produce the 1987 class. Table 12.2 shows that 1971 tenants became dispersed widely across the 1987 class spectrum. We see from Table 12.2 that 5 tenants became farmers, 6

Table 12.2
Class to Class Mobility
Nadur Village Kerala 1971 and 1987

| 1971 Class | 1987 Class | | | | | | | | |
|---|---|---|---|---|---|---|---|---|---|
| | Prof | Serv- ice | Craft | Farm- er | Trade | Recip- ient | Lab | Agric Lab | Total |
| Professional | **5** | - | - | 3 | - | 3 | - | - | 11 |
| Service | - | **2** | 2 | 1 | - | 2 | - | - | 7 |
| Craft | - | - | **10** | - | - | - | - | - | 10 |
| Farmer | - | 1 | - | **3** | 1 | 2 | 4 | - | 11 |
| Trade | 3 | - | - | 3 | **8** | 3 | 7 | - | 24 |
| Recipient | 2 | 4 | - | 2 | 2 | **8** | 7 | - | 25 |
| Labor | - | 1 | - | 2 | 2 | 4 | **29** | 5 | 43 |
| Agric Laborer | - | - | - | - | - | 3 | 2 | **2** | 7 |
| Landlord | - | - | - | 2 | - | - | - | - | 2 |
| Tenant | - | 1 | 1 | 5 | 2 | 4 | 6 | 1 | 20 |
| Partitions | 1 | - | 1 | 2 | 3 | 1 | 2 | - | 10 |
| Totals | 11 | 9 | 14 | 23 | 18 | 30 | 57 | 8 | 170 |

*Note:  Boldface type indicates numbers of households staying in same occupational class at both periods.*

dropped to laborer, 4 became recipients, 2 went into petty trade, and 1 each became service workers, craft, and agricultural laborer. No tenant household managed to join the professional class in the period between the 2 surveys.

The 1987 labor class illustrates the limits of class mobility during the period between the 2 surveys. None of its members derive from professional, service, craft, or former landlord households. Agricultural laborers are even more limited, deriving entirely from labor, agricultural labor, and 1 tenant household.

Table 12.2 illustrates the constraints on class mobility. What factors account for the constraints? In Chapter 5 we noted that caste traditionally held great sway over class access and income-earning potential. We see from Tables 12.1 and 12.2 that the craft class is highly constrained by its caste origins. Do other castes have an effect on class membership and mobility? Data for examining this question appear in Table 12.3, which shows that caste membership influences class position at both periods and that it thus constrains occupational class mobility. Nambudiris were the only landlords in 1971 and a large portion of the professionals at both periods. Pulayas moved only between the laborer and agricultural laborer classes except for one household that achieved recipient class membership. We will describe this household in the case studies (Case 21) later in this chapter. Craft households are the most stable, with all coming from the craft castes except for one Nair, one Ezhava, and one Mannan household that each sent an offspring for tailoring training. Tailoring with a sewing machine is the only apparent way into a craft position in Nadur (Case 22).

Service and farmer classes display limited caste variability. Nambudiri farmers went from 2 to 5, Nairs from 7 to 11, Muslims from 0 to 3, and Ezhavas from 0 to 2. Service households went from 4 to 8 among Nairs. Other castes were not involved in service or farmer classes, however. Among Muslims we see a lot of movement down from petty trade into the labor class (Case 8). Small-scale shops and brokering cattle or land sales are risky businesses from which many drop out and return to house compound or other rural labor.

Laborers increased substantially among Nair households as some tenants could not turn their land reform gains into adequate income from rice cultivation and coconut sales alone. They thus took in additional income from rural laboring. Among Ezhuthasan and Chetty households we see a stable pattern of labor income as with Ezhavas and Pulayas, two of the traditional field laboring castes. Only Nairs and Pulayas have households primarily dependent on agricultural labor in Nadur; the numbers are stable over the 16 year period between surveys.

Tables 12.1, 12.2, and 12.3 show substantial overall percentage movements among the occupational classes, but these movements are limited mostly to one notch up or down the class hierarchy and are constrained by caste.

## Income Mobility

The data on class mobility suggest that income mobility, too, will be limited. How much income mobility occurred? To answer this question, we have adapted the income quintiles presented in Chapter 6, Table 6.4. Comparing the quintile position of each of the 160 households for which we have data at both surveys, we find that 52 (32.5%) remained in the quintile in 1987 that they been in in 1971. We consider this a lack of income mobility. Another 52 households moved up or

Table 12.3
Class Membership by Caste
Nadur Village Kerala 1971 and 1987

| | Caste | | | | | | | | | | | | | | | |
|---|---|---|---|---|---|---|---|---|---|---|---|---|---|---|---|---|
| | Nambudiri | | Nair | | Craft | | Ezh/Chy | | Muslim | | Ezhava | | Mannan | | Pulaya | |
| Class | 1971 | 1987 | 1971 | 1987 | 1971 | 1987 | 1971 | 1987 | 1971 | 1987 | 1971 | 1987 | 1971 | 1987 | 1971 | 1987 |
| Professional | 5 | 3 | 4 | 4 | | | | | | | 1 | 1 | 1 | 3 | | |
| Landlord | 2 | | | | | | | | | | | | | | | |
| Service | 1 | | 4 | 8 | | | | 1 | | | | | 1 | 1 | | |
| Craft | | | | 1 | 10 | 11 | | | | | | 1 | | | | |
| Farmer | 2 | 5 | 7 | 11 | | | 1 | 2 | | 3 | | | | | | |
| Petty Trade | | 1 | 8 | 8 | | | 2 | 3 | 11 | 6 | 1 | 2 | 2 | | | |
| Recipient | 1 | 4 | 22 | 22 | | | | 1 | | 1 | 1 | 1 | | | 1 | 1 |
| Tenant Farmer | | | 17 | | | | 1 | | 1 | | 1 | | | | 1 | |
| Laborer | 1 | | 14 | 24 | | | 6 | 6 | 6 | 12 | 8 | 8 | | | 8 | 7 |
| Agricultural Laborer | | | 5 | 5 | | | | | | | | | | | 2 | 3 |
| Partitions | | 1 | | 2 | | 1 | | 1 | | 4 | | 1 | | | | |
| Totals | | 13 | | 83 | | 11 | | 13 | | 22 | | 13 | | 4 | | 11 |

down only one quintile. We shall consider this movement also to be an absence of mobility. Thus 104 households (65%) were non mobile.

Of the remaining 56 households, 25 (16%) dropped 2 or more quintiles. This we shall call downward mobility. The other 31 households (19%) moved up 2 or more quintiles—upward mobility. Income mobility by caste and class appears in Table 12.4.

Table 12.4 demonstrates that class mobility is a major factor in determining income mobility. Households remaining in the same occupational class had 10% drop 2 income quintiles or more and 12% rise 2 income quintiles or more, a total of 15 income mobile households or 22%. Class mobile households, however, had 19% drop and 25% rise, a total of 41 households or 44% of the category.

Table 12.4 shows fairly consistent patterns of income mobility by caste, 1971 class, and 1987 class. Among the castes, Nambudiris exhibit 17% both up and down. The 1971 landlord class remained in the same or adjacent quintile. Nairs display a 25% upward mobility rate, but also 16% downward. Their success in the land reform combined with educational advancement and entry into the service sector as was shown on Table 12.3.

The 1971 classes of agricultural laborers, craft households, and petty traders stayed in their relative income positions. The most income mobility from 1971 classes occurred among farmers, professionals, and recipients. Professionals could not move up much—they were already in the 1st or 2nd quintiles in 1971. Farmers experienced the greatest upward rise, followed by recipients who combined outside earnings, educational advances, and land reform gains to project themselves into several of the higher occupational classes as we can see from Table 12.2: 2 became professionals, 4 moved into service, and 2 remained farmers.

Looking backwards from the 1987 occupational classes, we see that laborers and professionals were the most stable. The greatest income mobility occurred in the service class where incomes increased substantially relative to other households during the period 1971 to 1987. Income-downwardly mobile households went mostly into farmer and recipient classes.

## Land Reform, Class Change, and Income Mobility

What features of the households characterize upward, downward, or non mobility by income? Table 12.5 presents evidence of the effects of the land reform.

Table 12.5 shows that income mobility is strongly related to land

Table 12.4
Quintile Change by Caste and Class 1971-1987

| | Down | | Same | | Up | |
|---|---|---|---|---|---|---|
| | Cases | Percent | Cases | Percent | Cases | Percent |
| **Caste** | | | | | | |
| Nambudiri | 2 | 17 | 8 | 67 | 2 | 17 |
| Nair | 13 | 16 | 48 | 59 | 20 | 25 |
| Craft | 1 | 10 | 8 | 80 | 1 | 10 |
| Ezhuthasan/Chetty | 3 | 25 | 7 | 58 | 2 | 17 |
| Muslim | 2 | 11 | 15 | 83 | 1 | 6 |
| Ezhava | 3 | 25 | 8 | 67 | 1 | 8 |
| Mannan | 1 | 25 | 2 | 50 | 1 | 25 |
| Pulaya | 0 | 0 | 8 | 73 | 3 | 27 |
| **1971 Class** | | | | | | |
| Professional | 4 | 36 | 6 | 55 | 1 | 9 |
| Service | 2 | 29 | 4 | 57 | 1 | 14 |
| Craft | 1 | 10 | 8 | 80 | 1 | 10 |
| Farmer | 2 | 18 | 5 | 45 | 4 | 36 |
| Petty Trade | 2 | 8 | 18 | 75 | 4 | 17 |
| Recipient | 3 | 12 | 15 | 60 | 7 | 28 |
| Laborer | 8 | 19 | 27 | 63 | 8 | 19 |
| Agricultural Laborer | 0 | 0 | 6 | 86 | 1 | 14 |
| Landlord | 0 | 0 | 2 | 100 | 0 | 0 |
| Tenant | 3 | 15 | 13 | 65 | 4 | 20 |
| **1987 Class** | | | | | | |
| Professional | 0 | 0 | 7 | 70 | 3 | 30 |
| Service | 0 | 0 | 3 | 33 | 6 | 67 |
| Craft | 2 | 15 | 9 | 69 | 2 | 15 |
| Farmer | 6 | 29 | 13 | 62 | 2 | 10 |
| Petty Trade | 1 | 7 | 10 | 67 | 4 | 27 |
| Recipient | 8 | 28 | 18 | 62 | 3 | 10 |
| Laborer | 7 | 13 | 41 | 75 | 7 | 13 |
| Agricultural Laborer | 1 | 13 | 3 | 38 | 4 | 50 |
| **Class Mobility** | | | | | | |
| Class Same | 7 | 10 | 52 | 78 | 8 | 12 |
| Class Changed | 18 | 19 | 52 | 56 | 23 | 25 |
| Totals | 25 | 16 | 104 | 65 | 31 | 19 |

Table 12.5
Land Gained or Lost by Mobile and Non Mobile Households
Nadur Village Kerala 1971-1987

|  | Land Gained or Lost in Acres by Mobility Pattern | | | |
|---|---|---|---|---|
| Characteristic | Down N=25 | Same N=104 | Up N=31 | All N=160 |
| Rice Land | -.05 | -.28 | +.42 | -.11 |
| Rice Land Owners Only | -.16 | -.68 | +.87 | -.11 |
|  | (N=7) | (N=33) | (N=16) | (N=56) |
| House Compound Land | -.25 | +.04 | +.52 | +.09 |
| All Land | -.30 | -.25 | +.95 | -.02 |

gained or lost since 1971. Upwardly mobile households gained rice land and house compound land totaling .95 acres. Downwardly mobile households lost land in both categories. Stagnant households gained an average of .04 acres of house compound land, but lost .68 acres of rice land.

Table 12.6 gives us more detailed connections between the household income quintiles and rice land ownership at each survey period. Both jenmy and owner-operator rice lands correlated highly with income: 90% of jenmied land and 83% of owner-operated land was held by households in the highest quintile. Jenmy land correlated 0.64** with income and owner-operated correlated 0.68**. Land held by tenants, by contrast, is rather evenly dispersed among the income quintiles and has a correlation coefficient of 0.02 with all households included.

In 1987 much had changed. There is still a correlation of 0.25** between rice land owned and household income, but it is much lower than previously. This fact is captured in part by the correlation of 0.20* (not shown on the table) between the change in land ownership and the change in income. When only 1987 rice land owners are counted (N=61), the correlations are 0.34** for income and rice land and 0.30 for income change and rice land change (N=56).[1]

Table 12.7 contains the parallel data for house compound land. Here

Table 12.6
Percent of Rice Land Owned by Income Quintiles
Nadur Village Kerala 1971 and 1987

| | 1971 | | | 1987 | |
|---|---|---|---|---|---|
| | Ownership Percent | | | Percent | Gain/Loss |
| | Jenmy | OwnOp | Tenant | Owned | Acres |
| **1971 Household** **Income Quintiles** | | | | | |
| Highest | 90 | 83 | 22 | (32) | -41.21 |
| 2nd | 0 | 11 | 13 | (13) | 3.06 |
| 3rd | 10 | 5 | 14 | (13) | .78 |
| 4th | 0 | 1 | 26 | (24) | 11.06 |
| Lowest | 0 | 0 | 25 | (19) | 8.68 |
| Correlation Coefficients | 0.64** | 0.68** | 0.02 | | |
| **1987 Household** **Income Quintiles** | | | | | |
| Highest | (80) | (74) | (28) | 39 | -30.36 |
| 2nd | (9) | (7) | (4) | 20 | 3.12 |
| 3rd | (3) | (19) | (22) | 16 | 1.85 |
| 4th | (8) | 0 | (14) | 15 | 2.65 |
| Lowest | 0 | 0 | (32) | 10 | 5.11 |
| Correlation Coefficient | | | | | 0.25** |

*Note: Numbers in parentheses in the upper right show how much land was owned in 1987 by members of the 1971 quintiles. Those below indicate what percent was held in 1971 by members of the 1987 quintiles.*

we see patterns similar to those of rice land. The correlation of change in income with change in house compound ownership is 0.21*, very close to that for rice land.

### Education, Class Change, and Mobility

We saw in Chapter 11 that educational advances took place in all castes and classes in Nadur between 1971 and 1987. How did these

Table 12.7
Percent of House Compound Land Owned by Income Quintiles
Nadur Village Kerala 1971 and 1987

| | 1971 | | | 1987 | |
|---|---|---|---|---|---|
| | Ownership Percent | | | Percent | Gain/Loss |
| | Jenmy | OwnOp | Tenant | Owned | Acres |
| **1971 Household** **Income Quintiles** | | | | | |
| Highest | 96 | 81 | 21 | (40) | -33.25 |
| 2nd Quintile | 2 | 7 | 25 | (18) | 13.04 |
| 3rd Quintile | 2 | 6 | 19 | (12) | 7.99 |
| 4th Quintile | 0 | 1 | 24 | (18) | 15.73 |
| Lowest | 0 | 4 | 12 | (13) | 10.43 |
| | | | | | |
| Correlation Coefficients | 0.68** | 0.66** | -0.02 | | |
| | | | | | |
| **1987 Household** **Income Quintiles** | | | | | |
| Highest | (73) | (51) | (24) | 37 | -15.53 |
| 2nd | (7) | (11) | (19) | 25 | 15.51 |
| 3rd | (18) | (31) | (21) | 13 | -5.46 |
| 4th | (2) | (1) | (19) | 12 | 9.00 |
| Lowest | 0 | (6) | (17) | 13 | 10.42 |
| | | | | | |
| Correlation Coefficient | | | | | 0.15 |
| | | | | | |
| Totals | 100 | 99 | 101 | 101 | 13.94 |

*Note: Numbers in parentheses refer back to former categories; that is, what percent of land was owned in 1987 by members of the 1971 quintiles; and, what former percents were owned in 1971 by members of the 1987 quintiles.*

advances affect class and income mobility? The data appear in Table 12.8 which shows that income-downward households had an educational increase of 1.8 years. Upwardly mobile households, by contrast, had the highest educational level in 1987 with 6.0 years and the greatest educational increase with 2.6 years.

If we divide the sample into class stagnant versus class mobile

Table 12.8:  Average Educational Levels  of Mobile and Non Mobile Households
Nadur Village Kerala 1971 and 1987

| Characteristic | Averages by Income Mobility Pattern | | | |
| | Down | Same | Up | All |
|---|---|---|---|---|
| Years of Education 1971 | 3.5 | 2.8 | 3.4 | 3.0 |
| Years of Education 1987 | 5.4 | 5.1 | 6.0 | 5.3 |
| Years of Education Change | 1.8 | 2.3 | 2.6 | 2.3 |
| **Class Same** (N=67) | | | | |
| Years of Education 1971 | 1.8 | 2.3 | 2.4 | 2.3 |
| Years of Education 1987 | 4.5 | 4.3 | 4.9 | 4.4 |
| Years of Education Change | 2.7 | 2.0 | 2.5 | 2.1 |
| **Class Changed** (N=93) | | | | |
| Years of Education 1971 | 4.2 | 3.3 | 3.7 | 3.6 |
| Years of Education 1987 | 5.7 | 5.9 | 6.4 | 6.0 |
| Years of Education Change | 1.5 | 2.6 | 2.7 | 2.4 |

households, the educational differences associate more clearly with the
class mobile and income mobile households.  Among the income-
upward households that also changed class, we see the highest average
years of education of 6.4 versus 5.9 for income-stagnant and 5.7 for
income-downward households.  These averages suggest a strong role for
education in propelling households up or down the income quintiles in
association with a change in class membership.

Correlation coefficients support the impressions given by these
averages.  For 1971, average years of education of the household correlated .41** with income; in 1987 it correlated .49**. The correlation of
change in education and change in income was .15 overall, but for
households changing class it was .26*.

## Land Reform, Education, and Mobility

How did land reform, education, and class change work out in the
individual households?  In Chapter 9, we examined four typical laborer
and agricultural labor household cases (Cases 1-4, pages 188-92). We
shall now consider 18 more cases with emphasis on household mobility.
These cases fall into four general types:  (1) the former landlords, (2)

illustrative cases of downward mobility, (3) cases to illustrate different aspects of income stagnation, and (4) illustrative cases of upward mobility.

### Case Studies: The Two Large Landlords

How did the Nadur sample's 2 large landlords fare during the period between the 2 surveys? Despite different experiences, both households started and remained in the top quintile.

*Case 5: A Former Landlord Combines Education with Remaining Land.* Krishnan headed the largest landlord household in the Nadur sample in 1971 with 32.42 acres of rice land and 39.15 acres of house compound. A few years earlier the family had 61 acres of rice land from which they were receiving rent of about 4,500 paras of paddy annually. In 1987 such a rent would have been worth Rs 76,500 or about 1.4 times by itself the total household income of the richest household in the sample in that year. The household lost 31.42 acres of rice land and 31.35 acres of house compound land as rental property, while retaining 1 acre of rice land and 7.8 acres of house compound. Krishnan manages the farming of the rice land for subsistence while 30 coconut trees on the house compound land produced more than 2/3 of the 1987 income. The household head supervises workers who have planted five acres in rubber which could yield big returns in the future. Although the household has lost income since the land reform, it remains in the top income quintile. The splendid mansion is maintained with its 17 rooms, a verandah and private well. Krishnan also owns four cows and several consumer items such as a radio, electric iron, fans, and books. The household educational level increased from 5.6 to 9.6 years on average. Two of the sons currently live outside Nadur where they earn good incomes from professional work, but the household claims it does not need or receive money from them. Vasudevan, another adult son, lives with the household. With his Bachelor of Science degree, he is able to bring in irregular but important income by tutoring students who need help in passing the SSLC exam. This Nambudiri landlord-turned-farmer household has received according to its own account about half the compensation owed to it from the land reform committees and former tenants; it is nevertheless surviving the loss of its once giant rental estates and doing well by local standards.

*Case 6: Landlord Losses Plus Bad Business Experiences Lead to Household Income Losses.* In 1971 Hari's household held 7.06 acres of rice land and 7.13 acres of house compound. The holdings had been far more extensive, but the household head began selling off land to tenants a few years before the land reform. We cannot say how much land was lost over recent decades. In 1987 the household retained 0.85 acres of house compound on which they lived in a decaying mansion. No rice land was left, but 50 coconut trees provided income along with payments for religious services to the household head and income from bank interest on a fund set up with the pre-reform sales of rice and house compound lands to tenants who perhaps feared that the reform would be prevented or that some other households might gain the land. Hari then began to experience a series of personal tragedies and business failures. One son went to work in the Middle East Gulf states and returned with a lot of money. But the tire retreading business he started failed as did investments in a bus and taxi. Serious health problems plagued Hari and several household members. Despite these tragedies, the household remains in the top income quintile with an income of Rs 10,000 from their coconut sales and from the household head's work cooking for weddings and other formal events—a specialty of many post land reform Nambudiri former priests. Several of the adult children have advanced educations but are unemployed.[2] Their educational level went from 4.8 to 8.3.

## Case Studies: Downward Mobility, Land, and Education

Downwardly mobile households include 2 rice land losers, 5 gainers, and 18 who neither gained nor lost rice land. Nine households from the top quintile in 1971 dropped in 1987 to the 3rd to 5th quintiles. Two of these were Nambudiri landowners with professional incomes in 1971 that were lost by retirement and not replaced. These two households also lost some jenmy holdings. Another was a Variar temple servant that supported the land reform movement politically and paid a price in land losses.

*Case 7: A Temple Servant Loses from Aging and the Land Reform.* Babu was a temple servant (*ambalavasi*) who cleaned and decorated the main Nadur temple for Rs 450 per year in 1971. The household lost .30 acres of 2-crop rice land in the reform, maintaining .70 acres for themselves. Officially they gained .20 acres in house compound for the site directly across from the temple where they live, but since they had worked for the temple, they did not pay rent previously, and thus gained nothing from the reform's provisions for house sites. Temple income declined greatly following the land reform. In 1987 Babu's wife Usha earned Rs 606 for the temple upkeep, an increase of only 35% in 16 years. Their daughter Susila married just after 1971, taking her Rs 200 per month teacher's salary to her new household. Babu and Usha now depend greatly on the tailoring work of their daughter Geetha who earns Rs 200 per month. Loss of rice land, loss of temple income, and loss of a high earner through the aging process of the household led to its decline from quintile 1 to quintile 3. The overall educational level went from 7.5 to 8.3 during the 16 years between surveys. Babu himself remains one of Nadur's most politically active persons, and is respected by fellow villagers for his principles and actions in the past in leading petition campaigns and demonstrations for more electricity and better roads. The household has received an electrical hook-up it didn't have in 1971, but the road in front of Babu's is unpaved and the house is in disrepair.

One of the worst-off groups in Nadur consists of the 7 households that dropped from petty trade to labor as the main source of income. Five of these households are Muslims and all 7 started and ended the study period with low educational levels, increasing only from 0.67 to 3.4 years average. These are households which in 1971 had bullock carts or engaged in buying and selling cattle, local fertilizer, or vegetables. They now subsist almost entirely from house compound labor supplemented with some agricultural field labor when available. None of them has any rice land. None has been able to garner government pensions or welfare beyond the ration shop and school lunches.

*Case 8: A Muslim Household Loses Income When Petty Trade Fails.* Mohammed and Sayinnu, their 3 sons, 2 daughters, daughter-in-law, and granddaughter depend for income mostly on the house compound labor of Mohammed and 2 of his sons. The sons get 120 days per year while Mohammed works about 60 days. Another son helps his father with the household's own .33 acres of house compound land on which they plant vegetables for home consumption and sales worth Rs 200 per year. They were not tenants in 1971 and have no rice land now. But in 1971 Mohammed was able to earn Rs 5 per day buying and selling wood. They went from petty trade to the labor class. Both Mohammed and Sayinnu are illiterate and no children have yet gone past the 7th standard. Overall the educational level of the household went from 0 to 0.9 and they dropped from quintile 2 to 4. Their 2 yielding coconut trees provide part of their food needs. Since 1971 they have managed to put a tile roof on their small, crowded, mud-walled house, but have received no loans for other improvements. Owing to their poverty, one older son, Ali, married but could not set up a separate household. They thus went from a nuclear to an extended structure to pool their meager resources. Mohammed's household has no obvious prospects for improved income in the immediate future.

Sixteen other households suffered downward mobility. They represent a cross-section of castes. Most stayed in the same occupational class or dropped one or more lower.

*Case 9: Land Reform Gain Is Undercut by Loss of Plowing Work.* Prabhavathy and her husband Sethu Madhavan, their 4 children and one grandchild make up a Nair household which received .80 acres of double crop rice land and .60 acres house compound in the land reform. Despite having the rents removed on their rice land, they were just breaking even with production costs in 1987. In 1971, the household head made Rs 200 from plowing the rice fields of others with his bullock team, but this work has been largely replaced by tractor plowing. In 1986-87 they produced 80 paras of rice worth Rs 1,360. This supplied half the needs of the household's 7 members. The household has begun planting vegetables for sale on their house compound land, but they derived only Rs 500 from this in 1987. The household was in the farmer class in both periods, dropping from quintile 2 to 5. The educational level increased from 6.0 to 7.6. The 2nd daughter, Janaki, completed 10 years of school. At age 17, she now studies tailoring, and could bring additional income to the household soon.

### Income-Stagnant Households

The 104 households remaining within the same quintile or moving only one quintile up or down represent a wide cross-section of caste, class, income, landholding, and educational levels. Some were wealthy and stayed that way, others were in the middle, and some languished in poverty.

*Case 10: A Mannan Professional Stays Wealthy.* In 1971 Sudhakaran headed a Mannan household in which the educational level was 7.4. His son Vasu was employed at an Ayurvedic medical research station in the next village and was earning Rs 300 per month. Since then, Vasu has become the head of the household and is now manager of a district medical office, earning Rs 1,500 per month. Both his educational and career advancements result in part from government programs to benefit members of former untouchable castes such as his. His household's educational level rose to 10.0 years in 1987. Despite his personal success, he has not lost his sense of caste and class solidarity with the most oppressed groups. During the interview, he expressed the unsolicited opinion that caste and class inequality are still among the "greatest evils in Kerala" and offered further the view that the government reservations policy should be extended into the sphere of private firms. Vasu's salary of Rs 18,000 supports him and his 2 children. The household remained in the 1st quintile at both surveys.

*Case 11: Land Reform Losses and Misfortune Offset a Nambudiri's Bank Holdings and Coconut Production.* Krishnan's household illustrates the tragedy that can befall the well-off when major earners die unexpectedly. In 1971 they held 3.5 acres of rice land from part of which they received rent and on part of which they managed the cultivation. In addition, the household head earned Rs 250 per month as the local school master. They lost 2.34 acres of rice land in the land reform but gained 5.05 acres house compound in a partition. In 1977 Krishnan's father Neelakhandan died. Then eldest son Hari died unexpectedly of a heart attack after the family had invested a lot of money in educating him to the level of engineer. A second son Narayanan also died without warning while conducting a Brahmin prayer service away from the village. Now third son Krishnan is not able to build a house or marry. He has an SSLC but works only as manager of the family's remaining 1 acre of 2-crop rice land and 7 acres of house compound. Krishnan's household has a small interest payment from a bank deposit made from the money they received as payment from land taken in the reform, and they produce coconuts on their house compound worth Rs 600 per year. In addition, they are able to produce all the rice for the household's own needs. The educational level of the household rose from 7.6 to 11.6 during the 16 year period between surveys, but 3 SSLC+ members are unemployed. The household dropped from the 1st to the 2nd quintile.

*Case 12: A Muslim Household Gains Land but Not Income.* Hansa heads a Muslim family that got 2 acres of single-crop rice land in the reform. The 180 paras of rice they produce provide 50% of their needs which they supplement with agricultural and garden labor to support their 8 members. According to their account, they paid 100 paras in rent prior to the reform. In 1971 the stone cutting work of father and son together along with banana sales from their house compound had made them 1 of 2 Muslim households in the top income quintile; now they are 2 of 8 Muslim households in the 2nd quintile. No Muslims are in the 1st. From total illiteracy in 1971 they have raised their average educational level to 1.3 years. The best educated household member is Muhammed, the 34-year-old eldest son, with 5 years of school. They have been able to put a tile roof on their house but have no electricity and still share their well with several other households. The well, however, is newly upgraded with a cement casing and a pulley system that makes it easier to draw water.

*Case 13: A Blacksmith Stays Even.* Raman was 55 years old in 1971. He made Rs 320 per month fashioning scissors, knives, and agricultural implements from iron. With his wife Sarojini, Raman and their 6 children and one grandchild lived as they do now in the artisan section of Nadur. Although a low caste enclave, it is well-situated, directly across the rice fields from the main temple. The colony receives cool breezes during the hot months of March to May and is also close to a year-round source of drinking water on the rice fields just below it. Now Raman is 71 and resides with 2 children, a daughter-in-law, and 4 grandchildren. His oldest son Kunaran, now 39, helps him in blacksmithing. The two men together bring in Rs 6,800 per year. Valli, one of the daughters, works in the spinning coop to bring in another Rs 1,200 per year. Since 1971 the house has acquired an electrical hook-up. It lies along one of the main village power lines. In 1986 Raman borrowed Rs 2,400 to purchase a grinding motor which will allow him and Kunaran to produce more iron implements than before. The household dropped from the first to the second quintile, but has a bright short-term future if Kunaran can get enough iron implement orders. The threat to blacksmithing is competition from cheaper industrial goods. Raman owns no rice land and holds only .10 acres in house compound on which he has planted 5 coconut trees, as many as the site can support. The educational level of the household increased from 4.9 to 6.0 years and 2 grandchildren are in 7th and 2nd standards respectively. Kunaran passed the SSLC exam. The household might hope for one of the grandchildren to go to a higher educational level.

Laborers and agricultural laborers were mostly a stagnant group in the 16 year period between the two surveys. Five laboring households increased the amount of agricultural work relative to house compound or other labor, while 2 went in the other direction. Two agricultural laboring households remained that, while 29 households stayed in the labor class. All three of these groups can be thought of as a single category of 36 households with 1971 years of education at about 2 increasing to about 3 in 1987. Average incomes for the group remained low. The caste composition remained mostly Pulayas, Ezhavas, and Sudra Nairs. This group absorbs most of the agricultural labor pensions and other forms of government welfare without which many of the households would be even more destitute.

*Case 14: A Nair Tenant Remains Poor but Transfers Gains to His Children.* In 1971 Ramakrishnan's household of 12 survived on farm labor and 1.95 acres of rice land held as tenants. Their Nambudiri landlord held title until 1973. Their 2 buffaloes plowed their fields and the fields of others, bringing in a good enough income to put them in the 3rd quintile. Ramakrishnan's household was poor but had the security of their jenmy's patronage.

In 1987 much had changed. Ramakrishnan, now 65 years old, had transferred the land received in the land reform to his older children. He and his 20-year-old daughter Vasantha work as servants to their former *jenmy*. They are paid Rs 40 per month altogether plus breakfast and lunch at the Nambudiri house for both servants on working days. Wife Radha and Vasantha also get 40 days of agricultural labor each year from their former jenmy.

The educational level of the household went up only from 4.4 to 5.0 years. Now the 6 household members are supported by the 2 servants' salaries, the limited agricultural labor, and Ramakrishnan's agricultural labor pension of Rs 45 per month. They have also received a low-interest loan to repair their small house which has mud walls and a tile roof. It stands on the house compound away from the larger and better built homes of the 2 children to whom the land reform gains were passed. Ramakrishnan's household remains in the 3rd quintile.

*Case 15: A Pulaya Agricultural Laborer Stays Impoverished.* Ayappan is a Pulaya farm laborer. His daughter's husband left a few years back to seek work outside the village. He has not contacted them since. The daughter Chakki now supports her two children with help from Ayappan and his wife Kali. Like Ayappan, the women are agricultural laborers with a small amount of house compound work. Ayappan and Kali are not yet old enough to receive agricultural labor pensions. They live a meager existence although the house does have a tiled roof. During much of the year they say they have too little income to feed themselves, and must depend on loans from the cooperative society, local merchants, and neighbors to get by. The educational level slipped from 1.0 to 0.7 years between 1971 and 1987. Only 19 households (12%) experienced a decline in average educational levels in the Nadur sample from 1971 to 1987. Ayappan's household languished in the bottom quintile at both survey periods.

### Case Studies: Upward Mobility, Land, and Education

Among the 31 upwardly mobile households are one rice land loser, 16 (52%) who gained, and 14 who neither gained nor lost. Six households gained one acre or more. Of these 6, 2 rose 2 quintiles, 3 moved up 3 quintiles, and 1 went from the 5th to the 1st quintile.

*Case 16: Two Professional Incomes—No Rice Land Needed.* Priyadatha, age 31, and husband Aryan, age 38, both teach in Nadur's school.

In 1971, before Priyadatha married and moved in, the household lived mostly from Aryan's work in a Bombay office. They lost 0.82 acres rice land during the period between surveys and do not engage in farming. This Nambudiri household takes in Rs 2,000 per month in professional salaries, resulting from the dramatic increase in educational level from 3.0 in 1971 to 14.0 in 1987. They have built a new house recently with a water tank on the roof and one of Nadur's few indoor plumbing set-ups, including a flush toilet. The house stands at the side of Nadur's main temple, and is a 5 minute walk from the school. Their 2 children, ages 8 and 6, both attend the school. Aryan and Priyadatha have planted 6 coconut trees on their .30 acres of house compound from which they meet home consumption needs. The household went from recipient to professional class and moved from the 3rd to the 1st quintile.

*Case 17: Land Reform, Education, and Caste Reservation Lift a Mannan Household Up.* The most spectacular case of upward mobility is Nanu's household which increased its income by 28 times between 1971 and 1987. The household moved from the 3rd to the 1st quintile. The already high educational level of 9 years did not increase, but Nanu and his wife Chandrika mustered several resources to put together their big income rise. First, .76 acres rice land had been purchased by the household even before the land reform. This land provides 50% of the basic grain needs of the household, equal to an after-cost income of Rs 1,437. In 1971 Nanu ran an ayurvedic pharmacy in a nearby town. On 20 cents house compound land received in the land reform, the household constructed a pharmacy alongside their large house. After studying Sanskrit and Ayurvedic medicine, Nanu became an ayurvedic physician who consults in the village in his office next to the pharmacy now owned by a brother. One of his daughters, Bina, is a nursing assistant while another has a government job as a block officer in Nadur. She earns Rs 1,000 per month. Finally, one grown son, Parameswaran, is a bus driver. These jobs all offer good salaries. They derive in large part —along with the educational facilities that made them possible— from the scheduled caste advancement programs of the Kerala State Government. Nadur's Mannans have made exceptional use of these programs.

*Case 18: Land Reform Combines with Gulf Remittances.* Three of Nadur's 1971 farmers stayed in that class. Jayan and Indira make up one of the two Nair households in this group along with their daughter Parukutty. The household had 2 buffaloes, tenanted land, and some owned rice land in 1971. They received 2.75 acres from the land reform and are able to supply 100% of their rice needs from the 2 acres now being farmed in rice. The other .75 acres was 1-crop land which did not yield well in rice. They are now using it as a vegetable garden. In 1986-87 the 2 acres of rice land yielded 380 paras worth Rs 7,177 of which Rs 1,500 were cash sales. The 75 cents single crop land yielded another Rs 1,500 in vegetables for sale. The youngest household member, daughter Amini, has not been able to translate her SSLC and typewriting training into employment, but remittances from two sons working in Bombay and the Gulf provide Rs 300 per month. With the land reform gains and the 2 remittances, the household rose from the 3rd to the 1st quintile despite stagnation in the overall educational level at 7.0 years for both surveys.

*Case 19: Big Land Gains Combine with a Construction Business.* Sankunny Ezhuthasan was the biggest single gainer in the land reform in Nadur. He is 38 years old. In 1971 he and his father Gopi supported the household off rice land tenancy and sale of bananas and vegetables from the house compound. Through the land reform Sankunny received 2.8 acres of rice land and 2.24 acres of house compound. The land was transferred partly in 1973 and partly in 1975, after which Gopi died, leaving the land reform benefits to his son. Despite its size, the house compound has only 4 coconut trees because the land is rocky and not well watered. On the 2.8 acres double-crop rice land, the household produced 440 paras (3,168 kg.) in 1986-87, of which 105 paras (756 kg.) were sold, and remainder used for local consumption worth a total net value of Rs 8,310. Without the land reform, Rs 2,767 would have gone to rent. In addition, the household runs a road repair contracting business that brings in Rs. 10,000 per year. Sankunny went past the SSLC to a pre-degree program and his wife Komalam has 10 years of education. The household changed from farmer to petty trade class membership. Land reform combined with investment in a lucrative small business to move the household from the 4th to the 1st quintile.

*Case 20: Remittances and a Land Purchase Raise a Pulaya Household.* Ayappan's house is located in a desolate colony of former untouchables. The household has increased its income by thirteen times since 1971, largely because it has acquired 1 acre of rice land through the efforts of one household member who worked in a Madras tea stall for many years. The rice land produced 90 paras (648 kg.) in 1987 for a net value of Rs 1,065. Ayappan and his wife Pariyani now supply half of their rice from their fields, a new development for Nadur's Pulayas.

The .10 acres of house compound contain 2 coconut trees. Agricultural labor still provides the main income. Four of the 9 household members work 20 or 30 days each rice season on others' fields and in house compounds. They earn Rs 5,000 per year from this work. Ayappan's 71 year old mother Kurumba receives an agricultural laborers' pension of Rs 45 per month. Their house has bamboo walls and a leaf roof. It lacks a latrine, electricity, or even a well. For drinking water members must catch rain in buckets during the monsoon and dig holes in the low area outside their compound in Nadur's long dry season. None of the older children has gone past the level of the village school even for technical training, so future prospects for the household are not as good as the recent mobility implies. Educational levels rose from illiterate to 4.4 years. The household went from the 5th to the 2nd quintile.

Case 21: Trade Union Work Moves a Pulaya Household Up. Karthyayani is a 74 year old widow. In 1971 her household lived off her agricultural labor and that of her now deceased husband Kunjan. One son then supported the household with Rs 50 per month from his work in Madras. Now two of her sons, Chakkan and Sankaran, have unionized jobs loading and unloading trucks. They bring Rs 300 per month to her. Most of their salary is spent outside Nadur, however, because they are often on the road for their jobs. Karthyayani also receives an agricultural labor pension of Rs 45 per month. The education of the household went from complete illiteracy in 1971 to an average 3.3 years in 1987. The sons have benefited not so much from government welfare programs as from their trade union. Recently Karthyayani received a grant to build a new home and will soon move from her thatched hut to a brick-walled structure with a tiled roof. She and her sons own no rice land for security and the .25 acres house compound are located on one of the most barren hillsides on the outskirts of the village, far from both electrical hook-ups and a safe water source. The household rose from the 5th to the 2nd income quintile.

Case 22: Tailoring and Land Reform Move an Ezhava Up. Sundaram is 67 years old and had only 2 years of school. His wife Suseela is illiterate. They are parents in an 8-member Ezhava household that got 0.70 acres of rice land and 0.60 acres of house compound in the land reform. In 1971 they worked the land as tenants, sold coconuts from the house compound, sold milk from their cow, and plowed with their 2 buffaloes. In 1987 they produced 90 paras (648 kg.) of rice from which they got a net return worth Rs 1,222. They also have 3 yielding coconut trees on the house compound. Suseela works as an agricultural laborer, but the main source of income is from their son Janardanan who has become a tailor. He earns Rs 5,000 per year. A daughter Ramani is a nursing student and Sundaram's sister Subhada receives a Kerala government agricultural labor pension. Suseela found 60 days of agricultural labor in the 2 1986-87 crop seasons. The future prospects for the household are pretty good if Ramani finds nursing work close enough to Nadur to live with Sundaram and Suseela. The educational level of the household rose from 3.6 to 5.3 years, while the transfer of resources in the land reform combined with access to skilled work to move the household from the 4th to the 2nd quintile.

## Household Life Cycle, Household Structure, and Mobility

The 18 cases described above along with Cases 1 to 4 in Chapter 9 illustrate the interplay of many factors in producing upward, downward, or non mobility. Measurable variables such as land reform gains, educational advance, access to special government programs, and income from absent workers combine with at least 2 other, less quantifiable factors: the household structure and its stage in the household aging process or household life cycle. These 2 factors are themselves related. In 1971 Aryan's household (Case 16) was headed by his 70-year-old father who was literate but had essentially Aryan's remittance from Bombay to support him and Aryan's 62-year-old mother. In 1987, 38-year-old Aryan and his 31-year-old wife Priyadatha were at the prime of their income-earning abilities. While much of the household's progress stems from the high educational levels of the two parents, their ages are also part of the success. In 27 years, Aryan will have to retire and his salary will drop significantly. The children may leave or may require major investments to help them marry and build their own houses.

Raman the blacksmith (Case 13) lived in an extended household both in 1971 and 1987. He was 55 in 1971 and 70 in 1987. The household had 9 members at each survey period. Mohammed and Sayinnu (Case 8), by contrast, pooled the resources of their 1971 nuclear household with 7 members to create a 1987 household with 9 members. The age of the household head went from 40 to 50 years. As the household continues to age, it may lose income since Mohammed will become less able to earn good wages and no prospects for additional incomes are apparent.

Prabhavathy and Sethu Madhavan (Case 9) also changed from nuclear to extended. The age of the household head increased from 38 years to 54. Household size went up from 6 to 7 members despite some children leaving the household. Without new income, the household may not have the resources to partition and will remain extended. Sundaram's household (Case 22) has a similar household life cycle trajectory, but the tailoring work of daughter Ramani moved the household economically upwards while Sethu Madhavan's dropped.

These examples from the selected case studies illustrate the many complex ways in which household aging, size, composition, and assets combine to foster mobility or stagnation along with the land reform, education, and occupational change. Indeed, class change itself derives partly from the life cycle of the household. Aging farm laborers do not become unionized truck loaders, but their children sometimes do (Case 21).

## Conclusions

From the data in this chapter we can see that land reform, education, and particular government programs, combine with many other factors such as age of household members at the time of the reforms, bad luck in falling ill or good luck in having land come on the market when one has money from outside labor, to produce the complex patterns of mobility in Nadur from 1971 to 1987. We cannot claim that mobility would not have occurred without Kerala's redistribution programs, but we can see that the programs fostered much of the mobility and created conditions for further mobility in the future.

But what of the overall standard of living? Whether households are moving up or down the hierarchy of classes and economic quintiles, are the lowest income groups improving their material lives? We turn to this question in Chapter 13.

## Notes

1. If we leave off ration shop, lunches, and welfare, the correlations are 0.28** for rice land owned and household income, 0.19* for change in both; for rice land owners only, 0.41** for income and rice land in 1987, and 0.30 for income change and rice land change.

2. Saradamoni (1983:88) offers the case of a Nambudiri widow apparently ruined by the reform, but her example shows that other forces combined with the reform. According to the widow's account, her sons had left the village and were not sending any money. Chasin (1990) gives a more comprehensive view on the relation between the land reform and women's work and roles.

# 13

## Is Redistribution
## An Effective Development Strategy?

In Chapter 1, we stated our hypothesis, made up of 2 main propositions. First, we asserted that Kerala's radical reforms led to major reductions in inequality in Nadur. We believe Chapters 6 through 12 have shown how Kerala's redistribution programs reduced income inequality, distributed land, provided basic old age pensions, guaranteed food, expanded education, and made possible a small amount of mobility in Nadur village. The evidence thus confirms the first proposition.

We are now ready to consider the second proposition of the hypothesis: did the redistribution result in improvements in the material lives of the poorest villagers? If we can confirm both parts of the hypothesis, we have an affirmative answer to the larger question posed in the first sentence of our study: is redistribution an effective development strategy?

In this chapter, we argue that it is. To evaluate our evidence accurately, we need to overcome the built-in tendency to see the standard of living directly from a rich-country perspective. Stores stocked with VCRs appear to indicate wealth. Tile roofs on the homes of the poor are quite a bit less glamorous. The country with one may be lacking the other. And those without the tile roofs will not be the ones purchasing the VCRs. Redistribution produces changes that may appear slow to those of us who conceptualize the standard of living primarily through consumer goods. It may seem faster to those whose needs are at a much lower level. An anthropological village study of development can describe changes often ignored by journalists, economists, government representatives, development agency officials, and national-level statisticians. In this chapter we shall look at the changes in Nadur's standard of living over the 16 year period between surveys and we shall attempt to show that modest improvements have occurred.

## The Standard of Living

We saw in Chapter 1 that Kerala's per capita income in 1986 was only $182. We saw in Chapter 6 that Nadur's average per capita income was only $40 (Rs 300/7.5) in 1971, and $86 in 1987 (Rs 1,117 + 13).[1] These data tell us that Nadur's people are doing better in 1987 than they did before. They also tell us that the sample households remain extremely poor by international standards.

### Redistribution and the Order of Development

How can we combine our findings on redistribution from Chapters 6 through 12 with the fact of such extremely low incomes? Could redistribution provide anything at such low income levels? One way to approach this problem is to conjecture an order in which very poor households might spend an increase in income.

Based on our reading of other poverty research in Kerala (Scott and Mathew 1983; 1985) and the fact that many redistribution programs in Kerala target certain improvements, we predict that the poorest households would advance themselves in approximately the following order as they augment their incomes:

1.  Replace leaf roofs with roofs of tile.
2.  Add rooms to their houses.
3.  Upgrade their latrines.
4.  Upgrade their drinking water source, especially in the dry season.
5.  Purchase basic furnishings for their houses, such as beds, tables, cupboards, and dressers.
6.  Purchase consumer goods such as radios, watches, and bicycles.

In addition, somewhere along the way, households will attempt to get electrical hook-ups, plant coconut trees on their house compounds, and purchase productive animals such as cattle, buffaloes, and goats. Nearly all households mentioned planting a coconut or mango tree on their property in recent years: in 1987 the 1,171 coconut trees made up 35% of all trees on the sample house compounds. Besides per capita incomes, other variables influence the order of improvements. These include distance from electrical lines, difficulty of getting water, suitability of house compound land for adding coconut trees, and individual household attitudes. Despite the many complicating factors, we can get a fairly clear picture of the standard of living and its rate of improve-

Table 13.1
Type of Roof and Number of Rooms
Nadur Village Kerala 1971 and 1987

| | Number or Percent of Households, Average, or Total | |
| --- | --- | --- |
| | 1971 | 1987 |
| Roof of Leaf or Hay | 60 | 15 |
| Roof of Tiles | 95 | 155 |
| Unknown | 5 | 0 |
| Percent Tiled | 59 | 91 |
| Average Number of Rooms per House Structure | 5.8 | 6.7 |
| Total Number of Rooms | 922 | 1,139 |
| Total Number of Persons | 917 | 1,035 |
| Average Number of Persons per Room | .99 | .91 |
| Number of Households Adding One Room or More | | 103 |

ment by using this model. Let us consider these improvements in our conjectural order.

*Roofs and Rooms.* The 1971 survey included a description of the houses with the type of roof and the number of rooms. In the 1987 survey we repeated this data on the assumption that house repairs and improvements would be one of the first priorities of households experiencing improved incomes. We can see from Table 13.1 that this is indeed the case.

Table 13.1 shows major improvements in housing in Nadur from 1971 to 1987. Sixty households tiled their existing roofs or built new houses with tiled roofs raising the percent of tiled roofs from 59% to 91%. Only 1 sample household built a house with a leaf roof between

Table 13.2
Distribution of Latrine Types
Nadur Village Kerala 1987

| Type of Latrine | Households | |
|---|---|---|
| | Number | Percent |
| Flush Toilet | 36 | 21 |
| Water Seal | 18 | 11 |
| Covered Pit | 81 | 48 |
| Open Air | 35 | 21 |
| Totals | 170 | 101 |

the survey periods. The data by caste and class reveal that improvements were still slow to reach the very poorest groups, however. Fifteen Nair households tiled their roofs while 2 stayed of leaf. Ten Muslims improved their roofs, while 4 could only retain the less durable and less healthy leaf. All 6 Ezhavas with leaf roofs shifted to tile. Among Pulayas, however, only 3 households went to tiles with 7 staying of leaf. Two Pulaya households were constructing new houses with tile roofs with government assistance at the time of the survey, however. Of the 4 agricultural laborer households with non tiled roofs in 1971, only 1 put on tiles, while 3 remained as before. The 2 tenant households with leaf roofs in 1971 both tiled them, however, as did 19 of 27 laborer households.

Table 13.1 shows an 8% improvement in persons-to-room ratios, from 0.99 to 0.91. This was accomplished by 103 households building 162 new rooms while 10 partitions built new houses with a total of 55 rooms. The average house was thus 1 room larger in 1987 and almost certain to have a permanent roof.

*Latrines.* Proper disposal of human feces is central to public health. Because we lack data for 1971, we cannot say how many new or upgraded latrines have been built. The findings for 1987 show 4 types of latrines in Nadur, as shown on Table 13.2

We see from Table 13.2 that 69% of Nadur sample households use covered pits or open air sites for defecation. These are far less sanitary than the flush toilet or the water seal latrine that has a sealed pit beneath

Table 13.3
Sources of Drinking Water by Seasons
Nadur Village Kerala 1987

| Source of Drinking Water | Rainy Season | | Dry Season | |
|---|---|---|---|---|
| | Number | Percent | Number | Percent |
| Piped Water in House | 1 | 1 | 1 | 1 |
| Shared Piped Water | 5 | 3 | 27 | 16 |
| Protected Well at House | 118 | 69 | 47 | 28 |
| Shared Well | 43 | 25 | 89 | 52 |
| Pond or Stream | 3 | 2 | 6 | 4 |
| Totals | 170 | 100 | 170 | 101 |

a cement-covered hole that one washes clear by pouring a bucket of water down it. The lack of adequate sanitation facilities in Nadur poses a potential health problem that is probably avoided only because the houses are far apart and the hilly environment and relatively low water table inhibit passage of infected material from one house site to another. The Nambudiris and the other high-income households have the best latrine facilities; Pulayas have the worst.

*Drinking Water.* The same hilly environment creates difficulties in getting safe drinking water. In Chapter 3, we described some of the hardships village women face during the long dry season from December to May. Table 13.3 indicates the sources of water in rainy season and dry season.

Table 13.3 shows that Nadur sample households have pretty good access to water in terms of safe wells. Many households have built protected wells at their house site in recent years. Even so, many depend about as heavily on location and nature as on technology. Several Muslim and Ezhava households with safe well water in the rainy season must shift to "shared piped water" in the dry season. This means that women walk up to 1 kilometer to the spigot at the roadside. The pipe runs through Nadur from west to east, but provides water only to the western end of the village where most Muslims and Ezhavas reside. Nair and Ezhuthasan households send women up to 2 kilometers to the wells on the edges of the rice fields facing the Nambudiri estates. Pulayas dig holes in stream beds below their rocky house sites. Filling the entire length of the pipe system along the village road with water or digging a well at the panchayat center would, as we noted in Chapter 3, dramatically improve dry season access to drinking water by the most deprived castes. Here is a redistribution program awaiting action.[2]

*Electricity.* In 1971 only 12 sample households (8%) had electrical hook-ups. Eight were Nambudiris; 4 were Nairs. In 1987, 41 households (24%) were electrified. Most were still Nambudiris, (11 of 13) and Nairs (22 of 83), but 5 of 11 craft households had also obtained access. This is important since the blacksmiths now can utilize electric grinding motors, and some are taking advantage of government programs to do this as we saw in Chapter 9. Two pappadam chetties and 1 Ezhava added electricity during the period between surveys, but all other low-caste, low-income households remain unelectrified. As we noted in Chapter 9, however, households without electricity do benefit from a larger ration shop allocation which includes the right to purchase kerosene at subsidized prices. In 1971, the average household income of those with electricity was 3.9 times that of those without; in 1987, the difference had declined to 2.1.

*Household Furnishings.* The level of poverty of Nadur's residents can be seen informally by passing their houses. Except for a few Nambudiri houses with their giant house compounds, most houses are set close to the road or paths. The passer-by can easily see inside. Many households do not even own beds, but sleep on mats on the earthen floors of their houses. Following poverty scoring techniques used by recent researchers (Scott and Mathew 1983; 1985), we rated households on a 4-point scale for furnishings. The results appear in Table 13.4

Table 13.4 shows that Nadur sample households own very little property within their house structures. Seventy-eight percent have only the simplest items, and only 3% enjoy furnishings sufficient for a physically comfortable home life.

*Other Property.* With low incomes and basic household structures and furnishings not completed, we would expect Nadur sample households to have few consumer items. The entire sample owns only 1 automobile (1 more is owned within the village as a whole), 1 motorcycle, 105 radios, 18 sewing machines, 57 electric fans, and scattered other items. The household with the 4th highest income in 1987 recently purchased a television, VCR, and refrigerator, the only such possessions in the 170 sample households. In keeping with Kerala's tradition of

Table 13.4
Household Furnishings
Nadur Village Kerala 1987

| Types of Households | Households | |
| --- | --- | --- |
| Household Furnishings | Number | Percent |
| 1. Cooking Utensils, Wooden Bench, a Few Stools | 72 | 42 |
| 2. Plus Some Chairs and Cots | 61 | 36 |
| 3. Plus a Table and Enough Cots for All Members | 32 | 19 |
| 4. Plus Spare Cots, Cushioned Seats, Dressers, Etc. · | 5 | 3 |
| Totals | 170 | 100 |

literacy and high interest in reading, however, 34 sample households subscribed to a total of 48 newspapers and 30 households claimed ownership of 1,396 books. Many households took in a movie in a nearby town from time to time and read popular soap opera and film magazines available in the tea shops and the library.

## Redistribution and the Rate of Development

We noted in Chapter 1 that growth-oriented development requires decades before improvements in the standard of living of the lowest income groups. Does redistribution improve living conditions more rapidly? Are 40 tiled roofs in 17 years more than sample households would have added had Kerala chosen a growth approach without redistribution? We cannot offer a direct answer to this question, but 3 observations may provide some insights.

First, we should not assume that growth will take place just because a growth approach is chosen. Many countries and regions have tried unsuccessfully to achieve rates of economic growth high enough to have an impact on the basic needs of the poor. Unsuccessful growth-alone strategies have been devastating for the poor as we are witnessing in Africa's massive starvation and Brazil's increased death rate for children despite 20 years of "economic miracle" rates of growth. Redistribution is always theoretically available and is therefore more reliable since nearly all communities in the third world have some households with substantial wealth.

Second, redistribution in a poor community is probably inherently somewhat slow, because the resources to be redistributed are somewhat limited. Let us imagine a trade-off that took place in Nadur: the 1 automobile not purchased by a Nambudiri former landlord household because it lost its fabulous rents in the land reform now appears as 6 tiled roofs on the homes of Ezhava former tenants and laborers. The abolition of rents made the roofs possible, but was not enough to produce greater changes in the standard of living of the 6 beneficiaries.

Third, as we noted at the beginning of this chapter, gradual improvements in house structures of the poor do not make flashy scenes. Redistribution brings improvements that we must seek out—that is why anthropological studies can be important to evaluating its impact. Anthropological studies can also give voice to the people experiencing redistribution. We present some of their voices in the next section.

### Attitudes Towards Life and the Future

Despite their lack of physical comfort and consumer properties, Nadur sample households have positive attitudes towards the changes since 1971. On the 1971 survey, respondents were asked whether they thought Nadur had experienced much progress. In 1987 we asked 2 similar questions: "Do you feel life is better for you than it was for your parents?" and "Do you think life will be better for your children than it is for you?" Results of these questions appear on Table 13.5.

We see that in 1971 only 26% of respondents felt progress had been made in Nadur since India's independence. The typical response was "There has been no progress in Nadur."[3] Even some of the "yes" responses were qualified as "some progress." Only a very few persons gave statements like "things have changed very much and much has been done against poverty and hunger. Today life of the common people is smoother and easier." More typical were the negative statements such as one respondent's:

> The rich are getting richer. The government tried to make life better for the poor but it has no effect. The state of low class people is worse. The benefits of progress are being reaped only by a few people.

Table 13.5
Attitudes Towards Progress and Life
Nadur Village Kerala 1971 and 1987

| | Number and Percent of Households | | |
| | 1971 | 1987 | 1987 |
| | Nadur Village Had Made Progress | Life Is Better Than For Parents | Life Will Be Better For Children |
|---|---|---|---|
| No | 100 | 55 | 13 |
| Yes | 42 | 100 | 120 |
| Other | 18 | 15 | 37 |
| Percent Yes | 26 | 59 | 71 |
| Totals | 160 | 170 | 170 |

*Note: Other includes no response, no children, and comments that could not be interpreted as either positive or negative.*

If we break down the responses by caste and class, we find that 9 of 12 Nambudiris were positive in 1971 while 10 of 11 Pulayas were negative. Twelve tenants were negative and 4 positive. All 7 agricultural laborers stated that no progress had been made as far as they were concerned.

By 1987 attitudes had become more positive. The caste and class trends reversed themselves. Fifty-nine percent of respondents thought their lives were better than those of their parents[4] and 71% expected life would be even better for their children. Among the negative responses for one's own life, we heard that

Father had less expenditure and more income.

We are poorer than was my mother.

In father's time we were jenmies and hence without any task. Father was getting very much income. Socially we were very high at that time.

Positive responses included mostly references to greater income, higher wages, or other economic factors.

I have a job and more income than father, and so life is a little better.

Now there are better wages. With the help of my sons I have a little more income.

Even though father had more land to cultivate, most of it went to the jenmy and wages were very low. Now my life is better.

My business is progressing because of the demand for more clothes than in the past. My son is a tailor and gets a better wage than an agricultural laborer.

Now we are working in the rubber estate and getting almost good wages.

For 1987, we find that 8 Nambudiri respondents were negative and only 2 were positive. By contrast, 10 Pulayas thought life was better than for their parents while 1 declined to comment. Muslims were negative by a margin of 10 to 8. Among the 1971 classes, agricultural laborers had been positive by 5 to 2 while the former tenants broke even at 9 each and 2 non-responses. The 1987 agricultural laborers were positive by 6 to 1. Only the farmer and petty trade classes had negative majorities in 1987 with 14 to 9 and 9 to 7 respectively.

Negative statements about their children's futures were based on the fear of unemployment or related problems:

Chances to earn an income are very poor.

We have not educated them well and so it is very difficult for them.

Our business is dependent on the customers and I don't think my children can get more customers.

The unemployment problem threatens them.

Positive statements were overwhelmingly about educational improvements coupled with hopes they would lead to higher incomes:

They can get more wages.

The children are having a permanent income.

Since they have more education, they can get better jobs.

> Since they have more education than me, I think they can get more income and have a better life.

> I am planning to give them more education to get a job.

Several of the responses we categorized as "other" were conditional on employment:

> If they get a permanent job, their life will be better.

> I can't say now until they get employment.

> I hope they can get some work and earn a better living.

Among the castes, 10 of the 13 negative predictions about children's futures came from Nairs, against 57 positive responses. All Pulayas, Mannans, Ezhavas, Muslims, Ezhuthasans, and Chetties were either positive or had no response. Five Nambudiris out of 13 declined to speculate or gave answers not clearly yes or no. They were apparently less optimistic than in 1971. Neither 1971 nor 1987 class membership indicated special trends on this question.

## Conclusions

Nadur's people have few material possessions. Their lives are difficult and their living conditions are harsh in many ways. But the data from Nadur show that redistribution can spread some of the resources of the wealthy few to the impoverished many. In the 16-year period between the 2 surveys, nearly every poor household in Nadur benefited in at least one way from at least one redistribution program. Almost all poor households made some improvements in their standard of living. While for many the improvements seem meager by rich-country standards, they remain beyond the reach of hundreds of millions around the world and in other parts of India where growth-only approaches have left the poor untouched. We consider the evidence sufficient to conclude that redistribution in Nadur has shown itself an effective strategy for development.

But what of the future? With little left to redistribute, what strategy can Nadur villagers employ to continue improving their standard of living? One consequence of the redistribution movements is difficult to quantify, but perhaps of great importance for the next stage. We are referring to the awakened political consciousness of Kerala's workers and peasants, of their access to ideas, experiences, and organizations with a potential to graft onto the redistribution movements new programs to enhance people's lives. In the final chapter, we shall ask what is the promise of what Kerala's Left Democratic Front has called "The New Democratic Initiatives."

### Notes

1.  We divided the rupees per capita by the US dollar exchange rate for the respective years to get the approximate dollar equivalents.

2.  In 1986-87, the People's Science Movement (KSSP) conducted a random survey of 10,000 rural Kerala households in which the source of drinking water was found to be distributed as follows: tank or pond, 7%, shared well, 27%, own well or public tap, 62%, piped water in house, 4%. No seasonal breakdown was given (Kannan *et al* 1991:33, 36). The latrine classification in the study (1991:35) does not compare directly with our categories in Nadur.

3.  Kathleen Gough (1965:363) found in 1964 that most people in Palakkara Village felt things were "as bad as ever" when compared with 1949, the year of Gough's prior research.

4.  We asked female respondents to compare life with that of their mother, males with that of their father. Women tended to be slightly more optimistic than men, but the difference was not great.

# 14

## Redistribution:
## Basis for Development?

In Chapter 1, we surveyed several features of inequality. Redistribution reduces inequality. Movements for redistribution are movements against inequality: when successful, they reduce inequalities in wealth and power as we have shown in this study.

But such movements have other consequences: by involving people actively in changing their society, they create the potential for involvement in further programs. In this final chapter, we shall look briefly at this potential at 3 levels: (1) Nadur Village in the 1980s, (2) Kerala State from 1987 to 1991, and (3) India and the larger world where we all confront inequality. Redistribution, inequality, democracy, and participation are issues for the present and future of all the world's people.

### Struggles to Improve Nadur Village

Nadur residents have used Kerala's radical political tradition both in struggles to get better government services and in community projects to improve the village.

In 1981, a local Communist leader organized a campaign to get a new electrical transformer. Although electricity hook-ups benefit only 24% of households, they also reach most tea shops and provide light along a few roads and pathways that make possible night shopping and chores for many households. The current was so weak that the official 220 volts were only enough to provide dim power to 110 volt bulbs until about 10:00 p.m. Then, when enough people in villages farther up the line had turned out their lights, Nadur night owls would have to unscrew the 110-volt bulbs and put in the proper 220-volt lights to avoid blowing the early evening bulb. Following a petition drive which got hundreds of signatures, Nadur residents held some demonstrations at regional offices. They finally got a transformer substation which improved the voltage. Even in 1987, however, the current was frequently off, and lights still burn very dimly until 9:00 p.m. Although there are a few barely glowing street lamps along the major asphalt road and at the intersections, night travel requires a flashlight on many of the village paths.

Following the transformer campaign, villagers engaged in a struggle for improved bus service in the early 1980s. At that time, only one bus served Nadur. Local transport officials were planning to eliminate that bus, bypassing Nadur on the local route so that villagers would have to walk 3 kilometers to a main road bus stop. The bypass plan came at the request of bus company owners who wanted to make more profits by streamlining their operation. Hundreds of villagers signed petitions demanding maintenance and expansion rather than contraction of the service. Then several people went to the Thrissur District office of the transport company more than 1 hour's ride away. At 6:30 pm. they *gheraoed* a number of officials until they received a promise of continued direct service with more buses. *Gheraoing* is a militant demonstration in which people encircle (gherao) officials, preventing them from leaving their offices until they sign written promises demanded by the demonstrators. A number of demonstrators were charged with criminal offenses and brought to court, but all were set free. They won their demand for more buses. The village economy benefited in at least 2 ways from this struggle. Better bus service makes it easier for children to go on to higher education. And, as we saw in Chapter 5, the number of bus drivers increased in the sample population from 1971 to 1987.

Finally, in 1986, just a few months before our arrival in Nadur, activists gheraoed village officials to force them to pave the main village road. The road was nearly impassable during the rainy season, and in the long dry period from December to May, according to one activist leader, "the road was covered with dust. Whenever buses or taxis came along, the dust would be everywhere. It would even go into people's houses." One day, 60 people encircled the panchayat officials in their offices and forced them to sign an agreement stating they would resign from office unless the paving was completed within 6 months. According to one *gherao* leader:

> We wouldn't even let them go to the latrine. We had to do this because we had suffered a lot. The road was so dusty that we couldn't even walk there or sit in our houses.

In addition to fighting for government to fulfill its obligations, Nadur villagers sometimes make improvements themselves. In one recent year an unemployed high caste man got together a group of friends to repair a portion of the local road that was chopped up and hard to use in the rainy seasons. They shoveled and raked all of one day —high-caste men whose parents had been landlords. They were joined by low-caste people as all worked together for a common public goal. A leaking water line still plagued vehicle travel in 1987, however, by filling a section of the road with deep mud. Repair of the water line would improve the road while extending the availability of drinking water to more village residents in the long December to May dry season.

While our 1987 survey was underway, villagers began a campaign to repair and upgrade the school. With 14 rooms for 27 classes, it is woefully inadequate, forcing a double shift. Sometimes teachers are also in short supply. "The first standard has only 1 teacher for more than 100 students," according to a third grade teacher-activist. He does not blame the local school headmaster whom he considers dedicated to the school, but the state and national governments which he feels do not properly fund or support village education.

## The New Democratic Initiatives

Can the experiences with organized struggle for redistribution and for better government services lead to further experiments in equality-oriented development? This question forced itself on the left parties in Kerala when they won control of the state assembly in the March, 1987 elections. With decades of redistribution struggles behind them, many organizers felt that few additional gains could come from further redistribution at the time. True, the Left Democratic Front (LDF) government expanded the school lunch program to standards 5 through 7 in June, 1987, 2 months after taking office. They also raised the agricultural laborer pensions from Rs 45 to Rs 60 per month and eased the process for acceptance, as we noted in earlier chapters.

Soon, however, intense debates developed within the several left parties, especially the Communist Party Marxist (CPM), the main party of the left with more than half the popular support of the entire LDF. How could production be increased? How could the land reform be made more valuable to the former tenants? How could the environment be protected? How could public health measures be implemented at the village level rather than through hospitals and health clinics only? How could people be brought into action on the side of the government instead of only in opposition? Could the energy of the *gherao* be channeled into direct action for development?

The LDF labeled its first experiments to answer these questions "The New Democratic Initiatives." The program contains several projects: elected District Councils, group management of rice and coconut farming, introduction of high-efficiency ovens (*chulahs*, Pillai 1992)) to reduce the cooking smoke breathed in by village housewives, and many others. We shall describe briefly 2 of the programs for which the most evidence is available—the Mass Action for Total Literacy, and the Peoples Resource Mapping Programme.

## Mass Action for Total Literacy

We saw in Chapter 1 that Kerala's literacy rate is the highest in India. We saw in Chapter 11 that in Nadur the youngest generation has achieved virtually total literacy. Many older adults, however, remain illiterate, as do some younger people. In December of 1988, the LDF government organized a campaign to establish full literacy throughout Kerala. The campaign was initiated in Ernakulam District, where 20,000 volunteer activists, led by the Peoples Science Movement (KSSP), organized *jathas*, meetings, drama presentations, and literacy classes in neighborhoods where illiterates were concentrated. They called their program the Ernakulam District Total Literacy Programme (EDTLP).[1]

The goals of the project were modest. The activists hoped to teach villagers to read in Malayalam at the rate of 30 words per minute, to copy a text at 7 words per minute, to count and write from 1 to 100, to add and subtract 3 digit numbers, and to multiply and divide 2 digit numbers. They also hoped to transfer some knowledge about the world through lessons on human basic needs, Kerala and India, public institutions the learners would have to encounter, food, the dignity of work, prevention of disease, equality of the sexes, the need for clean drinking water, India's freedom struggle, the nature of local government, the post office, fair price shops, oral rehydration therapy, how to read a clock, and what immunizations should be given to one's children at what ages (Tharakan 1990:44,60).

With few funds at their disposal, the activists had to solve problems through community participation. During the campaign, teachers discovered that lack of eyeglasses prevented many of the learners from reading no matter what efforts they put into the program. In one Muslim region, organizers responded with an appeal for local people to donate spectacles. During October through November, 1989, more than 50,000 pairs of eyeglasses were donated. These were matched to those who needed them by 40 volunteers who were given one-day training courses to work with doctors, medical students, and traditional Indian Ayurvedic physicians (Tharakan 1990:74).

In February 1990, the District Collector of Ernakulam declared the district 100% literate: 135,000 persons had learned to read and to write out of an estimated total of 174,000 illiterates in the district.[2] The 135,000 neo-literates had scored over 80% on a test given as part of the program; the other 39,000 had failed the test, but gained some literacy skills they could build on in the follow-up programs. An independent observer calculated that each student became literate at a cost of between Rs 205 and Rs 333 (Tharakan 1990:45; 81-82). The Rs 333 figure comes to less than US$26 per literate person.[3] In recognition of its work, the KSSP received the UNESCO literacy award (Gupta 1991:80).

The program was more than literacy and information, however. The campaign included several additional components. One was the pride of accomplishment of the mostly low-caste learners. Many of the older learners had fought in earlier years in the land reform struggles or had other long-term experiences with trying to change their lives. Learning to read and do arithmetic gave them the confidence to challenge government officials above them. As one journalist reported: "Collectors [high government officials] in Kerala say neo-literates are writing letters to demand better roads and health facilities" (Gupta 1991:80). These newly enfranchised villagers sound like those in Nadur who were ready to sign petitions one day and ready to *gherao* if necessary the next. Those who are literate and who have felt the power of learning know they have rights. They are willing to struggle for them. Such people constitute a democratic force which, even for a government ostensibly committed to their welfare, must pay attention or face their direct action. As reported by the EDTLP evaluator (Tharakan 1990:65),

> ...the immediate benefit of the EDTLP was in helping the neo-literates and instructors being better equipped as participatory citizens. Probably the most astounding example of such a development is from the Pongumchuvadu Tribal Colony where the learners with the help of instructors cleared two kilometres of road through the forest, organized a cooperative society, and organized a fair price bazaar for Onam.

The literacy campaign also furthered the breakdown of caste barriers. Teachers from generally higher castes learned to have close contact with adult students and their children from the lowest castes.[4]

Finally, the program seems to have awakened women to continue both their education and their meetings together. Where at first they were meeting to learn the alphabet, later they came to talk about their problems and their feelings. Their discovery of their abilities and of their solidarity with each other became a force in itself, motivating them to work for cleaner water, better transportation, and more responsible government officials, including those of the LDF who supported the program.

A follow-up of the program included publication of a special newspaper, *AKSHARAM*, for the neo-literates, and the promise of expanding the campaign to all districts of Kerala. Although the expansion was cut short by the conservative Congress Party victory in the June 1991 elections, the program remains a campaign pledge of the LDF for Kerala's next elections in 1996 or earlier.

## The Peoples Resource Mapping Programme

Can farmers raise productivity without waiting for outside technology? The 1987-1991 LDF ministry experimented in 25 villages where organizers worked with farmers—mostly former tenants who had gained their land in the land reform—to map local land formations, soil conditions, and water channels.[5] The farmers experienced seeing geographical and ecological zones as key elements of agricultural success rather than just their own individual plots of land. They also learned to see themselves as actors in changing the farming system rather than being instructed by outside experts. Government agents digitalized the maps the farmers produced and analyzed them with computers to produce models for the most efficient use of land and water resources. The outcome of the experiment was a strategy called "group farming," in which landowners pooled labor to organize better water and land use, but did not give up private ownership of their plots. They thus created cooperatives based on pooling resources whose scientific analysis they had partly carried out. Under the right circumstances, such a program might be welcomed in Nadur, where former tenants want very much to make their private plots more productive, but have few means to do so. Our questionnaires indicate that almost all of Nadur's 61 rice land owners desire better use of irrigation and better use of the land. They want the government to help them, but they do not know exactly what they or the government should do. Under the best circumstances, the resource mapping and group farming projects could become extensions of the land reform.

## Development, Redistribution, and Inequality

In Chapter 1 we introduced 3 themes together: development, redistribution, and inequality. What conclusions can we draw from our study? What is the larger meaning of the Nadur data?

We believe the Nadur experience supports 2 general propositions about development that are of great importance world-wide. First, *greater equality brings improvement in the living standards of the poor without having to wait for large-scale economic growth. Redistribution is theoretically available to people everywhere whatever their rate of economic growth.*

Kerala can be said to have passed through the redistribution phase of its development process. The state's experience, illustrated by the findings in Nadur, demonstrates this first general proposition.

In the process, Kerala's people have created organizations, institutions, and a cultural and ideological milieu in which people expect to be active and to struggle for their rights. This leads to our second general proposition: *greater equality makes possible meaningful democracy and participation in programs to make development sustainable in the long run.* With the new democratic initiatives, Kerala may have begun a second development phase in which the energy and organization used previously to wrest redistribution can be turned to increasing skill levels, raising production, and working to protect the environment—the latter issue now being forcefully brought to public attention by the Peoples Science Movement.

The Kerala experience lends support from the third world to recent progressive propositions in the developed countries as well. U.S. economists Bowles, Gordon, and Weisskopf (1990:192) have argued that there is a "logic to a democratic alternative" to corporate or government bureaucratic domination of the economy. Two major issues arise: the free market versus political intervention and the question of an equality-efficiency tradeoff.

Regarding the free market, Bowles *et al* (1990:193) argue that "... in many crucial areas markets will misallocate resources...." People must intervene politically to assure fairness which the market cannot arrange by itself. People must also intervene to protect the environment which also does not come automatically through the market. Kerala's radical movements have already shown that fairness can be largely achieved. The new democratic initiatives offer the promise of meeting the environmental challenge, but much hard work lies ahead for Kerala's people.

Bowles *et al* also contend that equality does not undermine efficiency. On the contrary, equality is likely to lead to greater rather than less productivity—for example, by ending racial and gender discrimination the U. S. would render *more efficient* its use of existing talents (1990:220). They also show (1990:223) that among advanced industrial countries both productivity growth and investment performance *are strongly and positively correlated with equality.*[6] These correlations dovetail with and support the associations discovered by Cereseto and Waitzkin which we referred to in Chapter 1: at any given level of income and production, the greater the equality the better the standard of living and the better the economic performance. Kerala and Nadur fit well with such findings.

Present world trends suggest the need for us to ponder Kerala's and Nadur's experiences. A recent study (UNDP 1992:36) reports that the world Gini index of income inequality rose from 69 in 1960 to an incredible 87 in 1989.[7] The richest 20% of the world's people by country in 1989 had 59 times the incomes of the poorest 20%. In 1960, the ratio had been 30 to 1. When inequality within countries is considered, the top 20% are estimated to have at least 150 times more than the bottom 20% (UNDP 1992:1). The poorest 20% of the world's people had an average GNP per capita in 1989 of $262 (UNDP 1992:98), more than Kerala's statewide average.

Does international development aid work to overcome this problem? In 1988, about 41% of bilateral aid from rich countries went to middle- and high-income countries. Only about 8% of U.S. aid in 1986 was "development assistance devoted to low-income countries". Israel, with a GNP per capita of $8,650 in 1988, received $282 per capita in aid while India with a GNP per capita in that year of $340, received $2.58 in aid (World Bank 1990:127-28). With 34% of the world's "absolute poor," India was receiving only 3.5% of overseas development assistance from the developed nations in 1989 (UNDP 1992:7). These figures are important to consider if one is thinking that Nadur and Kerala are utopian dreams opposed to the hard reality of standard development policies. Based on these figures, poor people in the poorest countries have little realistic hope of benefiting very soon from development aid.

And, as we noted in Chapter 1, the world economic problems of the late 1980s and early 1990s seem to suggest further deterioration and the strong possibility of marginalization of hundreds of millions of the world's poorest people—mostly third world farmers and farm workers —who may simply be allowed to remain unemployed, drop out of school, get sick without medical care, and die. The spreading AIDS epidemic and recurrent famines in Africa, cholera in Latin America, and many other events may be signs of this marginalization.

Within India, too, Nadur and Kerala hold out hope for an alternative to recent and current processes. Inequality in GNP per capita declined nationally in India between 1960 and the late 1980s. But most of the change seems to have occurred within the top and upper middle quintiles. The bottom 20% increased its share only from 7% in 1960 to 8% in the late 1980s (World Bank 1990a:143).

The most recent programs and policies of the Indian national government look like reversals of even this modest improvement. According to historian Stanley Wolpert (1989:423) from 1985 to 1989 Indian Prime Minister Rajiv Gandhi:

> ...cut the red-tape that had so long stymied Indian entrepreneurial initiative, abolishing licensing delays for the import of high-tech products, computers, color television sets, and VCRs—all the things Rajiv and his upwardly mobile generation of modern Indian managers coveted. He also cut taxes on wealth and inheritance, following the lead of Reaganomics in trying to lift India's lumbering economy out of its deep-rutted path toward Socialism and economic "equality" for all onto the smoother high road of "trickle down" opportunities for faster economic growth at the top.

Wolpert's approving summary of recent Indian policies ignores an important question: how well have India's poorest farmers and farm laborers fared? We do not have direct data at this time, but the world has seen 2 dangerous manifestations recently.

First, caste, ethnic, and religious violence in India appear on the rise. This seems unlikely if economic benefits were spreading to all sections of the society. The far-right BJP party has attracted growing numbers of followers based on caste and religious hatred.

Second, with the collapse of the Soviet Union, India may have lost its traditional bargaining power for some independence *vis à vis* western financial institutions such as the World Bank and the International Monetary Fund (IMF). The plans of these institutions for the Indian economy may require an increase in economic inequality. Such an increase would only exacerbate political tensions and could solidify the marginalization of millions of Indian farmers and farm laborers who would be left outside a development program oriented towards India's rich and middle classes.

A different outsider's view comes from Jeremy Seabrook. Referring to the IMF policies as a "reconquest of India," Seabrook argues (1992:1) that present policies make the better off better while making the worse off worse:

...the present policy...frees the possessing classes from constraints upon
their capacity for creating wealth; and, at the same time, it leads to
greater inequality, and hence, misery, for the already impoverished.

Recent cuts in government subsidies to the poor combine with
apparent attempts to break India's trade unions (Seabrook 1992:5; Birtill
1992) in response to IMF and World Bank dictates to make India's
economy more "efficient." Seabrook labels this obsession with the forms
of economic growth without regard to the ultimate goal of improving
the lives of ordinary people Western "monetary fundamentalism."

But will the opening of India's economy on IMF and World Bank
terms necessarily harm most ordinary farmers and workers?  In Chapter
1, we noted Cereseto and Waitzkin's findings that the degree of inequality is most significant the lowest levels of development:  the more inequality, the lower the access to basic needs of the majority of the population.  More recently, Dale Wimberley (1991:406) has found that the
degree of transnational corporate penetration of a third world economy
"has a substantial detrimental effect on food consumption which grows
with the length of the lag between penetration...."  India is one of the 60
countries in his sample.  Will India's opening to IMF and World Bank
strictures lead to a better for a worse life for its people?  Wimberley cites
several studies indicating that increased transnational investment leads
to increased inequality, via reduction of food subsidies and other forms
of government welfare along with breaking of trade unions so that "the
incomes of the more privileged clientele [the managers and consumers
of the companies and their products] are not taxed away and there is
greater pressure on workers to accept lower wages" (1991:411).  Using
food consumption as his dependent variable and transnational corporate
investment as independent variable, Wimberley concludes for the 15
year period of his study that "There is a predicted difference of 730 calories and 21 grams of protein consumed per person per day between
countries having the maximum and minimum levels of penetration..."
(1991:419). If Wimberley's analysis is even approximately accurate,
India's farmers and workers may face harsh times while so-called "structural adjustment" leads to a so-called "economic miracle." Brazil's poor
have suffered and died through such a miracle.

By contrast, Nadur's people have experienced a form of development which offers an alternative to increased inequality and hope
against misery in our increasingly unequal world.  May the experience
from this village in Kerala be a lesson and a gift to us all.

## Notes

1.  This program is the subject of a 30-minute video segment of *The Quiet Revolution* (produced by Jack Robertson), based on interviews with participants in a village in Alleppey.

2.  Another 60,000 illiterates above age 60 were counted in the district. Although some of these people learned through the program, the official success count appears to have involved only those in ages 5 through 60 (Tharakan 1990:50).

3.  Tharakan included estimated value of non-monetary inputs to produce a high figure so as not to exaggerate the effects of the program. Dr. K. Ekbal of the KSSP (Gupta 1991:80) estimated the direct money outlay at "Rs 50 per head."

4.  This aspect of the program is portrayed dramatically in *The Quiet Revolution* video where a college-educated Ezhava teacher comes to value her friendships with Parayas—former untouchables over whom she could have placed herself because of her education.

5.  Published information on this program appears unavailable at this time. We base our summary on an interview with Dr. Thomas Isaac of the Centre for Development Studies, Thiruvananthapuram, Kerala, who participated in the development of the program.

6.  Using average growth rate of GDP per worker for productivity growth and ratio of income share of bottom 20% to top 20% for equality, they found a correlation coefficient of +0.31. With gross nonresidential investment per GDP and income share of bottom 20% to top 20%, the correlation rose to +0.40.

7.  Using somewhat different data and methods, Berry, Bourguignon, and Morrisson (1991:72-73) arrive at the less drastic Ginis of 67 for 1950 and 69 for 1986. They report the same direction of movement, however.

# References

Alexander, K. C. 1980. Emergence of peasant organizations in South India. *Economic and Political Weekly* 15(26):A72-A84.

Attwood, Donald W. 1992. *Raising Cane: The Political Economy of Sugar in Western India.* Boulder: Westview Press.

Basu, Alaku Malwade. 1986. Birth control by assetless workers in Kerala: the possibility of a poverty-induced fertility transition. *Development and Change* 17(2):265-282.

Bello, Walden, and Stephanie Rosenfeld. 1990. *Dragons in Distress: Asia's Miracle Economies in Crisis.* San Francisco: Institute for Food and Development Policy.

Berg, Alan. 1987. *Malnutrition: What Can Be Done?* Baltimore: The Johns Hopkins University Press. Published for the World Bank.

Bernal, Victoria. 1991. *Cultivating Workers: Peasants and Capitalism in a Sudanese Village.* New York: Columbia University Press.

Berreman, Gerald D. 1981. Social inequality: a cross-cultural analysis, in Gerald D. Berreman, ed., *Social Inequality: Comparative and Developmental Approaches.* Pp. 3-40. New York: Academic Press.

Berry, Albert, François Bourguignon, and Christian Morrisson. 1991. Global economic inequality and its trends since 1950, in Lars Osberg, ed., *Economic Inequality and Poverty: International Perspectives.* Pp. 60-91. Armonk, N.Y.: M.E. Sharpe, Inc.

Béteille, Andre. 1969. *Caste, Class, and Power: Changing Patterns of Stratification in a Tanjore Village.* Berkeley: University of California Press.

Birtill, Paul. 1992. A note on foreign investment in India's 'new' economy. *Race and Class* 34(1):17-22.

Boone, Margaret S. 1989. *Capital Crime: Black Infant Mortality in America.* Newbury Park: Sage Publications, Inc.

Bose, Ashish. 1991. *Population of India: 1991 Census Results and Methodology.* Delhi: B. R. Publishing Corporation.

Bowles, Samuel, David M. Gordon, and Thomas E. Weisskopf. 1990. *After the Wasteland: A Democratic Economics for the Year 2000.* Armonk, N.Y.: M.E. Sharpe, Inc.

Cereseto, Shirley and Waitzkin, Howard. 1988. Economic development, political-economic system, and the physical quality of life. *Journal of Public Health Policy.* Spring 1988:104-120.

Chasin, Barbara H. 1990. Land reform and women's work in a Kerala village. Michigan State University. Working Papers on Women in International Development No. 207. East Lansing.

Cohn, Bernard S. 1971. *India: The Social Anthropology of a Civilization.* Englewood Cliffs, N.J.: Prentice-Hall.

Davis, Kingsley. 1953 [1966]. Reply to Tumin. *The American Sociological Review* 18:394-397. Reprinted in Reinhard Bendix and Seymour Martin Lipset, eds. 1966. *Class, Status, and Power: Social Stratification in Comparative Perspective.* Second edition. Pp. 59-62. New York: The Free Press.

Downie, N. M. and Robert W. Heath. 1983. *Basic Statistical Methods.* Fifth edition. New York: Harper and Row.

Drèze, Jean, and Amartya Sen. 1989. *Hunger and Public Action.* Oxford: Clarendon Press.

Étienne, Gilbert. 1988. *Food and Poverty: India's Half Won Battle.* New Delhi: Sage Publications.

Fawcett, F. 1985 [1901]. *Nayars of Malabar.* New Delhi: Asian Educational Services.

Foster, George M., Thayer Scudder, Elizabeth Colson, and Robert V. Kemper, eds., *Long-Term Field Research in Social Anthropology.* New York: Academic Press.

Franke, Richard W. 1988. *Height and Weight of Children: Nadur Village, Kerala.* Unpublished Manuscript.

_____. 1992. Land reform versus inequality in Nadur village, Kerala. *Journal of Anthropological Research* 48(2):81-116.

Franke, Richard W., and Barbara H. Chasin. 1989. *Kerala: Radical Reform as Development in an Indian State.* San Francisco: Institute for Food and Development Policy.

Fried, Morton. 1967. *The Evolution of Political Society: An Essay in Political Anthropology.* New York: Random House.

Fuller, C. J. 1975. The internal structure of the Nayar caste. *Journal of Anthropological Research* 31(4):283-312.

_____. 1976. *The Nayars Today.* New York: Cambridge University Press.

_____. 1976a. Kerala Christians and the caste system. *Man* (New Series) 11:53-70.

Geertz, Clifford. 1973. *The Interpretation of Cultures.* New York: Basic Books.

_____. 1983. *Local Knowledge: Further Essays in Interpretive Theory.* New York: Basic Books.

George, K. M. 1983 [1971]. *Malayalam Grammar and Reader.* Second edition. Kottayam: National Book Stall.

_____. 1972. *Kumaran Asan.* New Delhi: Sahitya Akademi.

George, P. S. 1979. *Public Distribution of Foodgrains in Kerala—Income Distribution Implications and Effectiveness.* Washington D.C.: International Food Policy Research Institute. Research Report 7.

_____. 1982. Agricultural price movements in Kerala, in P. P. Pillai, ed., *Agricultural Development in Kerala.* Pp. 142-57. New Delhi: Agricole Publishing Company.

Gilbert, Dennis, and Joseph A. Kahl. 1987. *The American Class Structure: A New Synthesis.* Chicago: The Dorsey Press.

Gopalan, C., B. V. Rama Sastri, and S. C. Balasubramanian. 1985. *Nutritive Value of Indian Foods*. Delhi: National Institute of Nutrition and Indian Council of Medical Research (ICMR).

Gough, Kathleen. 1952. Changing kinship usages in the setting of political and economic change among the Nayars of Malabar. *The Journal of the Royal Anthropological Institute of Great Britain and Ireland* 82(1):71-88.

_____. 1961. Nayar: Central Kerala; Nayar: North Kerala; Tiyya [Ezhava]: North Kerala; and Mappilla: North Kerala, in David M. Schneider and Kathleen Gough, eds., *Matrilineal Kinship*. Pp. 298-442. Berkeley: University of California Press.

_____. 1965. Village politics in Kerala. *Economic and Political Weekly* 17(8):363-372. Reprinted in A. R. Desai, ed., *Rural Sociology in India* (5th edition, 1969). Pp. 736-767. Bombay: Popular Prakashan.

_____. 1970. Palakkara: social and religious change in central Kerala. In K. Ishwaran, ed., *Change and Continuity in India's Villages*. Pp. 129-164. New York: Columbia University Press.

Government of India (GOI). 1932. *Census of India, 1931*. Volume 28: Travancore, Part I: Report. By Rao Sahib N. Kunjan Pillai. Trivandrum: Government Press.

_____. 1966. *District Census Handbook, 4, Trichur*. Census 1961, Kerala State. Ottapalam.

_____. 1967. *Census of India, 1961*. Vol. VII, Kerala. Part VI B: *Village Monographs, Palghat and Trichur Districts*. New Delhi.

_____. 1971. *Census of India 1971*. Delhi.

_____. 1983. *Census of India 1981*. Series 1, Part II B(i). *Primary Census Abstract: General Population*. Delhi.

Government of Kerala (GOK). 1980. *Kerala District Gazetteers: Trichur Supplement*. Shoranur: Kerala Government Press.

Government of Kerala. 1984. *Women in Kerala*. Trivandrum: Department of Economics and Statistics.

_____. 1985. *Selected Indicators of Development in India and Kerala*. Trivandrum: Department of Economics and Statistics.

_____. 1985a. *Report on Wage Structure Survey in Kerala: 1977-1982*. Trivandrum: Department of Economics and Statistics.

_____. 1985b. *Report of the Survey on Socioeconomic Conditions of Agricultural and Other Rural Labourers in Kerala: 1983-84*. Trivandrum: Department of Economics and Statistics.

_____. 1985c. *State Income and Related Aggregates of Kerala*. Trivandrum: Department of Economics and Statistics.

_____. 1986 *Kerala Economy 1986*. Trivandrum: Department of Economics and Statistics.

_____. 1988. *Economic Review: 1987*. Trivandrum: State Planning Board.

_____. 1989. *Economic Review: 1988*. Trivandrum: State Planning Board.

_____. 1990. *Economic Review: 1989*. Thiruvananthapuram: State Planning Board.

_____. 1991. *Economic Review: 1990*. Thiruvananthapuram: State Planning Board.

_____. 1992. *Economic Review: 1991*. Thiruvananthapuram. State Planning

Board.

Grant, James P. 1988. *The State of the World's Children: 1988*. Oxford: Oxford University Press. Published for UNICEF.

_____. 1989. *The State of the World's Children: 1989*. Oxford: Oxford University Press. Published for UNICEF.

_____. 1990. *The State of the World's Children: 1990*. New York: Oxford University Press. Published for UNICEF.

Gupta, Shekhar. 1991. Kerala: the literacy war. *India Today*, 31 August 1991:77 and 80.

Gulati, Leela. 1990. Agricultural workers' pension in Kerala: an experiment in social assistance. *Economic and Political Weekly* 25:339-343.

Gwatkin, Davidson R. 1979. Food policy, nutrition planning, and survival: the cases of Kerala and Sri Lanka. *Food Policy*, November 1988:245-258.

Harris, Marvin. 1979. *Cultural Materialism: The Struggle for a Science of Culture*. New York: Random House.

_____. 1988. *Culture, People, Nature: An Introduction to General Anthropology*. (5th edition). New York: Harper and Row.

Harriss, Barbara. 1991. *Child Nutrition and Poverty in South India: Noon Meals in Tamil Nadu*. New Delhi: Concept Publishing Company.

Herring, Ronald J. 1980. Abolition of landlordism in Kerala: a redistribution of privilege. *Economic and Political Weekly* 15(26):A59-A69.

_____. 1983. *Land to the Tiller: The Political Economy of Agrarian Reform in South Asia*. New Haven: Yale University Press.

_____. 1989. Dilemmas of agrarian communism: peasant differentiation, sectoral and village politics. *Third World Quarterly* 11(1):89-115.

Hurst, Charles E. 1992. *Social Inequality: Forms, Causes, and Consequences*. Boston: Allyn and Bacon.

Indian Council of Social Science Research (ICSSR). Central Statistical Organization. 1983. *Social Information of India: Trends and Structure*. Delhi: Hindustan Publishing Corporation.

Isaac, Thomas. 1983. The Emergence of Radical Working Class Movement in Alleppey (1922-1938). Trivandrum: Centre for Development Studies. Working Paper No. 175.

_____. 1984. *Class Structure and Industrial Structure: A Study of the Coir Weaving Industry in Kerala, 1859-1980*. Ph. D. Thesis, Jawaharlal Nehru University, New Delhi.

Isaac, Thomas, and B. Ekbal. 1988. Science for social revolution: experience of the Kerala Sastra Sahitya Parishad. Paper presented at the Peoples Science Congress. Cannanore, Kerala. 11-12 February 1988.

Iyer, L. K. Anantha Krishna. 1981 [orig. 1909] *The Tribes and Castes of Cochin*. New Delhi: Cosmo Publications. 3 vols.

de Janvry, Alain. 1981. *The Agrarian Question and Reformism in Latin America*. Baltimore: Johns Hopkins University Press.

Jayadevadas, D. 1983. *Working Class Politics in Kerala: A Study of Coir Workers*. Thundathil, Kerala: T. C. Lilly Grace.

Jeffery, Roger. 1988. *The Politics of Health in India*. Berkeley: The University of California Press.

Jeffrey, Robin. 1976. *The Decline of Nayar Dominance: Society and Politics in*

*Travancore, 1847-1908.* New York: Holmes & Meier Publishers, Inc.

_____. 1978. Travancore: status, class and the growth of radical politics, 1860-1940—the temple-entry movement, in Robin Jeffrey, ed., *People, Princes and Paramount Power: Society and Politics in the Indian Princely States.* Pp. 136-69, Delhi: Oxford University Press.

_____. 1987. Culture of daily newspapers in India: how it's grown, what it means. *Economic and Political Weekly* 22(14):607-611.

Jenkins, S. 1991. The measurement of income inequality, in L. Osberg, ed., *Economic Inequality and Poverty: International Perspectives.* Pp. 3-38. Armonk, N.Y.: M. E. Sharpe, Inc.

Jose, A. V. 1984. Agrarian reforms in Kerala: the role of peasant organizations. *Journal of Contemporary Asia* 14(1):48-61.

Joshi, Barbara, ed., 1986. *Untouchable! Voices of the Dalit Liberation Movement.* London: Zed Books, for the Minority Rights Group.

Kannan, K. P. 1988. *Of Rural Proletarians: Mobilization and Organization of Rural Workers in South-west India.* Delhi: Oxford University Press.

Kannan, K. P., and K. Pushpangadan. 1988. Agricultural stagnation in Kerala: an exploratory analysis. *Economic and Political Weekly* 23(39):A120-A128.

Kannan, K. P., K. R. Thankappan, V. Raman Kutty, and K. P. Aravindan. 1991. *Health and Development in Rural Kerala.* Trivandrum: Kerala Sastra Sahitya Parishad.

Kerbo, Harold R. 1991. *Social Stratification and Inequality: Class Conflict in Historical and Comparative Perspective.* New York: McGraw-Hill, Inc.

Kozol, Jonathan. 1985. *Illiterate America.* Garden City: Anchor Press.

Krishnan, T. N. 1976. Demographic transition in Kerala: facts and factors. *Economic and Political Weekly* 11(31-33):1203-1224.

_____. 1991. Wages, employment, and output in interrelated labour markets in an agrarian economy: a study of Kerala. *Economic and Political Weekly* 26(26):A82-A92.

Kumar, Gopalakrishnan, and Frances Stewart. 1987. Tackling Malnutrition: What Can Targeted Nutritional Interventions Achieve? Trivandrum: Centre for Development Studies. Working Paper No. 225.

Kumar, Shubh K. 1979. *Impact of Subsidized Rice on Food Consumption and Nutrition in Kerala.* Washington D. C.: International Food Policy Research Institute, Research Report 5.

Kuznets, Simon. 1955. Economic growth and income inequality. *American Economic Review* 45:1,3-6,17-26. Partially reprinted in Mitchell A. Seligson, ed., 1984, *The Gap Between Rich and Poor: Contending Perspectives on the Political Economy of Development.* Pp. 25-37. Boulder: Westview Press.

Lenski, Gerhard. 1966. *Power and Privilege.* New York: McGraw-Hill, Inc.

Lewis, John P. and Kallab, Valeriana, eds. 1983. *U.S. Foreign Policy and the Third World: Agenda 1983.* New York: Praeger Publishers. Published for the Overseas Development Council.

Lipton, Michael. 1977. *Why Poor People Stay Poor: Urban Bias in World Development.* Cambridge: Harvard University Press.

_____. 1988. *The Poor and the Poorest: Some Interim Findings.* Washington, D.C.: The World Bank. Discussion Paper No. 25.

Mahadevan, K. and M. Sumangala. 1987. *Social Development, Cultural Change and*

*Fertility Decline: A Study of Fertility Change in Kerala.* New Delhi: Sage Publications.

Maheshwari, Shriram. 1985. *Rural Development in India: a Public Policy Approach.* New Delhi: Sage Publications.

Majumdar, R. K., and A. N. Srivastva. 1987. *History of South India (with Special Reference to Karnataka).* Delhi: Surjeet Book Depot.

Mari Bhat, P. N., and S. Irudaya Rajan. 1990. Demographic transition in Kerala revisited. *Economic and Political Weekly* 25(35):1957-1980.

Mathew, Joseph. 1986. *Ideology, Protest, and Social Mobility: Case Study of Mahars and Pulayas.* New Delhi: Inter-India Publications.

Mencher, Joan. 1962. Changing familial roles among South Malabar Nayars. *Southwestern Journal of Anthropology* 18:230-245.

_____. 1965. The Nayars of South Malabar, in M. F. Nimkoff, ed., *Comparative Family Systems.* Pp. 162-191. Boston: Houghton Mifflin Co.

_____. 1966. Kerala and Madras: a comparative study of ecology and social structure. *Ethnology* 5(2):135-171.

_____. 1966a. Namboodiri Brahmins of Kerala: an analysis of a traditional elite in Kerala. *Journal of Asian and African Studies* 1:183-96.

_____. 1974. The caste system upside down: or, the not so mysterious East. *Current Anthropology* 15:469-478.

_____. 1978. Agrarian relations in two rice regions of Kerala. *Economic and Political Weekly* 13(6-7):349-366.

_____. 1980. The lessons and non-lessons of Kerala. *Economic and Political Weekly* 15(41-43):1781-1802.

_____. 1980a. On being an untouchable in India: a materialist perspective, in Eric Ross, ed., *Beyond the Myths of Culture.* Pp. 261-294. New York: Academic Press.

_____. 1982. Agricultural labourers and poverty. *Economic and Political Weekly* 17(1-2):38-44.

Menon, A. Sreedhara. 1979. *Social and Cultural History of India: Kerala.* New Delhi: Sterling Publishers Pvt. Ltd.

_____. 1984. *A Survey of Kerala History.* Madras: S. Viswanathan.

Menon, V. K. J. 1953. Geographical basis for the distribution pattern of rural settlement in Kerala. *Journal of the Maharaja Sayajirao University* 2:41-54.

Miller, Roland E. 1976. *Mappila Muslims of Kerala: A Study in Islamic trends.* Madras: Orient Longman Ltd.

Minhas, B. S. 1991. On estimating inadequacy of energy intakes: revealed food consumption behaviour versus nutritional norms (nutritional status of Indian people in 1983). *The Journal of Development Studies* 28 (1):1-38.

Mitra, A. 1985. The nutrition situation in India, in M. Biswas and P. Pinstrup-Anderson, eds., *Nutrition and Development.* Pp. 142-62. New York: Oxford University Press.

Moore, Barrington, Jr. 1966. *Social Origins of Dictatorship and Democracy: Lord and Peasant in the Making of the Modern World.* Boston: Beacon Press.

_____. 1978. *Injustice: The Social Bases of Obedience and Revolt.* White Plains, N.Y.: M.E. Sharpe, Inc.

Morawetz, David. 1977. *Twenty-Five Years of Economic Development, 1950 to 1975.* Baltimore: Johns Hopkins University Press.

Morris, David Morris. 1979. *Measuring the Condition of the World's Poor: The Physical Quality of Life Index*. New York: Pergamon Press. Published for the Overseas Development Council.

Morris, D. M. and Michelle B. McAlpin. 1982. *Measuring the Condition of India's Poor: The Physical Quality of Life Index*. New Delhi: Promilla & Co.

Mukherjee, Chandan. 1979. Lorenz Ratios for Distribution of Rural Ownership and Operational Land Holdings, India, 1971-72. Trivandrum: Centre for Development Studies. Working Paper No. 94.

Murthy, N. Anjneya, and D. P. Pandey. 1985. *Ayurvedic Cure for Common Diseases*. Delhi: Orient Paperbacks.

Nag, Moni. 1989. Political awareness as a factor in accessibility of health services: a case study of rural Kerala and West Bengal. *Economic and Political Weekly* 24(8):417-426.

Nair, P. R. Gopinathan. 1974. Decline in birth rate in Kerala: a hypothesis about the inter-relationship between demographic variables, health services and education. *Economic and Political Weekly* 9:323-336.

_____. 1979. Role of primary education in socioeconomic change: the Kerala case, in M. A. Oomen, ed., *Kerala Economy Since Independence*. Pp. 85-102. Delhi: Oxford.

_____. 1983. Educational Reforms in India: Universalisation of Primary Education in Kerala. Trivandrum: Centre for Development Studies. Working Paper No. 181.

_____, and D. Ajit. 1983. Parallel Colleges in Kerala: a Case Study of Their Structure in Terms of Enrollment Costs and Employment. Trivandrum: Centre for Development Studies. Working Paper No. 156.

Nair, R. Ramakrishnan. 1976. *Social Structure and Political Development in Kerala*. Trivandrum: St. Joseph's Press for The Kerala Academy of Political Science.

Namboodiripad, E. M. S. 1976. *How I Became a Communist*. Trivandrum: Chinta Publishers.

_____. 1984 [orig. 1967]. *Kerala Society and Politics: An Historical Survey*. New Delhi: National Book Centre.

Nayanar, E. K. 1982. *My Struggles: An Autobiography*. New Delhi: Vikas.

Nieuwenhuys, Olga. 1990. *Angels With Callous Hands: Children's Work in Rural Kerala (India)*. Ph. D. Dissertation. Free University of Amsterdam.

_____. 1991. Emancipation for survival: access to land and labour of Thandans in Kerala. *Modern Asian Studies* 25(3):599-619.

Ninan, K. N. 1986. *Cereal Substitutes in a Developing Economy: A Study of Tapioca (Kerala State)*. New Delhi: Concept Publishing Company.

Nossiter, T. J. 1982. *Communism in Kerala: A Study in Political Adaptation*. Delhi: Oxford University Press.

_____. 1988. *Marxist State Governments in India*. London: Pinter Publishers.

Oberai, A. S., Pradhan Prasad, and M. G. Sardana. 1989. *Determinants and Causes of Internal Migration in India: Studies in Bihar, Kerala, and Uttar Pradesh*. Delhi: Oxford University Press, for the International Labour Organization.

Oomen, T. K. 1985. *From Mobilization to Institutionalization: The Dynamics of Agrarian Movement in Twentieth Century Kerala*. Bombay: Popular Prakashan.

Padhi, Sakti Prasad, and K. N. Nair. 1992. Dynamics of Land Distribution: An Alternative Approach and Analysis with Reference to Kerala. Thiruvananthapuram: Centre for Development Studies. Working Paper No. 245.

Padmanabha Menon, K. P. 1986 [1937]. *History of Kerala*. Vol. 4. New Delhi: Asian Educational Services.

Panikar, P. G. K. 1975. Fall in mortality rates in Kerala: an explanatory hypothesis. *Economic and Political Weekly* 10:1811-1817.

_____. 1980. Inter-regional variation in calorie intake. *Economic and Political Weekly* 15:1803-1814.

_____, and C. R. Soman. 1984. *Health Status of Kerala: Paradox of Economic Backwardness and Health Development*. Trivandrum: Centre for Development Studies.

Panikkar, Gopal T. K. 1983 [1900]. *Malabar and Its Folk*. New Delhi: Asian Educational Services.

Panikkar, K. N. 1989. *Against Lord and State: Religion and Peasant Uprisings in Malabar, 1836-1921*. Delhi: Oxford University Press.

Parthasarathy, G. 1981. Integrated rural development: concept, theoretical base, and contradictions, in T. Mathew, ed., *Rural Development in India: Papers Presented at the National Seminar on Rural Development at the North Eastern Hill University April 1978*. Pp. 24-40. Delhi: Agricole Publishing Academy.

Paulini, Thomas. 1979. *Agrarian Movements and Reforms in India: The Case of Kerala*. Saarbrüken: Verlag Breitenbach.

Pedhazur, Elazar J. 1982. *Multiple Regression in Behavioral Research: Explanation and Prediction*. Second edition. New York: Holt, Rinehart, and Winston.

Pillai, C. Madhavan. 1976. *NBS Malayalam English dictionary*. Kottayam: National Book Stall.

Pillai, K. S. 1981. Fighting illiteracy in Kerala. *International Journal of Adult Education*. (42):3-6.

_____. 1984. Adult education in India: the task ahead. *International Journal of Adult Education* 45(5):3-6.

Pillai, P. Mohanan. 1992. Constraints on the Diffusion of Innovation in Kerala —A Case Study of Smokeless Chulahs. Thiruvananthapuram: Centre for Development Studies. Working Paper No. 248.

Prakash, B. A. 1989. Unemployment in Kerala: An Analysis of Economic Causes. Trivandrum: Centre for Development Studies. Working Paper No. 231

Prem, J. 1985. *Economics of Khadi Industry in Kerala: A Case Study of Trichur District*. M. A. Thesis. University of Calicut. Department of Economics.

Premi, Mahendra K. 1991. *India's Population: Heading Towards a Billion. An Analysis of 1991 Census Provisional Results*. Delhi: B. R. Publishing Corporation.

Pushpangadan, K. 1992. Wage Determination in a Casual Labour Market: The Case of Paddy Field Labour in Kerala. Thiruvananthapuram: Centre for Development Studies. Working Paper No. 244.

Radhakrishnan, P. 1989. *Peasant Struggles, Land Reforms, and Social Change: Malabar, 1836-1982*. New Delhi: Sage Publications.

Rajeev, P. V. 1983. *Economic Development and Unemployment: Relevance of Kerala Model*. New Delhi: Asian Publication Services.

Ratcliffe, John. 1978. Social justice and the demographic transition: lessons from India's Kerala State. *International Journal of Health Services* 8(1):123-144.

Reitsma, H. A. and J. M. G. Kleinpenning. 1985. *The Third World in Perspective.* Totowa, N.J.: Rowman and Allanheld.

Rouyer, Alwyn R. 1987. Political capacity and the decline of fertility in India. *American Political Science Review* 81(2):453-470.

Rudra, Ashok. 1989. Field survey methods, in Pranab Bardhan, ed., *Conversations Between Economists and Anthropologists: Methodological Issues in Measuring Economic Change in Rural India.* Pp. 218-37. Delhi: Oxford University Press.

Sankaranarayanan, K. C. and V. Karunakaran. 1985. *Kerala Economy.* Delhi: Oxford.

Sanoo, M. K. 1978. *Narayana Guru: A Biography.* Bombay: Bharatiya Vidya Bhavan.

Saradamoni, K. 1980. *Emergence of a Slave Caste: Pulayas of Kerala.* New Delhi: People's Publishing House.

_____. 1981. *Divided Poor: Study of a Kerala Village.* Delhi: Ajanta Books.

_____. 1982. Women's status in changing agrarian relations: a Kerala experience. *Economic and Political Weekly* 17(5):155-162.

_____. 1983. Changing land relations and women: a case study of Palghat District, Kerala. In Rekha Mehra and K. Saradamoni, eds., *Women and Rural Transformation: Two Studies.* Pp. 33-171, New Delhi: Concept Publishing Company.

Sastri, Nilakanta. 1966. *A History of South India.* Oxford: Oxford University Press.

Sathyamurthy, T. V. 1985. *India Since Independence: Studies in the Development of the Power of the State. Volume 1: Centre-State Relations, the Case of Kerala.* Delhi: Ajanta.

Schenk-Sandbergen, Loes. 1988. *Poverty and Survival: Kudumbi Female Domestic Servants and Their Households in Alleppey (Kerala).* New Delhi: Manohar Publications.

Scott, Wolf and N. T. Mathew. 1981. A development monitoring service at the local level. *International Social Science Journal* 33(1):82-90.

_____. 1983. *A Development Monitoring Service at the Local Level. Volume II: Levels of Living and Poverty in Kerala.* Geneva: United Nations Research Institute for Social Development. Report No. 83.2.

_____. 1985. *A Development Monitoring Service at the Local Level. Volume III: Monitoring Change in Kerala—the First Five Years.* Geneva: United Nations Research Institute for Social Development. Report No. 85.7.

Seabrook, Jeremy. 1992. The reconquest of India: the victory of international monetary fundamentalism. *Race and Class* 34(1):1-16.

Segal, Jerome. 1986. What Is Development? College Park, Maryland: University of Maryland Center for Philosophy and Public Policy. Paper No. DN-1.

Sen, Amartya. 1981. *Poverty and Famines: An Essay on Entitlement and Deprivation.* New York: Oxford University Press.

Shalom, Sephen Rosskamm. 1989. Capitalism triumphant? *Zeta Magazine* 2(4):92-98.

Shankman, Paul. 1984. The thick and the thin: on the interpretive theoretical program of Clifford Geertz. *Current Anthropology* 25(3):261-79.

Sivanandan, P. 1976. Economic backwardness of Harijans in Kerala. *Social Scientist* 4(10):3-28.

_____. 1979. Caste, class and economic opportunity in Kerala: an empirical analysis. *Economic and Political Weekly* 14(7-8):475-480.

Skocpol, Theda. 1979. *States and Social Revolutions: A Comparative Analysis of France, Russia, and China.* Cambridge: Cambridge University Press.

Slater, Gilbert. 1918. *Some South Indian Villages.* University of Madras Economic Studies 1. Madras.

Smith, David M. 1979 [1982]. *Where the Grass Is Greener: Living in an Unequal World.* Baltimore: The Johns Hopkins University Press.

Staal, Frits. 1983. *Agni: The Vedic Ritual of the Fire.* Berkeley: Asian Humanities Press.

Streeten, Paul, Shahid Javed Burki, Mahbub Ul Haq, Norman Hicks, and Frances Stewart. 1981. *First Things First: Meeting Basic Human Needs in Developing Countries.* New York: Oxford University Press. Published for the World Bank.

Subbarao, K. 1989. Improving Nutrition in India: Policies and Programs and Their Impact. Washington, D.C.: The World Bank. Discussion Paper No. 49.

Sundrum, R. M. 1987. *Growth and Income Distribution in India: Policy and Performance Since Independence.* New Delhi: Sage Publications.

Tharakan, P. K. Michael. 1990. *The Ernakulam District Total Literacy Programme: Report of the Evaluation.* Trivandrum: Centre for Development Studies.

Tharamangalam, Joseph. 1981. *Agrarian Class Conflict: The Political Mobilization of Agricultural Labourers in Kuttanad, South India.* Vancouver: University of British Columbia Press.

Tharian, George K., and Michael P. K. Tharakan. 1986. Penetration of capital into a traditional economy: the case of tea plantations in Kerala, 1880-1950. *Studies in History* 2(2):199-229.

Tumin, Melvin M. 1953 [1966]. Some principles of stratification: a critical analysis. *The American Sociological Review* 18:387-393. Reprinted in Reinhard Bendix and Symour Martin Lipset, eds. 1966. *Class, Status, and Power: Social Stratification in Comparative Perspective.* Second Edition. Pp. 53-58. New York: The Free Press.

United Nations (UN). 1975. *Poverty, Unemployment and Development Policy: a Case Study of Selected Issues with Reference to Kerala.* New York: United Nations Department of Economic and Social Affairs. Document ST/ESA/29.

United Nations Development Programme (UNDP). 1992. *Human Development Report 1992.* New York: Oxford University Press.

Unni, K. R. 1959. *Caste in South Malabar.* Ph. D. Dissertation. University of Baroda.

Varghese, T. C. 1970. *Agrarian Change and Economic Consequences: Land Tenures in Kerala: 1850-1960.* Bombay: Allied Publishers.

Venugopal, K. R. 1992. *Deliverance From Hunger: The Public Distribution System in India.* New Delhi: Sage Publications.

Wadley, Susan S. and Bruce W. Derr. 1989. Karimpur 1925-1984: Understanding rural India through restudies, in Pranab Bardhan, ed., *Conversations Between Economists and Anthropologists: Methodological Issues in Measuring Economic Change in Rural India.* Pp. 76-126. Delhi: Oxford University Press.

Westley, John R. 1986. *Agriculture and Equitable Growth: The Case of Punjab-Haryana.* Boulder: Westview Press.

Wimberley, Dale W. 1991. Transnational corporate investment and food consumption in the third world: a cross-national analysis. *Rural Sociology* 56(3):406-431.

Wolf, Eric. 1969. *Peasant Wars of the Twentieth Century.* New York: Harper and Row.

_____. 1982. *Europe and the People Without History.* Berkeley: University of California Press.

Wolpert, Stanley. 1989. *A New History of India.* New York: Oxford University Press. Third edition.

World Bank. 1988. *World Development Report 1988.* New York: Oxford University Press. Published for the World Bank.

_____. 1990. *World Development Report 1990: Poverty.* New York: Oxford University Press.

World Bank. 1990a. *Social Indicators of Development 1990.* Baltimore: The Johns Hopkins University Press.

_____. 1991. *World Development Report 1991: The Challenge of Development.* New York: Oxford University Press.

_____. 1992. *World Development Report 1992: Development and the Environment.* New York: Oxford University Press.

Zachariah, K. C. 1983. *Anomaly of the Fertility Decline in Kerala.* Washington D.C.: World Bank Case Studies of the Determinants of Fertility Decline in South India and Sri Lanka. Report No. 1 from RPO 671-70.

_____. 1983a. Kerala: solution or happenstance? *Populi* 10(4):3-15.

# Index